M

28 DAY BOOK

8/16 2H28

BRITAIN'S
MEDIEVAL
CASTLES

BRITAIN'S MEDIEVAL CASTLES

Lise E. Hull

PRAEGER

Westport, Connecticut
London

Library of Congress Cataloging-in-Publication Data

Hull, Lise.
   Britain's medieval castles / Lise E. Hull.
      p.   cm.
   Includes bibliographical references and index.
   ISBN 0–275–98414–1 (alk. paper)
      1. Castles—Great Britain.   2. Architecture, Medieval—Great Britain.   3. Great Britain—
   History—Medieval period, 1066–1485.   I. Title.
   DA660.H94 2006
   623'.1941'0902—dc22   2005020949

British Library Cataloguing in Publication Data is available.

Library of Congress Catalog Card Number: 2005020949
ISBN: 0–275–98414–1

First published in 2006

Praeger Publishers, 88 Post Road West, Westport, CT 06881
An imprint of Greenwood Publishing Group, Inc.
www.praeger.com

Printed in the United States of America

The paper used in this book complies with the
Permanent Paper Standard issued by the National
Information Standards Organization (Z39.48–1984).

10 9 8 7 6 5 4 3 2 1

Contents

CONTENTS

Illustrations

Acknowledgments

Developing a fascination with medieval castles was happenstance, born from a desire to experience as much of Britain's culture, countryside, and ancient and historic monuments as possible during the two and a half years I was assigned to the naval facility at Brawdy, Wales. Initially drawn to castle ruins by the romantic image they projected in the lush landscape, I actually wrote out a list of "must-see" sites that I wanted to visit before being sent to a new duty station. Progressively, I expanded my travels from Pembrokeshire to the rest of Wales, and then to England and the rest of Britain, ensuring I checked off several of my "must-sees" on each trip. Quickly, my casual curiosity gave way to understanding. I discovered I had acquired considerable knowledge about the archaeology and history of the sites. That awareness led to a lifelong passion, one that has taken me back and forth across Britain on countless excursions, to explore the castles and comprehend their place in the landscape and in history.

Along the way, I have met many intriguing people, such as the farmer whose intimate knowledge about the castle on his property rivals anything a professional could know, to heritage professionals, to the members of the Castles Studies Group, to the average British citizen, whose sense of place and national identity is palpable. Each has inspired and enriched my life and heightened my awareness of the importance of preserving castles of all types, not only those that produce tourism income but also—and perhaps even more so—the ruins and eroding earthworks that are the only surviving tangible links to the past at those sites.

Writing this book has helped me solidify my beliefs about Britain's medieval castles, what they were, what they are, what they are not—and what they were never meant to be. I have been mocked for claiming that there are no true castles in America. My research has bolstered that position, which is based on fact, not mythology. This book has evolved from my own research, both in the field and in resource materials. I have also benefitted enormously from networking with scholars in the field of castle studies and other aspects of British history and heritage, and with other castle enthusiasts who appreciate and promote their continued presence in the countryside.

I would especially like to thank the following people for sharing their knowledge and enthusiasm with me and for their support on this project:

John R. Kenyon, librarian, National Museum and Gallery of Wales, whose expertise and contributions to castle studies—and my own education— are immeasurable.

Heather Staines, senior acquisitions editor for Praeger, who enthusiastically encouraged me to run with this project and provided helpful guidance along the way.

Lisa Pierce, senior development editor for Praeger, whose responsiveness, advice, and excitement were sources of reassurance.

And Joseph Kaufmann, author and founder of Site O, an international research/discussion group for people who have an interest in fortifications and/or artillery (www.siteo.net) for connecting me with Greenwood Publishing Group in the first place.

Last, but by no means least, my enduring thanks is also extended to my husband, my family, and to M. J. Klimenko for encouraging my journey.

Introduction

WHAT IS A CASTLE?

Those of us who live in places where castles never thrived often grow up believing that Disney's Cinderella Castle, with its palatial staircases, spires rising to the skies, and pristine bejewelled furnishings fit for Prince Charming, firmly represents the medieval castle. The proliferation of photos of Mad Ludwig's Neuschwanstein in magazines, books, and even on jigsaw puzzle boxes reinforces that notion. So does bestowing regal names on buildings that are no more than grand mansions, like Hearst Castle at San Simeon or Belcourt Castle in Newport, Rhode Island. While such buildings were certainly pleasure palaces for their owners, built to impress their guests and passersby, none is a castle in the true sense of the term. None dates any earlier than the eighteenth century, and none of the builders intended them as military strongholds. Declaring their flamboyant homes as castles, men like Mad Ludwig of Bavaria, William Randolph Hearst, and Oliver Hazard Perry Belmont intended to send an unspoken message to the world: "Look at me! I am fabulously wealthy, incredibly important, and possess what you should covet but can only hope to achieve."

When arriving at an authentic castle, uninitiated visitors are sometimes disappointed. They expect to see an occupied, completely intact castle, like Windsor, with its State Apartments fitted for royalty, bearskin-topped guardsmen wearing scarlet jackets standing stoically at attention. Instead, they more often encounter crumbling masses of blocky stone, empty shells of structures whose original forms have decayed to the point that they can no longer be easily visualized, or grassy humps of bracken-laden earth surrounded by marshy fields and grazing cows. Some people recoil at the notion that indeed all three of these types of structure qualify as true castles, especially when they learn that palatial structures like Scotland's Balmoral Castle do not.

Chunks of broken-down rock may appear to be all that survives of a great stone fortress. In some ways, it seems understandable that the inexperienced onlooker questions that the substance is a castle. However, most ruined castles do retain some defensive and residential features that support their ongoing characterization as castles. Enclosing ditches, portcullis grooves, and drawbar holes all reveal a ruin's defensive nature, while foundations of buildings lining a curtain wall or fragments of decoration bespeak of past roles as halls, solars, or chapels. For example, almost completely demolished at the end of the English Civil War, South Yorkshire's Pontefract Castle may now seem devoid of the main features that contributed to its reputation as one of the Middle Ages' grandest fortresses. Yet, closer examination reveals a more glorious past, which featured a multilobed, three-storied, great tower encasing a substantial motte, a dungeon, the historic well chamber—reputedly Richard II's prison—in the outer bailey, and an encompassing ditch. Sometimes all that visitors need are a vivid imagination and some basic knowledge about castles in order to comprehend the enormity of such sites and how they were originally used. However, amateur detectives exploring Pontefract's castle will be able to identify evidence of its residential role, in the form of bread ovens, a hearth, latrine, foundations of a hall and two chapels, and even the discreetly placed well chamber.

Having grown up in the United States and developed an interest in archaeology and historic preservation before adolescence, I visited scores of historic homes, including the magnificent mansions in Newport, Rhode Island. I also wandered Civil War battlefields and explored National Monuments, saw several places where George Washington slept, and even participated in the excavation of a tannery site where Baylor's Dragoons were slaughtered and buried during the American Revolution. I attended lectures on archaeological findings at the Metropolitan Museum of Art in New York City and visited dozens of other museums. I studied archaeology in undergraduate and graduate schools, obtaining a master's degree specializing in Historic Preservation before entering the U.S. Navy in 1984. Up to that point in my life, my exposure to American "castles" had come in the forms of the Gingerbread Castle, in Hamburg, New Jersey, an early theme park based on the Hansel and Gretel fairy tale; Dick's Castle, then a derelict residence in Garrison, New York; the mansard-roofed Belcourt Castle, in Newport, Rhode Island; and, of course, Cinderella's dazzling castle in Orlando, Florida. Even though I recognized them as the classy structures they were built to be, I realized on a gut level that they were not really castles.

Spotting my first castle, Llansteffan, from the window of a passenger train as it loped along the Tywi estuary enroute my new military posting in Pembrokeshire in 1985, I felt an immediate surge of adrenaline. That view ultimately led me to jaunts throughout the countryside, initially as a casual visitor, awestruck with the visual impact castles had on me, their aging endurance and the romance they exuded. I could almost hear the stones speak. Soon, I took up full-time castle research and, to date, I have explored well over 300 castles in Wales, England, Scotland, Ireland, and Germany. I have explored most of the castles repeatedly and have gained a familiarity with them that verges on intimacy. I admit to having had my own set of preconceptions about castles, not so much based on the fairy-tale fantasies of childhood, but on what many movies suggest—that castles really had only one purpose: to keep out invaders and withstand sieges. However, as I became increasingly familiar with castle architecture, I came to recognize that certain basic features were common to all medieval castles: defensive structures, such as ditches or towers, and residential facilities, most notably, a hall and kitchen, chambers for the lord—and the occasional latrine. I also developed an understanding that, much more important to the castle-builder was the perpetuation of his control over an area and the maintenance of his lordship. The medieval castle fulfilled that goal, as readers will discover herein.

In countries studded with castles, such as Britain, nineteenth-century "Normanized" shams compete for attention with their medieval counterparts. Designed to mimic the mighty fortresses of old, grand residences like Penrhyn and Cyfarthfa castles in Wales are adorned with battlements, fitted with massive towers and neo-Norman interiors, and fronted with gatehouses that threatened and impressed all comers. Yet, transport them back to the Middle Ages, and neither castle would withstand a siege. They were never intended for that purpose. Rather, their owners, many of whom were rich industrialists who had gained their fortunes from the backbreaking production of laborers in coal mines, slate quarries, and ironworks, who earned a mere pittance of what their bosses earned, modeled their stately residences on medieval precursors, which exuded the power, wealth, and success that modern "barons" craved (and in some cases, achieved) during the Industrial Revolution. In Wales, ironmaster William Crawshay, for example, actually planted Cyfarthfa Castle on a grassy knoll near Merthyr Tydfil not only to overawe his workers, who lived in dilapidated cottages nearby, but also to physically remind them of their lowly position at his feet. Though these are majestic structures in their own right, the castellated residences of the eighteenth and nineteenth centuries are not real castles.

From the eleventh to fifteenth centuries, the British landscape sprouted castles almost as quickly as the wheat that sustained its burgeoning population. Ultimately, during its heyday of castle-building, Britain may have supported several thousand castles. Not all were necessarily active at the same moment in time. Nowadays, the remains of countless castles scatter the British countryside, towering over towns, hidden behind farmhouses and pubs, occasionally still barred from access to intruders, and sometimes still privately owned. No matter their present condition, each retains its own personality, its unique history and architectural tradition, and its distinctive reasons for being. Yet, every castle served the same two overriding purposes, one military, the other residential.

DEFENDED SETTLEMENTS

The phenomenon of fortification-building was not new to the Middle Ages. For millennia, humans have felt the need to protect themselves and their territory and have erected fortifications to provide safety and security from the elements and also from covetous neighbors. Well before the first castle arrived in England, fortified settlements occupied craggy hilltops and jutting coastal headlands throughout the British Isles. Many still dominate those sites and are easy to spot on a day's outing. Many, like Maiden Castle in Dorset, date to the Iron Age and have acquired place-names that imply a dual usage as a properly fortified military residence. In some ways, the military terminology can be extended to cover many of these fortifications. Nonetheless, these premedieval structures lacked the essential ingredient that would otherwise characterize them as true castles: private ownership.

The univallate and multivallate sites of prehistory offered substantial protection from an attack or prehistoric livestock rustling, functioning as fortified communal settlements (comparable to medieval walled towns) rather than individual ranches. The group's leader or chief probably lived in a separate, private dwelling at the site, but his home was just one part of the whole complex, which often formed a densely occupied settlement. Some hillforts and promontory forts, which guarded headland settlements, served as supply and distribution centers, granaries, animal pounds, and possibly as military establishments or ritual sites.[1] Many times, embedded rings of steep-sided earthen ramparts and deep ditches defended the entire settlement, sometimes cut into chalk-beds, buttressed with timber posts or compacted stone, and stockaded with timber palisades. Like medieval castles, many defended settlements were fronted with substantial gateways. However, these prehistoric earthwork forts were never intended exclusively for use as fortified private residences.

Arguably Britain's most legendary Iron Age fort, Cadbury Castle commands a hilltop overlooking the tiny village of thatched stone cottages in South Cadbury, Somerset. Long touted as the site of King Arthur's Camelot, archaeological excavations directed by Leslie Alcock from 1966 to 1970 targeted portions of the enormous multivallate fort, the summit of which covered 18 acres. The effort revealed that the fort was occupied as early as 3300 BC, during the Neolithic era, and that Bronze Age and Iron Age peoples added the defenses, lined the concentric ramparts with limestone slabs and deepened the ditches. By 100 BC, the entire set of four ramparts and ditches had been completed and small huts and storage pits filled the summit and accommodated the expanding settlement.

During the first century AD, the Romans devastated the hilltop settlement, the home of the Durotriges, members of the Celtic tribe based at Dorchester (then known by the Roman name, Durnovaria) who commanded at least twenty hillforts in southern England, including mammoth Maiden Castle. The bodies of thirty adults and children slaughtered by the Romans lay buried at the southwest entrance to Cadbury Castle until their discovery in the 1960s. In addition to collecting scores of pottery sherds imported from France and the Mediterranean, archaeologists discovered the remains of a large timber hall, dating to about AD 500.[2] Whether or not the man who spawned the Arthurian legends actually called this place his palace, someone of considerable status—perhaps a chieftain—decided the hillfort should be reoccupied and ordered the construction of the timber-framed structure. Perhaps, the leader administered justice and watched over the surrounding lands from this fine vantage point and guided his community into a period of sought-after calm after the Romans retreated from England. Some historians believe Cadbury Castle could very well have been the inspiration for Camelot.

At the time of the Roman invasion of Britain in AD 43, Iron Age hillforts teemed with activity. However, their defenses were no match for the technologically advanced outsiders, who swiftly devastated the fortified settlements and established their own encampments and military bases to keep order in the land. Like hillforts, Roman camps and forts were just that, military enterprises that provided soldiers with communal barracks and other facilities, which made life in the cool, damp British countryside as comfortable as possible. The basic Roman fort followed a standardized rectangular plan and had rounded corners. They were never intended to house kings or lords, but to accommodate military forces. In addition to their forts, the Romans enforced their conquest of Britain with other military engineering projects. Road networks linked smaller forts to the greater legionary fortresses at Chester, Caerleon, and York, and allowed the Romans to control passage through frontier regions (particularly between England and Wales) and to progressively expand throughout both areas.

Gradually, as the conquerors lingered in Britain, the indigenous populations either retreated to the fringes of their home territories or adapted themselves to the Roman ways. Many Romano-Britains built palaces and villas, like those at Fishbourne in West Sussex and Chedworth in Gloucestershire, both of which easily rivaled anything the Romans themselves constructed in Britain. However, some tribal groups, such as the Picts in Scotland, continued to threaten the foreigners and forced the Romans to take drastic action to prevent them from forcing their way into England. Intending to once and for all quash invasion from the north, Emperor Hadrian ordered the construction of a formidable barrier across northern England in AD 122, which expanded upon an already established line of forts stretching across what was known as the Stanegate area. Begun during the reign of Emperor Trajan, the Stanegate itself originated as a Roman road linking forts at Carlisle, Brampton, Nether Denton, Carvoran, Vindolanda, Newbrough, and Corbridge with smaller watchtowers and fortlets stationed in between.[3] However, the presence of the forts did little to dissuade the northern tribes from raiding the lands Rome considered its own. In response, Hadrian ordered the construction of a stone wall to fortify the Stanegate road.

Hadrian's Wall is, arguably, the greatest legacy left by the Romans to Britain. Running over 70 miles eastward from the Solway estuary, west of Bowness, to Wallsend, just east of Newcastle, the stone and earthwork fortification remains a monumental feat of engineering. Largely complete by AD 125, the ditch-fronted wall ran over craggy hilltops and plunged through valleys, connecting watch turrets to more substantial fortifications, like the huge fort at Housesteads in Northumberland, which the wall skirts on its northern perimeter and was designed to accommodate a garrison of 800 soldiers. With its ramparts, headquarters building, commandant's house, hospital, barracks, latrines, kitchens, storage facilities, and stables, Housesteads remains a classic example of a Roman fort, despite its now ruined condition.

Besides the major forts and a lengthy earthwork known as the "vallum," small walled enclosures with gateways on their northern and southern sides stood watch over the frontier along the wall's entire length. Positioned about every mile on the southern side of the wall, these simple "milecastles" were entirely military features, each garrisoned by twenty soldiers. Barracks and other facilities built nearby, but not inside, the enclosures met the men's basic needs.

The fortifications employed by the Romans throughout their empire cannot—and should not—be characterized as castles. True, they were fortified, and most contained residential buildings. But, their role within the empire was to reinforce the military supremacy of the Romans over their conquered subjects. They were public establishments founded to contain an army and provide soldiers with a moderate state of comfortable living and defensive muscle. Legionary fortresses, like Caerleon near Newport, also provided many of Rome's pleasures, including a baths complex for leisure time and a barracks fitted with latrines. Nonetheless, Isca, the fortress of the second Legion Augusta at Caerleon, was built solely to provide the basic needs of an occupying force and to establish an intimidating military presence on the southern Welsh border with England.

PRIVATE DEFENSES:
A MEDIEVAL PHENOMENON

What was new to the Middle Ages was the trend away from the fortified settlement that commanded an area toward the privately defended fortress, which served a variety of purposes but was owned and used by a single individual, a lord, monarch, or his representative. As early as 862, King Charles the Bald ordered a massive castle-building program in France to thwart invasions from the neighboring Normans. However, within two years, so many castles had been built that Charles ordered the demolition of all private castles, forts, and enclosures and required builders to first obtain a license before beginning construction. The oldest surviving castle, an earth and timber fortification known as a "motte," reputedly exists at Mont Glonne, on the River Loire, and dates to 990.

In addition to mottes, the French widely erected stone castles, the oldest of which include Peyrepertuse in the Pyrenees, Chateau de Coudray at Chinon, the castle at Rouen that replaced the motte built by a Viking named Rollo, and Doue-la-Fontaine. Fulk Nerra, Count of Anjou, was one of the most prolific castle builders in early eleventh-century France. He erected at least thirteen castles, including Chateau Gontier, Durtal, Bauge, Montlevrier, Passavant, Montreuil-Bellay, Faye-la-Vineuse, Montcontour, Mirebeau, Langeais, Montresor, Sainte-Maure, and Chaumont. Like the Normans in England, Nerra used castles as a conspicuous way to showcase his feudal authority within France.

For almost a century, historians have debated whether the Normans introduced the idea and practice of castle-building when they conquered England in 1066. We do know the Saxons built long dykes, earthen ramparts flanked by deep ditches that barred passage between regions. Of these, Offa's

Dyke is arguably the best known. Erected in the late eighth century by the king of Mercia, the linear earthwork stretched along the border between England and Wales and performed a defensive function. At least in theory, the earthen barrier prevented the Welsh in Powys from storming into England.

In addition to earthen embankments, the Saxons constructed other fortifications prior to the Norman Conquest. Excavations at some earth and timber castles in England, including Goltho and Stamford in Lincolnshire and Sulgrave in Northamptonshire, have revealed the presence of pre-Conquest timber halls fortified to some degree with earthworks underneath the Norman castles. Goltho, for example, may have been enclosed as early as the mid–ninth century with earthworks and a ditch. Whether or not the defended halls served the same function as the Norman castles that replaced them remains unestablished, yet it seems reasonable to presume that the homes of the leading Saxons would have required at least some form of protection, particularly from the Vikings, who were in full swing at this time, and also from regional rivals. These fortified halls may represent an early form of "castle" as defined in this book. Some historians characterize these sites as "burhs," individual structures that centered a Saxon lordship and where the local leader received payments and services from the populace;[4] others apply the term only to the fortified communal settlements occupied by the Saxons during the early Middle Ages.

The *Burghal Hidage*, written in the early tenth century, documents that Alfred the Great, King of Wessex from AD 871–899, established thirty-three burhs at a distance of 20 miles apart to prevent the Danes from taking over southern England.[5] The unusual record provides fascinating details of each burh, detailing its size, the length of the ramparts, and the number of men needed to garrison the site. Saxon builders often reused existing Roman walls as ready-made enclosures for a new burh, but also constructed timber-revetted earthen ramparts to defend the settlements. While some burhs primarily served a military purpose comparable to a Roman fort, many were noteworthy administrative or population centers. New inhabitants received land in the burhs in exchange for providing defensive support when necessary; the system seems notably similar to feudalism, the establishment of which historians generally credit to the Normans. The largest Saxons burhs included Wallingford in Oxfordshire, Southwark near London, Wareham in Dorset, and Chichester in West Sussex.

Considerable evidence also exists that the Saxons established a burh known as "Bircloyt" at Rhuddlan, in Denbighshire, which was later superseded by a motte castle, built by Robert of Rhuddlan to establish a Norman presence in an area long controlled by the Saxons. In short, even though archaeologists have unearthed evidence that the Saxon leaders may have erected private residences that were fortified to some degree, they apparently favored the defended community settlement, which confirmed their dominance in the area and also provided protection from outside attack. True castles, however, did not arrive in Wales until the Norman incursion after 1066.

In pre-Norman Wales, native Celtic rulers lived in large halls, known as "neuadd," protected by weakly fortified walls. Some, like Dinefwr in Carmarthenshire, were later rebuilt as stone castles. Royal courts evidently served as the main residence, the "llys" or royal palace, of the native princes. Like the neuadd, each llys was enclosed with a defensive wall. The llys at Rhosyr, near Newborough on the Isle of Anglesey, was only recently excavated. Notable finds included the foundations of two timber halls, lengths of the stone enclosure wall, and other structures. Such structures suggest functional similarities with medieval castles, in that the llys was a private residence with some degree of fortification and was used to carry out the business of the commote (or district) in which it was centered. However, at best, these structures should probably be classified more as residences than as fortified structures.

PRE-CONQUEST CASTLES

Inasmuch as archaeologists and historians still debate the exact timing of the introduction of castles into Britain, most now agree that at least three, and perhaps four, earthwork castles predate the Norman Conquest by more than a decade. Substantiated by entries in *The Anglo-Saxon Chronicle*, which record the existence of a "castle in Herefordshire" built by "foreigners" whose presence insulted the Saxons in 1051, and two others in 1052, known as "Pentecost's castle" and "Robert's castle,"[6] many castellologists speculate that the border castles at Hereford and Ewyas Harold represent the first two castles mentioned in the *Chronicle*, while the motte castle in Clavering, Essex, reputedly erected by Robert Fitz Wymarc, may have been the aforementioned Robert's Castle.[7] The fourth pre-Conquest castle is believed to have been Richard's Castle, a motte and bailey site on the border between Herefordshire and Shropshire probably erected by Richard FitzScrob, one of the Normans who arrived in England during the reign of Edward the Confessor.[8] In 1988, D. J. Cathcart King stated unequivocally that "Ewyas Harold, whether or not it can be identified as Pentecost's Castle, is the one certain pre-Conquest castle in England; it is described as having been refortified by 'earl William' (fitzOsbern, who reached the border in 1067, quitted England for ever in 1070, and was slain next year)."[9]

EWYAS HAROLD CASTLE. The tree-covered motte at Ewyas Harold on the English border with Wales in Herefordshire is one of only four castles in Britain that probably predate the Norman Conquest in 1066.

What makes these few motte castles particularly noteworthy is that they were built at least a decade prior to the Norman Conquest but were typically Norman in design. In a period when earth and timber castles had yet to make a significant mark on the British landscape but had been proliferating alongside stone castles in France for at least fifty years and had already made their appearance elsewhere in Europe, these three or four pre-Conquest castles are notably out of place. Though evidently erected by Norman followers (some of whom were also relatives) of Edward the Confessor, the reasons for their construction must have differed to some degree from what William of Normandy had in mind as he not only erected his own royal castles, but also as he parceled out the British countryside to his supporters, who built motte and ringwork castles and also began constructing them in stone. Rather than mechanisms of conquest, the pre-Conquest castles were early efforts to establish a Norman presence in the Welsh borders, and apparently also east of London, perhaps to display the Saxon king's affiliation with the French court, which he admired, perhaps to quell an imminent Welsh rebellion, or perhaps to reward his favorite supporters with lordships and land ownership. In any case, these four earth and timber structures appear to have been actual Norman castles; however, more detailed excavation is required in order to place them in their true medieval context.

FEUDALISM AND THE SPREAD OF CASTLES

Much more than merely being a medieval phenomenon, the appearance and proliferation of castles throughout Britain represented the enforced institutionalization of feudalism, which William the Conqueror imported from his homeland in Normandy. Feudalism originated in continental Europe during the latter stages of Carolingian rule, when the death of Charlemagne (Charles, King of the Franks and Holy Roman Emperor) in 814 resulted in political disunity. Civil war and widespread chaos highlighted by the invasion of the Vikings and other foreign raiders, led to the development of feudalism as a way to reestablish centralized governmental control, provide security, and stabilize the economy. Essentially consisting of a network of mutual obligations, feudalism was based on personal honor and professed loyalty, each participant exchanging specific services that ostensibly solidified their position within the feudal hierarchy.

Though evidently known to some degree in Anglo-Saxon England, feudalism was not systemically instituted in England and Wales until the decades immediately following the Norman Conquest, and castles played a key role in its implementation. The new sociopolitical order was predicated on the establishment of lordships. The monarch (initially by King William I but by later kings as well) granted parcels of land (fiefs) to individual lords (vassals, vassals-in-chief, or tenants-in-chief, later known as barons)[10] as rewards for military service and loyalty during the Conquest. The lords, in turn, either subdivided the fiefs and appointed lesser lords (also known as vassals) to manage them or kept the largest parcels for themselves, in order to govern the land and directly reap economic and other material benefits. In return for these grants of land, the vassals paid homage to the king, paid rent (taxes), and fulfilled military obligations, as and when required. Depending on their social status, vassals agreed to provide a specific number of men for an army or to serve in the castle guard; the number of men was calculated according to the extent of the lord's holdings.

According to R. Allen Brown, castles were the physical embodiment of the lordship: they "dominated the countryside in every way, militarily, socially, politically, administratively and economically, and all these potencies were integrated and combined in it, and given deliberate architectural expression by it."[11] Their commanding presence in the landscape and their unfamiliar, intimidating appearance provided the vehicle by which the Normans and later lords could clearly demonstrate their supremacy within their new territory and their complete control over the conquered populace. In short, castles functioned as centers of feudal power. Their owners intentionally planted them in the countryside, not solely as defensive structures which protected the lord and his household from rampaging subjects but, more so, as offensive strongpoints from which the lord and his garrison controlled a region. Indeed, among their other roles, castles were an in-your-face, ever-present enforcer of subjugation and an obvious reminder of feudal obligation.

Over time, control of a lordship or fief—and the associated castle—became hereditary; heirs not only acquired vast estates but also the laborers (serfs) bound to the land. Three of the most powerful Norman feudal lords—Hugh d'Avranches, Earl of Chester; Roger de Montgomery, Earl of Shrewsbury; and William FitzOsbern, Earl of Hereford—controlled the Welsh Marches, the border region between England and Wales, as unofficial kings in their own right. William the Conqueror not only granted them huge parcels of land to govern but also gave them the legal authority to enforce laws as if they ruled their own kingdoms. Such men used castles to demonstrate their newly acquired status within the feudal hierarchy.

In Scotland, the introduction of feudalism had less to do with conquest per se, but rather with the reigning monarch's interest in establishing a governing system that he would head. In the early twelfth century, having been educated in the courts of the Henry I, the Norman king of England, David I actually welcomed the Normans into his Scottish kingdom, encouraging their settlement with the establishment of lordships and the concomitant construction of castles. Among the Normans who migrated to Scotland and made names for themselves were the de Brus (or Bruce) family, the Comyns, Haigs, Hays, Ramsays, and Sinclairs, each of whom played significant roles in Scottish history and also erected several noteworthy strongholds, such as Blair in Perth and Kinross, Inverlochy in Highland, Neidpath in the Borders, and Dalhousie in Mid Lothian. Interestingly, unlike the situation in the rest of Britain, many of Scotland's pre-Norman population, including the Earls of Atholl, Fife, and Strathearn, also acquired feudal lordships.[12]

Not only did King David I and his grandsons Malcolm IV and William I (the Lion) invite notable Norman lords and their families to move to Scotland, they also encouraged several monastic communities from France to found abbeys and priories and to spread Roman Catholicism. The movement of Augustinian, Cistercian, and other religious orders into the Scottish Borders resulted in the construction of several major monasteries, including those at Kelso, Melrose, Jedburgh, and Dryburgh. In England and Wales, William I of Normandy and his heirs also welcomed the development of monastic communities, including several in North Yorkshire, such as Rievaulx and Fountains abbeys.

The rapid spread of motte, ringwork, and stone castles throughout the British Isles was the physical manifestation of the dramatically changing social order of the times, as the Normans progressively established power bases throughout England and Wales in the decades after 1066, and shortly thereafter moved into Scotland and Ireland.

DEFINING THE "CASTLE"

Plantagenet Somerset Fry's definition of a castle has long resonated with me: "the castle was a *properly fortified military residence*, which is as exact a definition as can be given."[13] R. Allen Brown puts forth the following definition: "Castles were not just fortresses but also residences, albeit the residences of the great. It is this *unique combination of the military and the residential functions* which makes a castle, and makes it differ from other types of fortifications of other periods, earlier or later."[14] Brown also emphasizes that the residential role of the castle had at least as much importance as its military role.

Certainly, Fry's and Brown's definitions complement each other; even the most ruinous of castles still retain evidence of these dual—essentially symbiotic—purposes. Eroded mottes continue to convey their importance as elevated platforms from which watchmen had distant views of the surrounding countryside and upon which timber towers or shell keeps occupied positions of relative safety. While the vast majority of timber towers do not survive, the flattened summits or keep fragments provide evidence of habitation. Over time, more complex stone fortresses either engulfed their earthen predecessors, motte and ringwork castles, or replaced them completely. For example, at Rhuddlan, the massive Norman motte, Twthill, which had previously superseded the Saxon burh, became obsolete when Edward I began to build the diamond-shaped concentric fortress several hundred feet to the north. Despite their eventual obsolescence, the earthen mounds and ringworks persist throughout the British countryside. Passersby not accustomed to recognizing the eroding mounds as castles may ignore them in their pursuit of stone fortresses, whose masonry towers and battlemented curtain walls, they believe, surely prove the power and grandiose lifestyles of their inhabitants. Yet, mottes and ringworks, and accompanying baileys, played the same basic roles for their builders that more formidable masonry strongholds also performed.

The diversity of castle design is striking. Not only did castles of the same type differ from each other, no two contemporary castles followed the same standard design. True, elements of every castle were standard; for example, all castles contained a living chamber and some sort of defense. Yet, their builders applied the same basic technology and building materials to create unique structures. As Robert Higham points out, "we should not view timber castles as a separate 'type' of castle, but rather as a variation on a theme. Castle designers aimed to meet similar requirements of defense and residence with whatever building technology and materials were available at their disposal. Timber might be chosen because no suitable stone was available, or because the builder could not afford to buy stone, or because speed of erection was essential, or because only short-term use for the site was envisaged."[15]

Clearly, their castles meant different things to different builders. They served much more than a basic "protect thy lord and his household" function. The extent of fortification, the layout of the internal structures, the choice of location, and the grandiosity of ornamentation all reflected the needs, expectations, and idiosyncrasies of the men who built and lived in them. Castles were much more than defensive structures built to protect the lord and residents. They were much more than grand homes for the monarch or regional ruler. Indeed, they were much more than merely functional facilities; otherwise, castles could have easily been built to a standard plan. While the structure itself was built to contain all the buildings the lord considered essential to the operation of his lordship, how the buildings were laid out—the image they presented to others—was as carefully, sometimes obsessively, contemplated as their ability to provide life's daily military and domestic requirements.

As society in the Middle Ages shifted and developed, so did castle-building. Advances in warfare technology also led to changes in castle design, the complexity of fortifications, and the role played by the castle in medieval society. The ultimate form a castle took was also dictated by the goals and personality of its builder. Many were more heavily defended, essentially more military, while others were primarily residential but also had defensive structures. Tower houses dominated the borders between Scotland and England and were also widespread in Ireland. Their thick, battlemented walls dutifully, though not necessarily comfortably, provided residents with their most basic needs: shelter and a sense of safety. They also symbolically displayed their owner's status, for, despite their simplicity and compact size, not everyone could afford to build a tower house. For those that could, the tower house filled a gap in the political order of the region. They were properly, albeit lightly, fortified residences that served an occasional military role.

Britain's medieval castles served individual overlords, who resided inside perhaps only part of the year but who retained control over the surrounding countryside, reaping the economic benefits of possessing the lordship and manorial estates. Only occasionally in times of war were these fortified private residences used as refuges for the local population. Not only did the construction of castles reiterate that the Normans now controlled the kingdom but their permanent presence in the landscape also emphasized the increasing responsibility placed on the individual leader as the commander of a region, whose separate status from the general populace and prestigious political position as the monarch's representative warranted a dwelling worthy of that status, one that provided distinct living arrangements as well as defensive might—the castle.

CHAPTER 1

Castles as Offensive Weapons

Castles: "the architectural manifestation of feudal society."
—R. Allen Brown, *Castles: A History and Guide* (1980), 16

It's simple enough to look at a castle, a fortified military residence built for private use in the Middle Ages, and make assumptions about its various functions, not only deciding what it meant to the owner-builder but also to society as a whole. Or is it? Castles must not be viewed in a vacuum. Rather than making judgments about their functions purely based on their exterior appearance, one must consider the context in which they were built: who built them, when they were built, what was happening in Britain at the times they were built, and what motivated their builders.

CONQUEST BY CASTLE

Among the relics of the medieval world, the Bayeux Tapestry ranks as one of its greatest treasures. Not only does the skillfully embroidered wall hanging remain in outstanding condition, the 230-foot-long series of panels vividly depicts one of history's most important events—the Norman Conquest of Saxon England. Chronicling the entire saga, from events leading up to the invasion, initial preparations and shipbuilding, to the Norman fleet's arrival in England, the construction of castles on both sides of the Channel, the Battle of Hastings, and William's coronation, the colorful masterpiece commemorates the victory of the Normans over the Saxons.

Probably commissioned in 1070 by Odo, the Bishop of Bayeux and William the Conqueror's half brother, and undoubtedly biased in favor of the Duke of Normandy, the wool-and-linen tapestry hangs in Bayeux in the Centre Guillaume le Conquérant. Historians, military enthusiasts, and craftspeople have studied and evaluated the magnificent creation for the authenticity of its details and its extensive insight into Norman military strategies, soldiers' garb, ship construction, and even castle construction. The tapestry reminded everyone that, after William's victory over the Saxon king, Harold II, the Norman kings dominated the English throne. During their reign, they implemented feudalism and introduced castles as one of their most powerful tools for wielding authority over their new subjects.

Besides depicting castles already in use in France, the Bayeux Tapestry illustrates the construction of several actual castles, including Dol and Dinan in Normandy, and Hastings in England, in a stylized yet easily understandable way. All were standard motte castles, mounds of layered earth topped with timber parapets, which the Normans built in their own homeland and introduced into Britain as a quick and effective means of subduing the English in the decades immediately after 1066. Between 1066 and 1215, approximately 700 motte castles and over 200 ringwork castles appeared in the English countryside,[1] and scores of others were erected in Wales. Scotland and Ireland received motte castles, but their differing political situations resulted in the greater construction of stone castles and tower houses. That is not to say that England and Wales did not receive their fair share of stone castles. Indeed, the Normans were busily building stone castles at the same time as the more primitive earth and timber strongholds. Among the most notable examples are Chepstow Castle in Monmouthshire, which is now believed to date to 1081, and the White Tower, which centers the Tower of London.

The castles of the Norman Conquest were largely offensive weapons used by the Normans to solidify control over the areas they progressively seized from the Saxons and the Welsh, and later from the Irish as well. The conquest of Britain was a piecemeal process, which began with the defeat of Harold Godwinson near Hastings and the coronation of Duke William of Normandy as King William I of England. However, even though William's men had slain the Saxon king, the Conquest was not yet complete. William recognized that his new subjects might well rebel against his authority—and, in fact, so they did. Consequently, he instigated a program whereby he erected castles in several of the larger Saxon towns, or burhs, in England, including not only the establishment of his capital in London but also the deliberate demolition of Saxon homes and the construction of castles in urbanized settlements, as at Nottingham, Warwick, Lincoln, York—and some forty other population centers in England.

WILLIAM THE CONQUEROR: BRITAIN'S FIRST CASTLE-BUILDING KING

Even though *The Anglo-Saxon Chronicle* offers evidence that the French (probably Normans) erected a few motte castles in the border region between England and Wales, and perhaps in Essex, prior to 1066 (see introduction), the vast majority of Norman strongholds appeared in the century immediately after the Conquest. Indeed, when Duke William of Normandy's army bested the Saxons in late 1066, his men had already erected a few simple earthwork fortifications in England, which displayed his power and foreshadowed the defeat of the Saxons. At Pevensey, in West Sussex, where William and his fleet first landed in September 1066, the Normans immediately constructed a castle inside the extant, albeit, crumbling defenses abandoned by the Romans six centuries earlier. Recognizing the need for speed as they began their march toward Hastings, William's men dug a ditch inside the Roman walls at Pevensey and piled the soil and rubble alongside to form an earthen embankment, or partial enclosure, which was probably topped with timber palisades. Only after becoming king did William grant Pevensey to his half brother, Robert, Count of Mortain, who refortified the stronghold with masonry defenses and began its conversion into a substantial fortress poised to defend the coastline from seaborne assault.

After his victory at the Battle of Hastings, William I ordered the construction of several fortifications not merely to form a barrier to protect London from outside attack but largely to provide himself with a significant power base from which to rule his new kingdom and consolidate the Conquest. Requiring brawn rather than skilled labor, raising earth and timber castles was a rapid, relatively simple, cost-effective way to establish a presence—and physically proclaim overlordship—in an area. While archaeologists have determined that the majority of Norman earth and timber castles featured a sturdy mound, a "motte," which supported a timber tower, and an adjacent "bailey," or defended enclosure, many of William's earliest strongholds in England were substantial earthen embankments fronted with a ditch, which enclosed an area. Inside the enclosure, soldiers and their commanders gathered, awaited orders, and prepared for their next foray into the countryside. Now commonly known as "ringwork castles," R. Allen Brown has characterized such structures as "enclosure castles" based on their plan,[2] while John

Kenyon describes them as "campaign castles,"[3] structures thrown up to quickly seize a spot during the initial stages of a military campaign.

Besides building the enclosure castle (a ringwork) at Pevensey and the motte castle at Hastings in Kent, which overlooked the Saxon town of the same name, just prior to the Conquest, the Normans swiftly planted an enclosure castle on top of the Saxon settlement at Dover and also added a ringwork castle inside the Roman fortifications at Londinium. The site became William's capital and the castle soon developed into one of the world's premier stone fortresses, the Tower of London. William I quite likely also erected earth and timber castles or reused Saxon fortifications when he stopped at Canterbury in Kent and Berkhamsted in Hertfordshire, prior to marching into London in 1066.[4] During William's absence from England in 1067, during which he returned to Normandy for ten months, the Normans erected a ringwork castle at Winchester, the Roman town that had been the Saxon capital. Upon the king's return later that year, he began construction on a ringwork castle at Exeter, another settlement established by the Romans and occupied by the Saxons.[5] A pattern was beginning to emerge as the Normans methodically entered towns and settlements previously dominated by the Romans or Saxons and supplanted the earlier sites with their own strongholds. Most Saxons had never seen such strange-looking earth and timber structures; the unfamiliar architecture served not only as an ever-present reminder of foreign oppression but also as a symbol of the new order.

Ideally, unskilled laborers could construct a ringwork in a matter of days in order to secure a spot and establish a concrete presence for the Normans within their new kingdom. The classic ringwork, or earthen enclosure castle, featured a mound of low to moderate size encircled with ditches and earthen banks, which were topped with timber palisades. The summit of the fittingly named stronghold was scooped out, so that the outer perimeter stood higher than the center of the mound. Unlike the motte and bailey castles, fewer ringwork castles acquired substantial stone structures, and many have long since been leveled. Some ringwork castles, like Castle Neroche,[6] were reused, converted into baileys to support adjoining mottes, the construction of which would have improved the offensive capacity of the site while creating a visible reminder of the Conquest. Besides Exeter, fine examples of ringworks reinforced with masonry structures can be found at Castle Rising in Norfolk and Restormel Castle in Cornwall and

GWERN Y DOMEN. One of Glamorgan's finest ringwork castles, Gwern y Domen retains its earthen embankments and associated bailey despite the encroachment of a railroad line and nearby roadworks.

Coity and Ogmore castles in Glamorgan. Other ringworks survive as well, for example, at Deddington in Oxfordshire, and Caerau and Gwern y Domen in Glamorgan.

A typical motte castle consisted of an artificially sculpted, flat-topped mound, packed with earth and often revetted with timber and stone. Rising well above ground level, mottes varied in height from as little as 5 or 6 feet to well over 50 feet, the diameters of their summits ranging from 20 feet to 380 feet across (as was the case with Norwich Castle, in Norfolk). Builders often reshaped natural hillocks for use as mottes or piled field stones or earth taken from what became the enclosing ditch onto the mound to create a usable foundation for timber (and, later, for stone) structures. Most motte castles were supported by at least one large rounded area, the bailey, which was enclosed by earthen embankments and defended with timber palisades. Construction required little skilled labor and could proceed quickly and inexpensively. While some historians allege that motte castles could have been completed in as little as a week, more than likely it took at least several weeks to months to finish each project. Nonetheless, along with ringworks, motte and bailey castles were the Normans' weapon of choice when it came to pacifying newly seized territory. Impressive examples survive at Berkhamsted in Hertfordshire, Pickering in North Yorkshire, Ewyas Harold in Herefordshire, Wiston in Pembrokeshire, and Tomen y Rhodwydd in Denbighshire.

For about a century, historians have varied in their estimates of the number of Norman motte and ringwork castles erected in England and Wales. This is not really surprising, as the historical record for the eleventh and twelfth centuries, when most mottes and ringworks were erected, is incomplete at best; likewise, the archaeological record is incomplete, for many earthwork castles have been demolished, plowed into oblivion or leveled to make space for other structures. Other structures once categorized as motte castles have been reclassified as ringworks, or other types of sites, including prehistoric barrows. Nonetheless, Richard Eales speculates that, given the historical and archaeological evidence and conclusions made by previous researchers, quite possibly some 950 to 1,150 "early Norman castles" existed in the landscape prior to 1200, with an average of between 500 and 600 in use at the same time.[7] Unfortunately, the high expense and considerable effort involved in excavating motte and ringwork castles have prevented researchers from making reasonably accurate conclusions on this issue.

Interestingly, the earliest ringwork castles appeared in Wales during the first decade of the twelfth century, about thirty years after the first mottes and stone castles were built, begging the question of the purpose they served for the Normans. Many were quickly reinforced with stone, as at Coity, Ogmore, and Newcastle Bridgend, also in Glamorgan, all of which were lordship centers, while still others were relatively modest sites, perhaps functioning as the defended residences of less wealthy individuals. Some historians speculate that, by this time, the choice of erecting ringwork or motte in a certain area may have been more a matter of the lord's stylistic preference or the condition of the terrain, rather than a decision based on offensive strategies.[8] With twenty-eight identified ringwork castles and another nine possible ringworks, Glamorgan contains the highest concentration of this type of earth and timber fortification in Wales. For example, all of Glamorgan's ringworks were constructed either in the Vale of Glamorgan or on the southern coast of the Gower, where geological conditions apparently interfered with motte construction. In northern areas, mottes were primarily built on glacial ridges, which could be easily reshaped into defensive mounds. Some ringworks also incorporated glacial drift; however, in the main, ringworks were centered in low-lying areas underlain by limestone where glacial deposits did not exist.

CHOOSING THE RIGHT LOCATION

In addition to building their castles on sites long recognized for their strategic value, access to waterways and roads, and for their symbolic meaning, the Normans shrewdly chose to place their castles in locations that suited their political aspirations and military priorities—which, of course, meant the ongoing oppression of their subjects. While many castles, like Bamburgh in Northumberland, Stirling in Stirling, and Dinas Bran in Denbighshire, were situated on prominent hilltops or ridges that commanded attention and respect from miles away, many others occupied low-lying landscapes, marshy riversides, and peninsular sites. Castles were generally sited for the convenience of the lord and his household, so that they could efficiently administer the lordship during peacetime and also ensure replenishment and access for reinforcements during wartime. Castles acted as offensive staging points from which mounted and armed knights could conduct sorties or fully organized sieges against an enemy or launch sudden forays into the local countryside to swiftly quell a rebellion. Therefore, the area a castle controlled was directly proportional to the distance a group of soldiers could safely travel in a day (estimated to be about 10 miles)[9] and then return to the castle. Those castles placed along major communications routes, overlooking fording points, or in mountain passes commonly used to traverse a region could be expected to block unwanted or suspicious movement through an area, but only if that movement passed close enough to the castle that the garrison could catch sight of the activity and have enough time to organize and rush to the spot.

Just as the Saxons recognized the strategic importance of controlling the borderland between England and Wales and constructed lengthy earthwork barriers between the two countries and the Romans dealt with the vulnerability of the northern frontier of England by constructing Hadrian's Wall, the Normans likewise acknowledged the necessity to command the same areas, which remained sources of contention long after 1066. In fact, along the Welsh borders, also called "the Marches," scores of Norman-built earth and timber castles still dot the landscape. Throughout their history, both well before and long after the Norman Conquest, the Welsh had internal problems that diverted their attention from the encroachment of the Normans in the Marches. Their lack of unity, discussed below, not only created a power vacuum, which the Normans used to their advantage to move farther into Wales, the discord actually reinforced the Welsh sense of national pride and provoked rebellion after rebellion, the storming of castles, thirteenth-century conquest, the Act of Union in the sixteenth century, and an uneasy coexistence with England. While most of the earth and timber castles in the Welsh Marches have extensively eroded and lost their original timber or stone structures, many developed into formidable fortresses, like Ludlow in Shropshire, and Raglan and White Castles in Monmouthshire. Even in ruin, these three castles still command respect. Others Marcher castles, like those at Chirk in Wrexham, Shrewsbury in Shropshire, and Powis in Powys, have survived the ages little worse for the wear, having been continuously occupied and repaired by their owners. Marcher lords were men with regional power on a scale comparable to the king's, who collected rent, administered the regions' system, doled out punishment, and waged war as necessary.

Not only did the Anglo-Normans build Marcher castles to dominate the native Welsh population, they also raised frontier castles to establish control over their own countrymen. For example, Morlais Castle played a key role in the conflict between Gilbert de Clare II, Earl of Gloucester and Lord of Glamorgan, and his neighbor, Humphrey de Bohun, Earl of Hereford and Lord of Brecon, in the late thirteenth century. The site marked the borderland between the two lordships. When de Clare began building his new frontier castle, he was well aware that he would incite de Bohun to the brink of battle. Probably thrown up by de Clare in about 1288 on the site of an earlier Iron Age fort, the diamond-shaped castle occupied a limestone ridge that commanded the border between the two lordships. In January 1292, after both men had repeatedly led incursions into each other's territory, King Edward I threw them into the Tower of London and imposed hefty fines. Even though de Clare retained rights to the castle, his victory over de Bohun was short-lived. In 1294–1295, Madog ap Llywelyn led a Welsh attack on

Morlais Castle, after which it disappeared from the historical record. In the end, Humphrey de Bohun had the last laugh, for Gilbert de Clare died in late 1295, three years before the Lord of Brecon.

The sociopolitical structure in Scotland produced a different kind of relationship between the Scots and the English, which led to the rise of Robert the Bruce and the Stewart dynasty and resulted in centuries of almost constant feuding and warfare, in which castles played central roles. In the border region linking the two nations, the Normans erected a scattering of perhaps less than thirty motte and ringwork castles, far fewer than in the Welsh Marches, where researchers have estimated as many as 500 timber castles once existed. Nonetheless, the Normans recognized the importance of controlling the border with Scotland; in time, northern England—and southern Scotland—acquired scores of stone castles. Some were complex strongholds like Warkworth in Northumberland and Carlisle in Cumbria, which originated as motte castles; others, known as "pele towers" in England and "tower houses" in Scotland, resembled the typical Norman rectangular keep, the self-sufficient stone strongpoint erected inside the castle walls which also provided accommodation for the lord and his family. In time, Northumberland acquired more castles than any other part of England.

The chaotic political relationship between Scotland and England frequently sparked warfare, as one nation's army crossed the border into the other nation and attempted to seize wide swaths of countryside commanded from castles. For centuries, for example, the Scots waged sieges against the powerful Northumbrian castles at Warkworth, Alnwick, and Bamburgh, endeavoring to gain a foothold in northern England; for centuries, the English garrisoned the castles and fought to keep the Scots at bay. These border fortresses were prized possessions. Those who controlled them, controlled the region and wielded considerable power within the kingdom.

The real value of the border castles became obvious after 1296, when Edward I used them as bases from which to stage his assault on Scotland. Ironically, the great warrior-king was unable to conclude his conquest of Scotland before his death in 1307. Later monarchs, like Edward III, followed his example, and the border castles continued to play a central role in the ongoing strife, which ended only with the coronation of Scotland's James VI as James I, king of England, in 1603.

The strategic wisdom of locating castles in border regions cannot be understated. Clearly, attackers viewed the structures as physical symbols of outside oppression, objects to be seized or destroyed as opportunities presented themselves. During the 1090s, William (Rufus) II of England erected the first castle at Carlisle, an earth and timber fortress strategically situated some 10 miles from Scotland. Not surprisingly, the Scots repeatedly targeted the stronghold, which encroached upon their homeland and commanded the River Eden, which flowed from England into the Solway Firth and, beyond, to the Atlantic Ocean. Between 1173 and 1461, they besieged Carlisle Castle nine times, but managed only once to capture it.[10] Over time, Carlisle Castle acquired more powerful masonry defenses, which not only enhanced the garrison's ability to defend itself during a siege but also reemphasized the fact that having a strong castle to dominate the area could keep the local populace under control while also providing the owner with considerable authority and influence in royal circles.

CASTLES AND THE HARRYING OF SAXON ENGLAND

As William I anticipated, many Saxons did not readily accept their new king nor his Norman deputies. Rebellions continued to take place throughout England, in Hampshire and Kent, and moved northwards into Durham and Yorkshire. Consequently, in 1068, William instigated an extended program of "pacification," which he enforced by building ringwork and motte castles and simultaneously implementing feudal law. In fact, it took several decades for the Normans to subdue the populace in portions of the country, and some parts of the kingdom were never completely subdued. Castle construction spread northwards from London, as the Normans launched the "harrying of the north," ravaging the countryside, torching crops, and destroying houses intending to once-and-for-all conquer the still-rebellious Saxons, who were then led by Earls Morcar, Edwin, and Gospatric.

Just as Duke William of Normandy replaced the Saxon king, Harold II, many of King William I's new castles stood squarely on top of settlements formerly occupied by the Saxons, and even earlier, by the Romans. He undoubtedly recognized the psychological and symbolic impact such construction would have on his new subjects and intentionally reused Roman tiles and other building materials to establish associations with this powerful past civilization and to demonstrate Norman ascendancy. In London and its immediate environs, which served as the king's primary power base, William ordered the construction of three strongholds along the Thames, at Baynard's Castle, southwest of the city, and north of London, at Montfichet. Individual lords managed the latter two castles on behalf of the monarchy. Then, as the Normans made their way through the Saxon countryside during the harrying from 1068–1071, seizing the lands and killing their opponents, they erected motte castles at Warwick, York, Lincoln, Huntingdon, and Cambridge, and an enclosure castle at Nottingham. Each of these earth and timber castles had historical associations not only with the Saxons but with the Romans as well.

MOTTE AT WARWICK CASTLE. Even though the later masonry additions to Warwick Castle overshadow the simple earth and timber site, the motte still survives as a key part of the great stone enclosure castle in Warwickshire.

Scores of Saxon houses were destroyed to make way for the castles: in Norwich, the Normans demolished 98 houses, while, in Lincoln, 166 houses out of a total of 970 were torn down to make way for motte castles.[11] Certainly, the Normans knew how to impose themselves on native communities: seize the area, devastate the countryside when necessary, destroy a large number of houses, and erect a castle over them. At Cambridge, they built their castle over a Saxon graveyard.[12] The symbolism of that act could not have been more clear.

THE NORMAN "CONQUEST" OF WALES

The Norman "conquest" of Wales differed in many ways from the effort in England. Unlike Saxon England, which was administered from several urbanized centers, Wales was largely a rural country, divided into a series of small "kingdoms" ruled by long-standing families, including the Houses of Gwynedd, Powys, and Deheubarth. Initially, the Normans chose to remain on the English side of the border with Wales and erected a scattering of motte castles to consolidate their control over the lands they progressively seized. Encouraged by William I and William Rufus during the early phase of feudalism in Britain, they established three major Marcher lordships, essentially miniature kingdoms with their own set of laws and authority, and numerous lesser lordships not only in the Marches but throughout Wales. Content with managing affairs from England, the Normans only sporadically forayed into Wales. William FitzOsbern, Earl of Hereford and vice-regent of England in William the Conqueror's absence, was a particularly prolific castle-builder who not only erected motte castles at Berkeley in Gloucestershire, Monmouth in Monmouthshire, and Clifford and Wigmore in Herefordshire, but also rebuilt Ewyas Harold Castle on the English side of the Marches.

During the eleventh century, the Welsh were immersed in a series of struggles of their own. Periodically, a strong charismatic leader would take charge of large portions of Wales, if not its entirety, but a unified Wales remained an elusive prospect. When the head of a dynastic family died, his holdings were equally divided amongst his sons, according to the law of partibility. Consequently, elder brothers might fight younger brothers to wrest control of a region. Such was the case in 1093, after the death of Rhys ap Tewdwr, Prince of Deheubarth, when a power vacuum occurred in West Wales. During the first two decades after Hastings, the Normans only made casual inroads into that part of Wales; in fact, William I met with Rhys just once, in 1081, reputedly during a pilgrimage to St. David's Cathedral. In return, Rhys paid homage to the new king and established a truce of sorts with the Normans. With the exception of occasional raids into West Wales, which increased in frequency when William the Conqueror died in 1087, the Normans stayed away from southwest Wales until 1093, when the Welshman's heirs battled for power over what they perceived as their rightful inheritance.

Taking advantage of the chaos, Roger de Montgomery, Earl of Shrewsbury, sent his son, Arnulf, with an army of Norman soldiers into Pembrokeshire, where they pushed the Welsh to the fringes of the former kingdom of Deheubarth and established an earth and timber castle on the River Pembroke. Pembroke Castle swiftly became the seat of the powerful Earls of Pembroke and developed into one of the realm's mightiest stone fortresses. Despite frequent raids on many of the Norman castles that dotted Pembrokeshire, the native princes never fully regained control of the area.

Within fifty years of the arrival of the Normans in Pembrokeshire, a line of earth and timber castles stretched along the southern side of the frontier delineated by the inhospitable Preseli hills, which separated the Englishry and the Welshry and reinforced the physical and political separation of the Welsh from their Anglo-Norman overlords. A second group of earth and timber castles, each bearing Welsh names and located in Welsh-speaking areas, marked the northern side of the Preselis. In time, the divide between the Welshry and the Englishry became known as the "landsker line," and was fortified with several substantial stone castles and earth and timber strongholds, including the now-vanished motte castle built by the Fleming, Letard Litelking, at Letterston, and Pointz Castle, a substantial motte possibly erected by another Fleming named Pons, Ponce, Punchard, or Punch. The walled castle town at Tenby was especially favored by the Flemings, where they prospered as merchants and tradesmen.

THE INVASION OF IRELAND

The Norman strategy in the decades immediately following the Battle of Hastings was to seize and occupy England and Wales. Even though the Normans erected numerous castles to control the border between England and Wales, they also used them as bases from which to push farther into Wales, progressively, albeit sporadically, wresting control of vast parcels of land from the native princes. As they extended their hold on the landscape, the Normans erected more castles and used the strongholds not only to physically overawe the local populace but also to graphically display their lasting presence. When it came time to cross the Irish Sea and invade Ireland in 1169, the Anglo-Normans employed the same tactics, which had worked so successfully against the Saxons and the Welsh.

The Norman lord, Richard (Strongbow) de Clare, Earl of Pembroke, sailed from his base in West Wales to instigate the "conquest of Ireland," took advantage of the tumult that afflicted rival Irish families, and erected earth and timber castles, many of which, like Trim and Carrickfergus, were soon reinforced with stone and converted into Ireland's most powerful fortresses. Of Ireland's earth and timber castles, the mottes were thrown up almost entirely in the eastern half of the island;[13] the identification of ringworks, on the other hand, is complicated by the proliferation in Ireland of a class of structures known as "raths" or "ringforts," which appeared in the countryside as early as the Iron Age, but persisted into the early Middle Ages. By 1186, the Anglo-Normans had permanently entrenched themselves in Ireland, building both timber and stone castles to consolidate their control over the Irish.

NORMAN INVOLVEMENT IN SCOTLAND

As mentioned in the introduction, medieval Scotland acquired a number of earth and timber castles; however, rather than being used as instruments of conquest, the Normans built their castles after being welcomed into Scotland. During the early twelfth century, King David I not only built his own motte castles but also encouraged Norman lords and Flemish settlers to move into his kingdom, construct castles, and spread feudalism. The new settlers effectively forced the native Gaelic-speaking populace northwards into the hinterland. By 1250, more than 200 substantial motte castles occupied the countryside. The most impressive examples include Duffus in Moray, Bass of Inverurie in Aberdeenshire, and the Mote of Urr in Dumfries and Galloway. As elsewhere in Britain, masonry castles appeared alongside earth and timber strongholds. Reputedly built in the early twelfth century, Scotland's earliest recorded stone castle is Sween, in Strathclyde.

SIEGE-CASTLES AND ANARCHY

Some military structures used for offensive purposes during wartime have been designated as "siege-castles." Like Kenyon's "campaign castles" mentioned above in the discussion of ringworks, these earthwork fortifications were erected when speed was of the essence. However, their usefulness was temporary, for they were directly related to the conduct of a siege. Many historians describe siege-castles as purely defensive structures, with their combined earthen embankment and fronting ditch thrown up to protect the besieged laying in wait inside. But they were in fact the tools of aggressors, who used the fortifications to entrench themselves near the castle they were preparing to besiege but keep far enough away to be out of firing range. When the siege ended, so usually did the need for the siege-castle; and, even though a few were reused, in most cases they were abandoned and allowed to decay. Consequently, since most of these strongholds never served as a fortified military residence for a lord, but rather as defended settlements of sorts, they should be characterized as "siege-forts" or "siege-works," terms which thereby eliminate misguided interpretations that they were castles.

Historically, the Norman kings of Britain used siege-works to besiege several castles. Some historians believe the fort named "Malvoisin" (or "bad neighbor"), which was reportedly erected by William (Rufus) II to besiege Northumberland's Bamburgh Castle in 1095, may actually have been an earth-and-ditch fortification, whereas others contend that the Malvoisin was actually a timber siege-tower, or "belfry," which the king's soldiers erected as a shield to gain proximity to the castle.[14] During the 1102 siege of Bridgnorth in Shropshire, Henry I ordered the swift construction of an earthwork fort, which acquired the name "Panpudding Hill." Also known as "Oldbury," the fortification (which has been classified both as a ringwork and a motte) may have been used to stage sieges in 1155, 1321, and 1646. England's National Monuments Record classifies the site as a ringwork and bailey.[15]

Constructing siege-works was a common tactic during the "Anarchy," the Civil War fought between King Stephen and Empress Matilda, both of whom claimed the throne as their rightful inheritance after Henry I's death in 1135. As his nephew, Stephen was Henry's closest living male heir. Matilda, on the other hand, was Henry's only legitimate daughter, and also the widow of the German emperor Henry V, who died in 1125. Just west of the mighty stone fortress at Corfe in Dorset, Stephen erected siege-works still known as "The Rings" to stage his successful siege in 1139. Still clearly visible from the ruined castle, the well-preserved earthworks resemble a classic ringwork castle and are arguably the best surviving example of their kind in England. Stephen also used siege-works to great effect when assaulting Exeter.[16]

EDWARD I: CASTLE-BUILDER, WARRIOR-KING, CONQUEROR

While one can argue with considerable justification that William I brought large-scale, methodical castle-building to the British Isles, his program was not based on a carefully planned system for effecting the Conquest. Castles were erected largely as needed, to establish a Norman presence not only in Saxon settlements and cities like London but also in the borderlands. Because earth and timber fortresses aided in the rapid subjugation of a town or an area, quite visibly establishing Norman dominance, it is not surprising that the Conqueror planted many of his new castles in urbanized centers. Scores of castles also appeared in the countryside and were used as staging points for sorties intended to expand and consolidate Norman control throughout Britain. Wherever the king distributed lands to his subordinates, more than likely a castle arose shortly thereafter. Not only did they visibly remind everyone of the presence of the Normans in a locality, castles also demonstrated the personal power of the individual who controlled the newly formed lordship and the inferior status of the local populace subject to that lord. In rural locations, the Normans generally chose the sites upon which to build their castles based more on the terrain, the extent of natural defenses it afforded, the availability of a reliable water supply, and ease of access to other parts of the realm.[17]

Despite the lack of a well-honed system, the Normans effected the conquest of Saxon England with relative ease. The subjugation of Wales was never to be as smooth. It would take almost 200 more years for an English king to finalize the "conquest" of Wales, for, despite the presence of castles and the arrival of Norman and other outsiders in Wales, the Welsh never fully gave up their fight for independence.

In many ways, Edward I was Britain's greatest castle-building king, although the Welsh might beg to differ. As a prince, Edward had witnessed firsthand the strategic value of castles not only at the sieges of Kenilworth and Lewes, during the barons' rebellion in the 1260s, but also while making a name for himself as a skilled fighter in the Holy Land, during the Crusades. Between 1277 and 1294, as King of England, Edward put into practice the technology he had seen in action at home and abroad and inaugurated a monumental building program in Wales, the likes of which has never been replicated. Using the most advanced castle-building technology of the times and the engineering talents of some of the world's most creative architects, including Master James of St. George, whose prowess as a castle-designer was widely acclaimed in Savoy, France, Edward I established a circuit of strongholds and walled towns around Wales that, at least for a time, quelled his subjects' rebellious ambitions. In 1986, four of Edward's great castles achieved international acclaim for their "outstanding contribution to humanity," when UNESCO designated the castles and town walls at Conwy, Caernarfon, Harlech, and Beaumaris as World Heritage Sites. His efforts at the Tower of London also directly contributed to that castle's selection for the World Heritage List in 1988.

Unlike in Saxon England, the native population in Wales continued to be ruled by the heads of dynastic families. Unity in Wales was elusive at best and infighting was frequent; however, the Welsh continued to view their Norman overlords and planted settlers, such as the Flemings, as their common enemy. Periodically, they banded together to assault castles and burn towns, and at times regained control of portions of their homeland from the Anglo-Normans. The thirteenth century saw the rise of great Welsh leaders, Llywelyn ab Iorwerth, who unified Wales and led assault after assault against the Normans, and his grandson, Llywelyn ap Gruffudd, whom Henry III officially recognized as Prince of Wales with the Treaty of Montgomery in 1267. Despite this proclamation, Henry III's son, Prince Edward, continued to clash with the Welsh prince. Eventually, the rivalry would erupt into full-fledged warfare between the Welsh and Plantagenet prince, but not until Edward had gained the English throne and all the power that accompanied it.

In 1277, Edward I led his army on his first campaign against the Welsh, implementing a three-pronged strategy that involved attacking Wales from English bases at Montgomery in Montgomeryshire, Carmarthen in Carmarthenshire and Chester Castle in Cheshire.[18] Within ten months, the English forced the Welsh to admit defeat, and Edward swiftly established a massive castle-building program in Wales. Not only did the king use innovative design plans to build four new royal fortresses at Flint (Flintshire), Rhuddlan (Denbighshire), Aberystwyth (Ceredigion), and Builth (Powys), his Marcher lords also erected notable castles at Ruthin (Denbighshire) and Hawarden (Flintshire) and refortified the Welsh-built castles at Dinas Bran,

RHUDDLAN CASTLE. The course of the River Clwyd was rechanneled to support Edward I's twin-towered stone fortress at Rhuddlan in Denbighshire.

Dinefwr (Carmarthenshire), and Carreg Cennen for use as English-occupied fortresses. Rhuddlan and Aberystwyth were fitted with concentric defenses, while Edward's riverside castle at Flint featured four corner towers, one of which functioned as a massive donjon, or great tower.

For Edward, sea access was paramount when situating castles so that his men could conveniently obtain supplies and reinforcements. Not surprisingly, he deliberately chose sites that gave his men maximum advantage during a siege. If the route of the river was insufficient, he knew he had the option of redirecting it—at an enormous cost. At Rhuddlan in Flintshire, Edward's workforce rechanneled the direction of the River Clwyd to ensure it flowed immediately alongside his stone castle, which he erected a short distance away from the massive Norman motte and bailey castle, Twthill. One of Edward's most innovative ventures, the 2-mile-long canal partially filled the moat and also providing a deep-water channel for ship movement between the castle and the Irish Sea. An average of seventy-seven men worked six days a week for three years straight to complete the project,[19] which also included the construction of a dock and dock gate to safeguard the ships, crew members, and passengers.

Even though Edward I took for granted that he had conquered the Welsh in 1277, they stunned him five years later with yet another rebellion.

Once again, England's warrior-king, nick-named "Longshanks" for his powerful stature, systematically assaulted the countryside. After his men killed the Welsh leader, Llywelyn ap Gruffudd, at Cilmeri, near Builth, the rebellion began to unravel in late December. With the capture and brutal execution of Llywelyn's brother, Dafydd, who had actually instigated the rebellion, Edward proclaimed himself victorious and initiated his second campaign of castle-building in Wales. This time, he enforced the subjugation of the Welsh not only with huge castles but also by appropriating the palaces of the native princes of Gwynedd and seizing Castell y Bere and the castles at Criccieth and Dolwyddelan, which he repaired and strengthened for his own use. The deliberate replacement of Welsh-built sites with English structures and the enclosure of North Wales with a ring of impregnable fortresses to keep the Welsh in check, physically and symbolically demonstrated England's complete command of Wales.

TWTHILL, the substantial Norman motte castle at Rhuddlan, was probably erected close to or over part of the Saxon burh that originally occupied the area.

Royal castles on a scale never before seen in Wales arose in Conwy, Caernarfon, and Harlech. Each fortress was strategically placed for seaborne access and to demand submission from onlookers. Of these, Edward chose Caernarfon as his imperial headquarters. Designed to display Edward I's supremacy over the Welsh and create subliminal links to the Holy Roman Empire, Caernarfon Castle was deliberately modeled on the walls of Constantinople. In 1284, Edward I solidified his conquest of Wales by signing the Statute of Rhuddlan and establishing his infant son, Edward, who was born at Caernarfon, as the first English Prince of Wales. The unforgiving king believed his second phase of monumental castle-building would completely overawe the Welsh. Fortifying his grip on Wales with the construction of planted towns and the deliberate settlement of English residents inside the castle towns, Edward I intended to intimidate the Welsh into complete submission and thereby firmly conclude his conquest of Wales. Lordship castles were likewise repaired or constructed anew at Caergwrle (Flintshire), Holt (Wrexham), Ruthin, and Denbigh, which Henry de Lacy, Earl of Lincoln, enclosed with an extensive masonry wall, fragments of which survive. Should the Welsh choose once again to rebel, the king undoubtedly assured himself, the upstarts would be met with such impenetrable obstacles that they would surrender with little more than a whimper.

LOOKING TOWARD the upper bailey at Caernarfon Castle. Powerful polygonal towers dominate Edward I's imperial castle at Caernarfon, in Caernarfonshire, which he designed to resemble the great circuit of walls at Constantinople, now in modern Turkey.

Though quieted for almost twelve years, the Welsh proved to their English overlords that they had not yet been conquered. Much to Edward I's chagrin, Madog ap Llywelyn led a well-organized rebellion throughout Wales, during which the Welsh revolted against the intolerable conditions they endured under English rule and stormed some of Edward's most formidable castles, including the invincible Conwy. At Conwy Castle, the mighty warrior-king, then in residence, became a prisoner in his own fortress. Food and water supplies dwindled until reinforcements finally arrived by sea from Ireland and forced the Welsh to retreat in the spring of 1295. Again, Edward responded with the construction of another castle, this time on the Isle of Anglesey, where he forcibly relocated the native residents of Llanfaes to a new location, appropriately named Newborough, before beginning his final masterpiece, the great concentric castle at Beaumaris, which he erected on top of the vacant Welsh settlement. Even though the English never completed the work at Beaumaris and Edward I focused his aggression toward the conquest of Scotland, the warrior-king had stymied the Welsh fight for independence.

Ironically, even though he was also known as the so-called Hammer of the Scots, Edward I never completely conquered his northern foes. Successfully besieging a number of powerful Scottish castles, such as Caerlaverock in Dumfries and Galloway and Stirling, Edward I made significant inroads toward his goal. However, rather than instigating the same monumental castle-building program in Scotland that he had used to such great advantage against the Welsh, Edward chose to refortify many Scottish castles, including Selkirk in the Scottish Borders and Dumbarton in West Lanarkshire, and to also seize the castles at Bothwell in South Lanarkshire and Stirling, garrisoning them all with English troops. Unlike in Wales, Edward erected only a few, poorly defended castles of his own in Scotland.[20] Not surprisingly, the Scots took matters into their own hands.

In 1306, the Scots crowned Robert Bruce as king and fought back against Edward I, who died the next year. They then managed a series of unexpected victories against the outlanders, now ruled by Edward II, an ineffectual ruler with few of the fighting skills his father prized so highly. In 1328, a year after Edward II's murder at Berkeley Castle, his son, Edward III, signed a treaty that returned control of Scotland back to the Scots. Nevertheless, Robert Bruce ordered the methodical destruction of many of his country's castles, so that the English could never again be able to use them against the Scots. Another 275 years would have to pass before the Scots and English would unite under a single monarch, James, the son of Mary Queen of Scots.

PLANTATION: CASTLES, COLONIZATION, AND PLANNED TOWNS

The systematic settlement of English, Flemish, Bretons (French emigrants from Brittany), and other colonists in England, Wales, and Scotland followed quickly after the Conquest and the spread of Norman castles. The Norman and Scottish monarchs justified the colonization of England, Wales, and Scotland with foreigners as a way to expand commerce, and, at least in Wales, to demonstrate the benefits of an anglicized lifestyle so that the locals would quickly assimilate and become a part of the new kingdom rather than continuing to resist Norman domination. As in Saxon England, the widespread construction of castles reinforced the notion that the Normans were there to stay and that the locals were better off acquiescing rather than resisting. However, the plan was flawed, and, as has been discussed above, both the Welsh and Scots rebelled repeatedly throughout the centuries after 1066.

After a devastating storm ravaged Flanders in 1106, Flemings emigrated in droves from their homeland in Flanders, now part of Belgium, at the invitation of Henry I, who offered them financial inducements and land grants to resettle in Britain. Skilled weavers and craftsmen, the Flemings moved into southwest Wales and parts of the Scottish Borders, erected castles, farmed the land, and established villages in the shadow of their castles.

As early as 1107, Henry I deliberately encouraged the Flemings, and English settlers from Devon and Somerset, to move into the Welsh lands in Pembrokeshire. By the beginning of the thirteenth century, the fully anglicized Flemings provided a buffer zone between the region's administrative center, the castle at Pembroke, and the local Welsh population. The intrusion of the Flemings and English outsiders was vigorously supported by the Norman king and forced the Welsh inhabitants into the northern fringes of Pembrokeshire and beyond. With the Welsh went their language, and English—with a strong Flemish dialect—became the dominant tongue. The area also acquired the appellation, "Little England Beyond Wales." More than likely, the Flemings were responsible for building Wiston Castle and the first castle at Haverfordwest and probably initiated construction on both sites shortly after their arrival in the area.

Wiston Castle was first mentioned in historical records in about 1147, when the Welsh, led by Cadell, Maredudd, and Rhys, sons of Gruffudd ap Rhys ap Tewdwr, and Hywel ab Owain, stormed the motte and bailey stronghold. However, the earth and timber castle probably dates to the start of the twelfth century, when its original owner, a Fleming named Wizo ("Gwys" in Welsh), settled the land, having received the Lordship of Daugleddau from Henry I. The Flemish settlement became known as Wizo's town, or Wiston.

For years, the identity of the original castle-builder at Haverfordwest has been hotly debated. For a time, historians had decided that Gilbert de Clare,

WISTON CASTLE. The massive motte at Wiston, in Pembrokeshire, is one of the finest examples of its type in Wales. Erected by the Fleming, Wizo, the mound was once crowned with a shell keep, the remains of which still survive.

Earl of Pembroke, was the most likely candidate to have ordered the castle's construction, even though there are no records to substantiate this claim. In fact, the earliest records referring to Haverford Castle date to the late twelfth century, when Gerald of Wales chronicled his journey through Wales. However, most researchers presently accept that it probably was Tancred, a Fleming, who began building Haverford-west Castle in about 1110. Married to Gerald's aunt, Tancred (or Tancard) also had ties to the villages near Hayscastle, called Upper and Lower Tancredston and Tancredston Bridge, still located about 5 miles north of Haverfordwest, and his children intermarried with several local families.

Tancred's castle at Haverfordwest (then known as Haverford) dominated the hilltop overlooking the Western Cleddau at the river's highest tidal point. At one time, ships could safely sail inland to the town's quay. Located just 153 feet from the river, the Fleming's castle probably featured earth and timber defenses, which were eventually replaced with stone. The basic plan of the original castle is easy to identify in the current remains. Initially, villagers may have lived in thatched huts on the hillsides close to the castle, whereas the wealthiest residents occupied prime property just beyond the castle walls.

Like his Norman predecessors, Edward I also recognized the strategic value of colonizing newly conquered lands with his own supporters. Not only was he responsible for Britain's greatest castle-building achievements, the warrior-king also founded several fortified castle towns, which he populated with foreign settlers, including English merchants and craftsmen. And, just as William I devastated many Saxon communities, Edward ordered the demolition of Welsh homesteads and the destruction of settlements in order to create English boroughs, the layout of which followed a strict grid plan.

One of the identifying traits of many medieval castle towns is their formal grid plan. At least one main street, commonly called High Street, stretched away from the castle. Small plots of land and minor lanes projected at right angles from the main street. Symmetry and order were carefully marked out and many medieval towns were enclosed with towered stone walls or earthwork embankments, as at Pleshey in Essex, where the well-preserved earthen bank still rings much of the present village. Over time, as the towns expanded, new streets widened the grid pattern, but the castle generally remained the focal point.

Standing atop the great round keep at Pembroke Castle, for example, one can easily identify the town's medieval grid plan. Projecting almost due eastwards from the castle gateway, the main street runs the length of the town before it circles back toward the castle. Around the circuit, remnants of the substantial towered, multigated town wall survive. Not only did such walls protect the colonists from assault and encourage trade amongst the residents, they also prevented the Welsh from participating in commercial ventures within the walls. Within the masonry walls, the new settlers, the English, Flemings, and Normans, conducted the daily business of life, and also maintained their own residence near the castle. Populated with English and other settlers, the new planned towns functioned as strategically located administrative centers whose residents would loyally serve the monarchy, stimulate trade, and keep the native populace in check.[21] In most cases, the settlers agreed to fight when called upon or to provide the garrison with supplies in exchange for the grants of land.

Other noteworthy medieval planned towns include Edward I's projects at Flint, Aberystwyth, Caernarfon, and Conwy. To accomplish the ambitious construction of these castellated towns, Edward I often ousted its prior residents, regardless of their professions. In 1284, Edward was so insistent on occupying land held by Cistercian monks at Conwy, that he moved the entire monastic community at Aberconwy to Maenan to make space for what would become his grandest planned castle town, Conwy, where the entire ¾-mile circuit of towered and gated walls are one of the best examples of their kind still extant in Europe.

The deliberate plantation of foreign settlers in Ireland, not only by the Normans but by postmedieval monarchs as well, changed the course of Irish history and also the appearance of the landscape. Throughout the sixteenth and seventeenth centuries, England's monarchs consistently supported a policy of sending English and Scottish families to Ireland to colonize the countryside. As in Wales, the goal was not only to populate Ireland with residents loyal to England, but also to change Irish culture and impose Protestantism on the island nation by seizing and redistributing their land to English and Scottish immigrants. The colonists agreed to build fortified houses and castles, provide men-at-arms when necessary, and abide by several strict rules, which, amongst other requirements, forbade them to employ Irish men or women not born in the immediate locality or to marry them. The English subtly but persistently conquered the native population.

The first plantation was organized by Henry VIII, who became King of Ireland in 1541. The English king decided to enforce a policy of "surrender and regrant," which allowed several leading Irishmen to rise within the English peerage if they acknowledged the English king as the head of Ireland as well as the head of the Church (Henry had established the Protestant Church of England by this time), and also adopted English laws and customs. In essence, the Tudor king forced the Irish hierarchy to give up their heritage in exchange for retaining ownership of their own lands. Properties seized by the king were then parceled out to English settlers, known as "planters" or "undertakers," who were expected to carry out (or "undertake") the king's policies and, in effect, civilize the Irish. By 1592, after the plantation of Offaly, Leix, and Munster, only about 1,300 planters occupied Ireland.[22] Failing miserably to impose their way of life on the local populace, many planters chose to intermarry and instead adapted to the Irish lifestyle.

The most vigorous effort to colonize Ireland began in the early seventeenth century, during the reign of King James VI of Scotland, who also ruled as King James I of England. Again, colonists from Scotland and England were enticed to Ireland with the promise of land in exchange for constructing castles and stone or brick homes equipped with "bawns," or fortified enclosures similar to baileys. They were also required to provide soldiers for an army or garrison.[23] For about ninety years beginning in 1607, Ulster witnessed the plantation of some 200,000 Scottish settlers, who erected castles, established Presbyterian churches, and outnumbered English planters by about twenty to one. Plantation castles sprang up throughout northern Ireland, where the Scots modeled their new castles on Scottish designs, most notably emulating the rectangular tower house, which is discussed in chapter 3. More compact than the medieval stone fortress, tower houses were multi-level, self-sufficient strongholds designed to establish a presence in a region, such as in the Scottish Borders, and to thwart sudden raids. Tower houses were not built to withstand a prolonged siege by an organized army.

The remains of plantation castles, like Monea, Tully, and Parke's castles, still scatter the Irish countryside. Located west of Enniskillen in Fermanagh, Monea Castle is arguably the best preserved of its kind. Built by the Reverend Malcolm Hamilton in 1616, in its heyday, Monea Castle consisted of a three-story tower house which measured 54 feet long by 20 feet wide. It also had what appears to be a typically Scottish bartizan at one corner and two rounded towers on the opposite side. The castle also featured a 9-foot-high bawn and a 300-foot-long enclosure wall. Interestingly, Monea Castle had a thatched roof. During the mid–eighteenth century, a fire ravaged the structure, which was then abandoned.[24]

The castle at Tully, north of Derrygonnelly and also in Fermanagh, was structurally quite similar to Monea Castle but had a single square wing projecting outwards from the center of the southern side, which created a T-shaped plan. Built by Sir John Hume between 1612 and 1615, the castle, which is also classified as a "stronghouse," was abandoned in 1641 after the violent assault by the Maguires, which not only devastated the castle, but also led to the slaughter of eighty-five Protestant planters—men, women, and children—on Christmas Day.

Parke's Castle, located near Dromahaire in County Leitrim, was another typical Irish plantation castle. Erected by Robert Parker in about 1610, the site superseded an earlier castle built by the O'Rorkes and had a five-sided bawn.[25] In recent decades, the castle has undergone an extensive rebuilding program, which has largely restored its original appearance.

The seventeenth-century plantation of Ireland also involved the construction of twenty planned towns, including Belfast. Rather than being laid out on the straightforward rectilinear grid plan employed in medieval England and Wales, these plantation towns contained square- or diamond-shaped centers, which housed their marketplaces, and widely spaced streets lined with tall houses radiated outward at regular intervals.

MAINTAINING THE LORDSHIP

Imposed as they were upon the populace, Britain's medieval castles functioned as "the headquarters for local government, whether royal or seigneurial."[26] Their ongoing presence in an area ensured the survival of the feudal lordship (at least in theory) and the monarchy (again, in theory). The lords who built and occupied Britain's properly fortified military residences generally gained the right to do so by a grant from the reigning monarch, who retained the power to wrest back control from his subordinate rulers on as little as a whim. Feudal authority passed from the monarch to the lord, who paid homage and owed allegiance in the form of knights service, who fought alongside the king when called, and who were expected to offer sound advice. In return, the king granted lords large tracts of land and expected them to erect a castle and properly govern the territory in his name.

As the administrative center of a lordship, a castle provided a place for the lord to carry out several official duties, which were critical to the maintenance of the estate and also to his ongoing control of an area. Indeed, the castle and its surrounding estates—and the people who worked them—formed a symbiotic relationship, one often known as a "manor." Despite the fact that a lord and his subordinates were essentially intruders occupying the region, in order to retain power, the lord had to successfully administer his lordship by establishing a tolerant and tolerable working relationship with the peasants who lived on and farmed the neighboring fields, with the people who worked inside the castle, and with those who paid rent in the form of goods, military service, or money. Not only did the lord expect (and need) support from the populace to keep a foothold on his lordship and its castle—the lord's residence and the symbol of his power—his subjects likewise expected and needed support from their lord.

Consequently, castles became the seats of local government. From them, law and order were dispensed; at them, local residents could register civil complaints and receive satisfaction—or the occasional favor from the lord himself. During wartime, the surrounding population could also expect the lord and his men to protect them. The monarch could also administer royal power and justice from these lordship castles, if and when a situation required his intervention.

In fact, the most powerful lords usually owned several castles that centered large estates and bound them together into a far-reaching power base. Some lords acquired so much power by accumulating landed estates that they actually threatened the king's authority, in psychological terms, if not in intent. Warfare often resulted from the uneven balance of power between the lords of the realm and their monarch. Castle-building decisions were directly influenced by these situations. For example, in the late twelfth century, Henry II intentionally built Orford Castle in Suffolk to reassert his authority over the Bigods, Earls of Norfolk, who controlled several castles in southern Norfolk and northern Suffolk, and also over William de Blois, King Stephen's son and later the 4th Earl Warenne, who held castles in Norfolk. Neither had supported Henry's mother, the Empress Matilda, in her struggle against Stephen for the English crown. In fact, years earlier, in 1148, Hugh Bigod had invited King Stephen to meet with Theobald, Archbishop of Canterbury, the Bishops of London, Chichester, and Norwich, and several noblemen at Framlingham Castle, also in Suffolk, in an effort to forge peace between the king and the leaders of the Roman Catholic Church.[27] When Henry became the first Plantagenet king in 1154, he felt the urgency to establish a physical presence in the region. Building Orford Castle about 13 miles from Framlingham, Henry II intended to squelch any ambitions held by either Bigod or de Blois to seize the throne.

Even though the monarchy maintained several castles for its own specific use, including Windsor, which still functions as an important royal residence (but has lost its military fortitude), the Tower of London, Edinburgh and Stirling in Scotland, and Caernarfon and Conwy in Wales, most of Britain was controlled by lords and landed gentry, men who often behaved as kings in their own right, wielding military power, collecting rent and taxes, and meting out their own interpretation of justice. During the fourteenth century, after the death of Gilbert III, the last de Clare Lord of Glamorgan, Caerphilly Castle passed to Hugh le Despenser, one of the realm's most despised noblemen, whose control over the king, Edward II, ultimately led to both men's deaths. As the administrative center of the much larger manor of Caerphilly, the castle functioned as a prison and an "estate office," from where the constable collected revenue from levies on local markets and fairs, rents, fisheries, and court fines, which he amassed when exacting justice within the manor.[28]

By the mid-fifteenth century, Sir William Herbert, Lord of Raglan (1465), Earl of Pembroke (1468), Sheriff of Glamorgan, Constable of Usk Castle, Chief Justice of North Wales (1467), and Chamberlain of South Wales (1462), had established his main base at the majestic residential fortress at Raglan. From there, Herbert capably managed the lordship, which was considered equivalent to a royal holding, where "no justices, stewards, escheators, coroners, ringilds or other officers or ministers of the King shall interfere."[29] Besides spearheading the stronghold's transformation into one of medieval Britain's most impressive palatial castles, among other tasks undertaken by the lord of Raglan Castle, Herbert also organized a force of 200 Yorkist soldiers to march from Raglan to Carreg Cennen Castle to receive the Lancastrian garrison's surrender and carry out the castle's demolition[30] during the Wars of the Roses. Clearly, Herbert had assumed a role befitting a man of considerable stature and influence within royal circles, and he ensured his palatial fortress displayed that status.

Many lords administered justice and collected revenue while seated in their majestic great halls, as at Oakham Castle in the County of Rutland, where the fine furnishings and elaborate architecture would have easily overawed their subjects and symbolically reinforced the lord's power and control over the region. Centering the manor of Oakham, which was controlled by the Ferrers, Earls of Derby, the freestanding hall served as a convenient venue for the collection of tolls, payments, and levies, which were taken by the Ferrers themselves or by their bailiffs. Curiously, at Oakham, an unusual tradition was established whereby tolls were presented in the form of horseshoes, scores of which now adorn the walls of the well-preserved great hall.[31]

Medieval castles frequently acquired special facilities, courthouses, or secondary halls, inside of which the lord, the constable, or another castle official would handle the day's business. Inside the inner ward at Pembroke Castle, William de Valence, Earl of Pembroke during the late thirteenth century, erected a courthouse alongside the great round keep. From there, the Earl or his representatives met with complainants, administered justice, and collected their income. Today, the rectangular structure is little more than a shell, but, during the Middle Ages, it would have provided more than ample space for the lord or his constable.

THE RUINED COURTHOUSE at Pembroke Castle. Now little more than an empty shell, the medieval courthouse at Pembroke Castle, in Pembrokeshire, stood alongside William Marshal's formidable round keep in the inner bailey.

Castles that centered an entire lordship, such as Chester Castle, tended to overshadow the castles of the lesser lords in the same region. As the seat of the Earls of Chester, the establishment and expansion of the original Norman castle within the remains of the great Roman fortress known as Deva not only emphasized the builders' political power but also allowed them to command the borderland between England and northeastern Wales. The

huge area under the control of the Earls of Chester was given a special designation as a "county palatine," which meant that these lords were answerable only to the King and could rule the countryside essentially as they saw fit. Chester Castle quickly became the administrative center of the lordship, and the great (shire) hall served as the hub of activity. Today, the Crown Courts still dominate the site. Besides being an administrative and legal venue where trials were routinely conducted, Chester Castle also functioned as a mint and a grim, disease-ridden prison.[32]

While some ringworks, such as Castle Rising in Norfolk, acquired strong masonry structures and developed into formidable castles that centered significant lordships, others were administrative centers for minor lordships. Even though lesser lords, such as Maurice de Londres, who erected the ringwork castle at Ogmore, were subordinate to men such as the Lord of Glamorgan, whose main base was at Cardiff Castle, both castles served as seats of government and both contained facilities for that purpose. During Robert Fitzhamon's tenure as Lord of Glamorgan in the late eleventh century, Cardiff Castle fulfilled a variety of roles: it was the "comitatus" or county court, the exchequer, the chancery, and the prison, and probably held the mint as well. The castle also functioned as a key administrative center from 1217 to 1314, while the de Clares served as Lords of Glamorgan.

Now little more than a shell, a structure purported to be a courthouse stands in the outer bailey at Ogmore Castle. Dating to the fourteenth century and rebuilt in the mid–fifteenth century, the roofless rectangular building has a simple doorway flanked by two large chambers, and was probably the third building to occupy the spot. The remains of a thirteenth-century building are evident closer to the river, while a well-preserved lime kiln peeks out from beneath the southwestern angle of the so-called courthouse. Apparently, the lime kiln was built over the thirteenth-century building, and the courthouse was then added on top of the lime kiln. The building, which some researchers believe may have been a chapel, was used at least until 1631.

MAINTAINING ROYAL CONTROL

Throughout the course of British history, different monarchs favored different types of castles as their main residences. Their choices were guided as much by their situation as by the castle's physical power, residential capacity, or visual splendor. Over the course of its lengthy history, for example, Edinburgh Castle has functioned as a royal residence, a military citadel and store for royal artillery, a treasury, a prison, and a repository for the government's records. Yet, despite Edinburgh's position in the Scottish capital city, the Stewart monarchs actually preferred Stirling Castle as their primary fortress.

EDINBURGH CASTLE. Scotland's royal stronghold at Edinburgh has capably served the monarchy over time as a privately fortified military residence. Changing repeatedly over the course of its history, the castle features a wide range of structures, and today still provides a home to the military while also allowing public access.

Like Edinburgh, Stirling stood atop a plateau of volcanic bedrock; however, it also controlled passage between northern and southern Scotland and access to the North Sea. The castle's substantial defenses and impressive royal buildings created the clear impression of noble dominance, almost as if the entire site had erupted from the bedrock just to command the region. Scottish rulers made extensive use of Stirling Castle as a royal administrative center and held Parliament and State ceremonies inside the great hall.

The "Royal Palace and Fortress of the Tower of London" has stalwartly performed a variety of functions during the ten centuries of its existence, including acting as an impregnable fortress, a prison, and as the king's zoo (Henry III established a royal menagerie inside the castle to house an elephant, bears, lions, and other exotic animals presented to him by the crown heads of several European nations). Edward I built a royal mint inside the castle and added a treasury to house the Crown Jewels. The Tudors expanded the castle's role as a prison and staged scores of political executions both on Tower Green and on Tower Hill, where 125 prisoners lost their lives. During the seventeenth century, the castle acquired a heightened military role with the occupation of the Office of Ordnance, which established munitions stores, military workshops, a barracks for the permanent garrison, and gun batteries at the site. The Tower of London also contained two armories. In the 1840s, the army transferred the mint, zoo, and records office elsewhere, but the formidable castle still ensures the security of the Crown Jewels, which are stored in vaults and displayed in the Jewel House.

CENTERS OF ECCLESIASTICAL POWER

Rivalling Britain's secular lordships, the medieval religious hierarchy also controlled huge parcels of land and built great palaces and formidable castles to house themselves and perpetuate their position within a region. For example, the Bishops of St. Davids, who were the most powerful and prosperous ecclesiastical lords in West Wales, functioned as secular lords in their own right. Imbued by the English king with the proper legal authority, the bishops held courts, filled prisons, and maintained a gallows. As mobile bishops, they kept residences and facilities throughout southwestern Wales, as at Llawhaden, where they located their administrative center at the barony's castle, and at Lamphey, a manor hubbed by its own bishops' palace. Featuring a twin-towered gatehouse, a towered curtain wall, a steep-sided encompassing ditch, and a dungeon, Llawhaden Castle was as much a fortified residence as any of its secular counterparts.

Further east at Cardiff, the Bishops of Llandaff also constructed a castle that overlooked the River Taff and served largely to provide defensive strength for the neighboring Llandaff Cathedral, just a few hundred yards to the north. From Llandaff Castle, the bishops could watch over the activity in the cathedral's precinct. The twin-towered castle gatehouse contained a prison in the eastern tower and guardrooms and living chambers in the western tower. Inside the gate passage, an arrowslit, portcullis, and heavy timber doors safeguarded the clerics and their staff.

CASTLES AS PRISONS

Popularized in movies and literature and by marketing representatives as places of torture, imprisonment, and disease-ridden hell, the dank underground chambers traditionally associated with medieval castle prisons most often served a temporary need, housing important hostages or prisoners of war while the captors awaited the payment of ransom or the settlement of a dispute. In reality, not every castle contained a dungeon, and most castles never functioned as prisons. However, the presence of a prison within the thick masonry walls would certainly have deterred the local populace from rebelling and given them temporary pause before violating the law.

The word "dungeon" actually derives from the French "donjon," a medieval word itself deriving from the Latin "dominium," meaning "lordship," which was used to identify the keep, the self-sufficient great tower that simultaneously functioned as a castle's internal strongpoint and the lord's residence. While the basement or lowest level of some keeps held the prison and guardrooms, not all did. Indeed, many ground level and underground chambers were actually used for storage. Frequently, the castle's prison was located near or inside the main gatehouse along with the guardrooms, to prevent the enemy from gaining access into the interior. This also allowed the guards to keep a close watch over their captives. Historically, as castle architecture evolved and many castles acquired gatehouses, owners often converted the donjons into prison towers—hence, the name "dungeon"; eventually, the term was used to designate any chamber that served as the castle's prison. A few castle keeps, such as the cylindrical great towers at Flint Castle in Wales and Bothwell Castle in Scotland, are still known as donjons—they were never intended as prisons.

Even though it seems reasonable to assume that castle-builders would situate their prisons away from the castle's vital inner core, many dungeon towers actually stood well inside the walls. At Pembroke Castle in Wales, the cylindrical dungeon tower erected by William de Valence, Earl of Pembroke during the late thirteenth century, was intentionally located close to the great keep along the perimeter of the inner bailey. The tower resembles those erected along the outer curtain wall and around the town of Pembroke itself. Accessible only from inside the inner bailey, the dungeon tower rose three stories. The basement level contained the dungeon itself, a small, poorly lit chamber known as an "oubliette" that was probably entered only via a trapdoor in the ceiling. A spiral staircase at the first-floor chamber led to the uppermost levels, which reputedly served as fighting platforms should an enemy breach the great gatehouse and storm the outer bailey. Interestingly, despite the existence of this prison tower, medieval graffiti cut in the form of crosses and heraldic shields suggests that prisoners may also have been held in a small chamber in Monkton Tower, which formed part of the curtain wall and guarded the water gate on the opposite side of the outer bailey from the dungeon tower.

One of the strangest locations for a prison tower can be found at Conwy Castle, Edward I's mammoth fortress in North Wales. There, the dungeon was accessible only from inside the great hall. On the southern side of the hall, a discreetly placed doorway in one of the window embrasures opened into a short mural passage. From there, a set of steps led to an adjoining room at about 4 feet above ground level. Unwary visitors might suddenly find themselves falling down onto the floor, and then, perhaps, through the trapdoor and into the pit-prison below. Once in the oubliette, they had no easy way out.[33]

One can only speculate as to why Master James of St. George designed the castle so that the prison was positioned immediately alongside the great hall. Perhaps he assumed the king's guests would be too preoccupied with the evening's entertainment to be aware of the plight of the prisoners nearby. Perhaps the dungeon's presence forewarned them to act with a degree of decorum when dealing with the warrior-king. Or, perhaps the tower's physical location outside the town itself made it the only reasonable place for a prison.

An oubliette (from the French "oublier" meaning "to forget") must have been an incredibly brutal place for confinement, with or without the physical tortures that may have accompanied imprisonment. Known throughout Europe and even in the Middle East, these early pit-prisons were usually shaped like slender cylinders. The only entrance into the windowless chambers was through a trapdoor in the ceiling, which opened from the floor of the guardroom above and was placed too high for the prisoners to grasp in an escape attempt. Guards tied doomed prisoners to a rope and then lowered them into the oubliette. They likewise used ropes and baskets to lower food to the prisoners. Some oubliettes were below ground level; on occasion, these filled with water seeping in from the ground, which made survival almost impossible.

The earliest-known medieval oubliettes survive at Pierrefonds in France, and at the Bastille, in Paris. The eleventh-to-twelfth-century Black Tower at Rumeli Hisari, in modern Turkey, contains an unusual variation. Guards forced unsuspecting prisoners along a long, dark passageway that ended above an opening in the floor through which they tumbled, never again to see the light of day. The Scots, on the other hand, fancied the bottle dungeon, a particularly unpleasant type of oubliette shaped like a bottle so that the prisoner could never lie down.

Newark Castle in Nottinghamshire was especially well equipped with four oubliettes. Probably added in the early fourteenth century during the castle's third major building period, the hexagonal northwest tower contained a round prison chamber and a beehive-shaped chamber known as a bottle dungeon. Ventilated by a slender slot in the exterior wall, the bottle dungeon was situated immediately alongside a square oubliette, which was embedded in the base of the west curtain wall. Further along this western wall, a three-sided tower held two more prisons, one a simple chamber, and the other, yet another oubliette. One of the many castles William the Conqueror erected shortly after seizing the English throne, Newark Castle's lengthy history included the destruction of Saxon houses and a cemetery to make way for the construction of a Norman earth and timber castle in 1069.[34]

Contrary to popular belief, relatively few people endured lingering deaths in pit-prisons. Imprisoned in Berkeley Castle in Gloucestershire by his wife, Queen Isabella ("the she-wolf of France"), and her paramour, Roger Mortimer, in 1327, the deposed King Edward II was forced to endure his final days confined to a small chamber on the first floor. Not as comfortable at it may seem, this chamber was located next to the opening of a 28-foot-deep cesspit (the pit-prison). Normally, guards dropped human prisoners onto a mass of animal flesh already decaying in the oubliette; but, as a royal, Edward was spared this fate. Aware that rotting carcasses emitted toxic fumes, Isabella's guards believed that the king would die if merely exposed to the malodorous vapors. However, Edward did not die. The king's surprising fortitude forced a creative response from the queen's henchmen—they allegedly murdered him with a red-hot poker. Edward III, the son of Edward II and Isabella, then became the King of England. For his mother's part in the deposition and death of his father, Edward committed Isabella to what amounted to house arrest at Castle Rising, in Norfolk. Allowed to come and go as she pleased until her death in 1358, the dowager queen frequently moved between Castle Rising and her castles at Mold and Hawarden, in the Welsh Marches, and Mere and Hertford, in England;[35] however, she lost all authority to influence royal decision-making.

When their medieval roles as fortified military residences became obsolete or their owners moved elsewhere, many British castles experienced a rebirth as prisons. Some continue in that capacity today. As early as 1195, Lydford Castle in Devonshire supported a "strong house" for prisoners, probably the masonry keep that still dominates the spot. By the fourteenth century, the castle served as the county prison and courthouse. From Lydford Castle local authorities enforced stannary law in wild Dartmoor, a major tin-mining region in England, until the county moved the prison to the much larger and more isolated Princetown, which was constructed in the nineteenth century to confine prisoners during the Napoleonic Wars.

In 1780, construction of a new county jail was completed inside the grounds of Haverfordwest Castle. The work entailed the conversion of several medieval structures. Placed along the southern wall of the inner ward, the compact prison building measured about 13 feet by almost 7 feet and had brick flooring. Lead doors prevented escape. Among the most notable inmates were French prisoners of war seized during the so-called last invasion of Britain in 1797. In 1816, a debtors' prison was added along the wall between the North Tower and the governor's house, which occupied the site of the original inner gatehouse. In 1820, an even larger, three-story jail was added to the outer ward of the castle, which contained some 110 cells, a chapel, a small courthouse, and eight wards fitted with male and female workrooms, dayrooms, and airing yards. To keep the prisoners gainfully occupied, two treadmills (one for men and the other for women) were installed inside the inner ward on the site of the medieval chapel to produce flour for their own bread. The jail finally closed in 1878.

Begun in the twelfth century but extensively modified in the late eighteenth and early nineteenth centuries, Lancaster Castle (Lancashire) has a lengthy history of use as a state prison and a courthouse. It boasts a reputation for sentencing to death more prisoners than any other English court. Besides the great keep, which still serves as one of Her Majesty's working prisons, Lancaster Castle features the Gaoler's House, erected in 1788; the prison for female felons, begun in 1792; the men's prison, begun two years later; a debtors' prison; the shire hall and crown court, also added in the 1790s; and the female penitentiary, built in 1821. The "drop room" confined convicted prisoners prior to their execution by hanging.

Although castles were not built to serve strictly as prisons, some housed royal prisoners in relative comfort and others were sites of bloody executions. Some prisoners, such as Queen Isabella, Edward III's notorious mother, and Mary, Queen of Scots, who were under house arrest, could generally come and go freely, as long as a guard accompanied them. In fact, castles played a crucial role in almost every event of significance in the Scottish queen's tumultuous life. In 1567, Mary found herself in a desperate and unhappy situation, married to the ruthless, ambitious, and notoriously unpopular James Hepburn, Earl of Bothwell. When Mary's supporters finally betrayed their queen, she and Bothwell fled to Borthwick Castle, south of Edinburgh, where their adversaries caught up to them. Hoping to quell the rebellion, Mary approached the rebels, but they promptly seized their queen and took her to Loch Leven Castle in what is now Perth and Kinross, the first of a series of castle prisons used to confine the Queen of Scotland. Bothwell, on the other hand, escaped, fleeing first to Crichton Castle in Mid Lothian and then on to Dunbar in East Lothian, where he had arranged to meet Mary. The meeting never took place.

At Loch Leven, Mary reputedly occupied the third floor of the main tower, perhaps in the range of rooms above the hall. No one can truly claim that the queen suffered during her confinement, except initially when her health failed her. Inside these chambers, Mary not only signed abdication papers and relinquished the throne, but she also danced, embroidered, had the companionship of her ladies-in-waiting, and gradually regained her health. Disguised as a servant and crouching down in the rescuing boat, Mary escaped from Loch Leven Castle on May 2, 1568. At Niddry Castle, West Lothian, she reclaimed the monarchy and gained a new following of supporters. However, as on so many other occasions, the Scottish queen made a misguided decision and headed into England to beg for Elizabeth's support. She promptly found herself back in prison.

On May 18, 1568, Mary was again under house arrest in the English border castle at Carlisle. Two months later, she was moved to Bolton Castle, in North Yorkshire, where she lived in relative comfort once she had obtained the proper furnishings, like special Turkish rugs that kept out the cold. In early 1569, she was sent to Tutbury Castle, in Staffordshire. Twice imprisoned at Tutbury, Mary hated the inhospitable place, which was already five hundred years old, dank, and partly ruined when she arrived. She again became ill and was transferred to the more comfortable Wingfield Manor, a fortified mansion in Derbyshire, and then to Chatsworth, where she regained her health, albeit tenuously. Other prisons included Sheffield Castle and Sheffield Manor in South Yorkshire, and Chartley Hall and Tixall in Staffordshire.

On September 21, 1586, Mary left Chartley Hall for yet another prison. Though probably reconciled to her fate by this time, the former Queen of Scotland had no idea that Fotheringhay Castle in Northamptonshire would be her final home. On February 8, 1587, Mary, Queen of Scots, bowed her head on the executioner's block in Fotheringhay's great hall and died. Some historians claim Mary's heart was buried at the castle, but it has never been found. The remains of the extensively ruined motte and bailey castle belie its momentous role in British history.

While some political prisoners had the freedom to roam the passages of their castle prison, some, like Henry Marten, the convicted regicide who signed King Charles I's death warrant, were largely restricted to a prison tower for the balance of their lifetime. Renamed for its most notable prisoner, the heavily defended Marten's Tower at Chepstow Castle was built in the late thirteenth century to house important guests. Imprisoned in 1660, Marten spent the remaining twenty years of his life under house arrest. Living with his wife on the first floor of the tower, their servants occupying the second floor, Marten not only received guests, but from time to time he was also able to visit associates in the local community.[36] Henry Marten died at the castle in 1680, at the age of 78.

Arguably the best known of Britain's medieval castle prisons is the Tower of London. Altered frequently over time, the 90-foot-high White Tower, or great keep, initially provided accommodation for the king and the castle's constable but also housed important prisoners, such as the Duke of Orleans, in its lavish upper levels. The basement, with its 15-foot-thick walls, was occasionally used to contain less savory characters. Over time, successive monarchs expanded and upgraded the castle and its defenses, transforming it into one of the world's most impressive concentric castles. The Tower of London provided palatial accommodation, but also imprisoned many historic figures,

MARTEN'S TOWER, Chepstow Castle. Probably constructed to provide Roger Bigod III, the lord of Chepstow Castle, with well-defended private accommodation, the battlemented Marten's Tower retains substantial spurred buttresses, which helped prevent collapse and thwarted undermining.

including Sir Walter Raleigh; Sir Thomas More; Welsh Prince Gruffudd ap Llywelyn; John Balliol, briefly the King of Scotland in the late thirteenth century; George, Duke of Clarence; two Earls of Essex; and Edward V (age 12) and his brother, Richard, Duke of York (age 9), now traditionally known as the "Princes in the Tower." Executions took place both inside the castle, where the likes of Queens Anne Boleyn and Katherine Howard lost their heads, and on Castle Hill, just north of the castle. The Tower of London continued to serve the monarchy as a state prison, confining Jacobites in the 1740s and German prisoners of war, including Rudolf Hess, in the 1940s.

CONCLUSION

Looking at a classic stone castle, like Dover, Caerphilly, or Warwick, one can spot an array of defensive mechanisms: impenetrably thick stone walls; tall crenellated towers spaced at intervals, which served as observation posts, places from which to fire upon an enemy below, and to block unwanted access; and twin-towered, battlemented gatehouses equipped with movable drawbridges, spiked portcullises, heavy timber doors, which could be barricaded with stout iron bars, murder holes and machicolations ideally poised above the gate passage and used to drop missiles or water upon attackers or douse burning timbers, and arrowslits, slots in the masonry behind which defenders could target the enemy and fire at them without being hit in return; and an enclosing moat or dry ditch, deep enough to test the mettle of the fittest soldiers and wide enough to limit an onslaught by even the most powerful of siege engines.

The casual observer can reasonably conclude that these mechanisms were developed and installed to protect a lord, his household, and his pocket of land from seizure. The conclusion seems logical; yet, upon closer inspection of a castle's physical makeup and history, one cannot help but realize that the properly fortified military residence served much more than a defensive role in medieval society. Indeed, a castle's defensive purpose was largely secondary to its offensive, aggressive role as a subjugator of a populace, a vehicle by which conquest could be solidified, and a structure that commanded a region with military license and its dominating physical presence.

CHAPTER 2

Castles as Defensive Strongholds

Shutting oneself up in a castle was not an attempt to avoid conflict, but a maneuver to make the enemy fight at a disadvantage.
—Philip Warner, *Sieges of the Middle Ages* (2000), 2

The intrusion of the Normans and their followers into Britain inevitably brought about a number of sociopolitical changes. Much of the populace rejected outside control, and rebellions against the new overlords continued. Consequently, castles appeared throughout the countryside. Initially erected to effect the Conquest, earth and timber castles were fairly simple structures with limited defensive capabilities. The goal of their builders was to establish a presence in a region. Some motte and ringwork castles featured steeply banked mounds topped by timber palisades and surrounded by dry ditches, which made scaling their walls a strenuous effort for even the most able-bodied of soldiers. The Normans swiftly recognized the fallibility of their earthwork castles, which burned easily and were prone to rot. They either refortified many of them with masonry walls and towers, as at York, or constructed completely new strongholds.

Increasingly equipped with more sophisticated defensive mechanisms, such as arrowslits, portcullises, and machicolations, Britain's castles took on a dualistic military role. Not only were they offensive strongholds intended to subjugate a population and dominate a region, castles were also intended to withstand peasant revolts, assaults by besieging armies, and trickery by ostensibly loyal subjects. Castle-builders, the kings, lords, and barons of the land, required defensive might for two crucial reasons: to protect themselves, their families, staff, and garrison during a siege; and to defend the lordship, prevent the seizure of land, and maintain an offensive posture in the region.[1]

BESIEGING A CASTLE

The medieval siege was a complex process that ended with a castle assault only when other tactics failed to force a surrender. Because the cost of besieging a castle was incredibly high, in terms of assembling and paying an army and gathering enough supplies and hauling them to the site, and also in terms of the time, effort, and lives involved, military leaders normally did not rush into battle. Indeed, if the besieging army lost too many men in an initial onslaught, they were often forced to retreat or give up the siege completely. Further, if they were successful enough to gain control of the castle, the now-weakened troops might not be capable of repulsing a renewed attack by forces sent to relieve the wounded garrison. Consequently, the full-out siege was normally a last resort, unless, of course, the attacking king or lord had a particular investment in breaking his opponent.

Although directly influenced by the Romans, medieval warriors devised their own procedures for carrying out a siege, often responding to developments in castle architecture, the defenses of which became more and more complex as siege technology improved. Initially, their assaults mainly concentrated on towns or major cities, which were often fortified, rather than on individual castles.[2] Until about 1100, siege tactics consisted mainly of using firepower to break through the castle's physical defenses or starving out the defenders.[3] During the twelfth and thirteenth centuries, siege warfare became increasingly sophisticated and, by the mid–fourteenth century, engines of great power, such as the ballista and trebuchet, became the mainstay of virtually every siege. At the same time, specific conventions for conducting a siege became well established.[4] The most practiced soldiers followed traditional protocol, which allowed honorable negotiation and surrender before resorting to pummelling the garrison into submission.

Just journeying to a castle site to lay siege involved meticulous planning. First, commanders had to devise an overall strategy for taking the castle.

Thought had to be given to where the best archers, skilled carpenters, black-smiths, sappers, and engineers could be drawn; to which lords owed knights' service to the king (if the king were waging the battle), and how many knights they would provide (knights normally were obligated to do forty days' service during the course of a year); to how much timber, lead, tools, nails, food, drink, livestock, and other provisions were required, and from where they could be acquired; and to the timing involved in assembling the massive entourage and moving the entire siege train—at an average rate of 9 miles per day[5]—across the countryside.

Given the huge effort involved in coordinating a siege and assembling an army, potential besiegers made at least cursory efforts to convince the garrison, the constable, or the lord of the castle to surrender peaceably. The besiegers would first send a herald or messenger to the castle to an-nounce the impending siege and propose that the defenders surrender or re-quest a truce for a specific period of time. Defiant garrisons often responded to the besiegers' effrontery by killing the herald and tossing his head or body over the battlements. On rare occasions, opposing leaders might meet in the open field to discuss terms, but generally they preferred their underlings to handle the face-to-face discussions.

When the prospect of surrender seemed unlikely, the attacking forces would begin their trek to the siege site, where they set up their encampment and constructed some basic defenses of their own not too far from the cas-tle's walls. Specialists would also begin erecting bulky, intimidating siege en-gines. Other soldiers fomented dissent in the surrounding countryside in an effort to recruit supporters and seize control of crops and other resources—assuming landowners and peasants had not already torched them. In fact, it was common for inhabitants of an area to use a "scorched earth" policy to sabotage an impending siege. After gathering food, livestock, and other items for their own use, they would intentionally burn their own lands to prevent the enemy from gaining any benefit from them. Oftentimes, the re-sulting famine left the besiegers no alternative but to retreat.

Surrender under honorable terms was a common way out of a siege. In many cases, the besiegers allowed the defenders a period of time, ranging from a week to forty days, to decide whether or not to give in. Truces effec-tively delayed a full-blown assault, so that the constable could contact the lord for directions on how to handle the situation or to gain assistance at the castle. In cases where supplies and reinforcements failed to arrive in time to bolster the garrison, they would fly a white flag as a sign of surrender. How-ever, lengthy truces could also lead to the deterioration of the attacking army, particularly when each knight's forty-day service obligation neared comple-tion and no reinforcements showed up to replace them. If a beleaguered garrison knew they had enough food and drink to carry them at least forty days or had notice that relief was on its way, they could survive the siege unscathed.[6] Truces also gave the defenders time to construct their own siege engines, shore up their defenses, and build wooden hoards (fighting platforms) on the battlements.

If the garrison refused surrender demands, the siege began with an overt act, a symbolic sign of intent. At times, attackers threw javelins or shot crossbows at the castle gateway to signal their intentions. On occasion, siege engines hurled missiles. By the late Middle Ages, cannon fire signaled the beginning of battle.

In order to ease access to the castle, attackers might first fill in the encompassing dry ditch or wet moat with vegetation, tree branches, gorse, heather, loose earth, or whatever was available locally and not needed for other purposes. Alternatively, they might use a barge to sail to the base of the curtain wall. Once the ditch could be crossed or the moat forded, the initial offensive could proceed rapidly. Often relatively mild, the early assault primarily consisted of an escalade (using ladders to scale the curtain wall) and small-arms fire, employing crossbows, long bows, and slings.[7] Scaling ladders frequently consisted of a single timber pole with footholds or pegs projecting outward. Rope-ladders used leather thongs and were equipped with grappling hooks that latched onto the castle wall. Other ladders had iron spikes at their bases to secure them into the ground, or used wooden wedges to remain upright. Still others used straps and buckles.[8]

The key to a successful escalade was for the aggressors to climb the ladders as quickly as possible, leap onto the battlements, and then immediately begin fighting any number of defenders. During this effort, besieging archers and crossbowmen outside the castle shielded themselves behind screens known as "pavises," and provided protective fire for their comrades while also attempting to kill the fighters on the battlements. The onrush would take place at several spots along the curtain wall in the hopes of splitting up the garrison, diverting their attention, and gaining access somewhere.

The besiegers simultaneously assaulted the main gate's heavy timber doors, timber fighting platforms, and timber rooftops shielding the castle towers, setting them afire or battering them with axes. They might also begin hammering the masonry defenses with picks, iron bars, and other tools, while being protected inside a hide-covered timber-and-iron framework, known variously as a "cat," "rat," "tortoise," or "turtle,"[9] and also as "sows," "weasels," and "mice."[10]

Of course, the defenders made every effort to thwart the escalade, by shoving ladders away from the walls, shooting at the besiegers and dropping stones, quicklime, or hot liquids upon them. They also attempted to douse any fires. It took nimble, sure-footed, quick-thinking men to maneuver their weighty armor and weapons and scale the walls successfully.

Some escalades actually succeeded in defeating a castle's garrison. In 1140, attackers seized the outer defenses of Devizes Castle, in Wiltshire, by using rope-ladders; however, the defenders managed to resist the siege for some time afterwards.[11] In 1327, the garrison at Norham Castle in Northumberland was victorious against an escalade.[12]

If the escalade successfully breached the castle's walls, the besiegers would chivalrously offer the garrison a final chance to surrender with honor or to call a temporary truce. On the other hand, when the escalade failed to make a serious dent in the defenses, the attackers intensified the onslaught. They also began constructing siege-works or a siege castle in preparation for a prolonged conflict. Then, they would man their most destructive weapons—the siege engines.

No two sieges were ever conducted in exactly the same way. How the assault took place depended on the strength, size, and resources of the attacking army, the condition and complexity of the castle's fortifications (some castles were easier to take than others), its armory and supplies, as well as the resolve of the besieged. Consequently, an army might employ several different types of siege engine, such as belfries, mangonels, ballistas, and trebuchets, to bring down the battlements, while also attempting to force surrender by other, perhaps less sensational, means.

If a castle was strong enough to withstand the pounding of the siege engines and if the garrison refused to surrender, the commander of the besieging army still had several options rather than giving up the fight. The next weapon employed would be the "sappers," skilled fighters capable of digging tunnels, propped up with timber frameworks, underneath castle walls and towers. Once the miners reached their destination, they filled the tunnel, sometimes called a "sap,"[13] with flammable materials, tar-soaked beams, branches, and vegetation, and set them alight. If things went according to plan and the flames consumed the timber props inside, the tunnel would promptly collapse, taking with it whatever stood on the ground overhead, and opening a breach in the curtain wall for the besiegers to storm through. To determine if a mine was being dug, defenders placed bowls of water on the castle walls and watched for ripples. The tiny waves indicated that sapping was underway, and the garrison then had a chance to respond. Sometimes, they dug countertunnels and surprised the sappers with defensive fire, floods, or thick smoke before the walls collapsed.[14] Undermining was not without risks, and miners were sometimes killed when a tunnel collapsed too early. Yet, the technique remained an effective tactic for sieges and capably brought down many powerful fortresses.

While sappers busily dug mines, other attackers would roll one last siege engine up to the castle walls—the siege tower, or "belfry." Used by the Romans, the belfry was a feat of engineering creativity, a multipurpose machine built to reach the battlements of the castle so that the men secreted inside could safely climb over the walls or utilize a series of weapons, like battering rams and mangonels, from positions of relative safety. The wheeled wooden tower normally stood at least three stories high. At the top, a strategically placed drawbridge opened to allow the attackers to scramble onto the battlements. Some belfries rose well over 90 feet high and were crowned with a mangonel or ballista. To protect the belfry from fire and the men inside from being shot, animal hides soaked in mud and vinegar covered the framework.[15] On rare occasions, iron plates also offered protection. The mechanism itself might carry scores of soldiers, who used ladders to move between levels. A belfry at the siege of Kenilworth Castle (1266) held 200 archers and 11 siege engines.[16]

Each man had a particular role to play in operating a siege tower. Some men were responsible for moving the clumsy structure into place; others stood poised with containers of water to keep fires at bay. The ground level often contained a ram, which swung on ropes or chains from the ceiling, and also held sappers who dug under the castle foundations. Archers, crossbowmen, gynours, and armored knights manned upper levels, firing at the defenders while waiting to pounce upon them when the belfry reached its destination.

Moving the belfry into position was no mean feat. Attackers first had to ensure the moat or ditch was filled in and the ground surface relatively smooth so that forward progress would not be impeded. Then, it took strong, persistent men—and sometimes oxen—to haul the unstable, heavy tower into place at the foot of a curtain wall. Windy weather posed problems and the defensive actions of the soldiers on the battlements could also thwart attackers' efforts.

Henry III employed two enormous belfries during the siege of Bedford Castle to tower over the battlements and shelter archers firing at the garrison. Unfortunately, almost nothing survives of this once-mighty castle. The siege itself was well documented by contemporary writers, and certainly the castle must have been a formidable foe in order to precipitate such an extensive and expensive undertaking. When finished, along with the execution of eighty men, the king ordered the complete demolition of the castle, the remnants of which survive about 55 miles north of London.

Given the destructive power of the war engines, the devastation that mining could cause to a castle, and the determination of the attacking army, one would expect a breach in the castle's walls or the surrender of the garrison during the later stages of a siege. But, as often as not, the besiegers had to resort to a final tactic to force capitulation. With the attackers already in place around the castle, and much of the land scorched, the likelihood was poor at best that reinforcements and additional supplies would safely reach the besieged. The besiegers could easily apply starvation tactics at this point.

Blockading the castle and adopting a wait-them-out attitude might come early in a siege, if the attackers believed the garrison had few resources to defend themselves. Then, a blockade might save lives on both sides of the fray, while also conserving the resources available to the besiegers if they decided to push ahead with a full-scale assault. However, when used as a tactic late in a siege, the blockade was intended to lower morale inside the castle and to starve the garrison into surrender. As food and drinking supplies dwindled, disease often spread rampantly, thanks to the catapulting of carcasses into the castle or the poisoning of the water supply with dead bodies or deadly chemicals, like sulfur.[17] Sometimes, garrisons held out for months during blockades and forced the besiegers to retreat when their supplies ran out.

As soon as a garrison surrendered, arrangements were made for the movement of captives and the payment of ransom, and the victors were expected to keep up their side of the bargain. A variety of solutions might be debated, including banishment, relinquishment of all personal property, or the symbolic humiliation of the captives. Not surprisingly, defeated leaders were often imprisoned or swiftly and brutally executed. It was clearly to their advantage to have in place as efficient, powerful, and complex a set of defenses as time, money, and technology allowed.

THE SIEGE WEAPONS

Medieval siege engines originated in Greek, Roman, and ancient Chinese warfare. In fact, Archimedes was responsible for advancing siege technology, which the Greeks had introduced to the world before the fourth century BC. The renowned mathematician and engineer actually developed several engines as early as 213 BC, when the Greeks fought the Romans at the siege of Syracuse. His prototypical "petrariae" (or "great stone-throwing engines") were copied and modified by the Romans and, later, used throughout the medieval world.

The Romans bequeathed two important siege engines to medieval warriors. The "onager," meaning "wild ass," consisted of a heavy timber trestle mounted midway on a horizontal timber frame. Operated by as many as ten men, the stone-throwing torsion machine capably projected stones and other missiles weighing 12 pounds or more for a distance of up to 500 yards. The onager's shooting motion, similar to what happens when children fling peas with a spoon, hurled the missile in an overhead arc. When fired, the engine's rear kicked upward, hence the descriptive name.

The onager's medieval counterpart, the mangonel, featured long-timber arms or beams, with large cuplike scoops affixed to one end to hold missiles or incendiary devices. "Gynours" ("gunners," the engine operators) pulled back the heavy beam and used skeins of twisted rope (the Romans supposedly used human hair) to hold it in place while they readied the missile. Then, they released the firing arm, which sprang into action. "Mangonel" apparently means "stone-thrower" and may derive from the Greek "mangano," meaning "crush" or "squeeze."[18]

Despite the inherent inaccuracy of this torsion-operated machine, which is sometimes called a "catapult," the mangonel could effectively break through stone walls or knock down a castle's battlements. Occasionally, mangonels projected dead carcasses over the battlements in an effort to spread disease into the castle. In response, defenders sometimes used their own siege engines to toss back one of the besiegers, if they had managed to capture him during the escalade, or a messenger who carried unacceptable surrender terms.[19]

Used in battle across Europe and the Holy Land, mangonels saw action when the Vikings besieged Paris (885), at the siege of Acre (1191), and at the siege of Chateau Gaillard, in France (1203–1204), where King Philip of France successfully used petraries, mangonels, mantlets (protective wooden screens), and siege towers (belfries) to defeat the English. Mangonels were also on hand in 1216, when France's Prince Louis besieged mighty Dover Castle, on England's southeastern coast.[20] Despite Louis' greatest efforts, which included a battery of siege engines and other tactics designed to take even the strongest of castles, he failed to breach Dover's formidable defenses (it is, arguably, England's mightiest castle).

Prior to the siege of Bedford Castle, Henry III requisitioned "petrarias," "mangonillos," and "berefridum cum balistis," or petraries, mangonels, and belfries with ballistas, and used them to great effect.[21] From June 22 to August 15, 1224, a petrary and two mangonels fired at a tower on the eastern wall, two more mangonels shot missiles at the western tower, and other mangonels aimed at the northern and southern sides of the castle.[22]

The Romans modified a modest Greek siege engine known as the "scorpion" into a horrific dart-firing machine called the "ballista," which was later used during the Middle Ages. Like the mangonel, the ballista was also powered by twisted skeins of rope, hair, or sinew, but, rather than firing its missiles in an overhead arc, the ballista projected its heavy stones, bolts, and spears along a horizontal path. Easy to fire accurately, smaller ballistas were effective antipersonnel weapons that skewered warriors to trees, while large field ballistas capably crushed castle roofs, as they would have done during the siege of Bedford. Ballistas could project a 60-pound stone at least 400 yards.

A variant of the ballista was a tension-driven device called the "springald," which closely resembled a crossbow in form and function. Used to project javelins, the springald had a vertical springboard fixed at its lower end to a timber framework.[23] Soldiers manually retracted the board, which moved like a lever. When released, the springboard smacked the spear or bolt projectile and thrust it toward its target. Springalds also made excellent defensive weapons: at Chepstow Castle, Wales, Roger Bigod mounted four springalds on the corners of the great keep to keep the enemy at bay. Although the springalds no longer survive, the platforms on which they stood are still visible.

While their comrades busily managed the engines, other besiegers used battering rams or bores (chisel-like poles) to pound the main gateway and crash through the walls. Rather than soldiers simply grabbing a giant log and repeatedly thrusting it at castle gates or stone walls until they broke open, the battering ram involved a sophisticated device operated from inside a timber framework called a "penthouse" or "pentise." Used in warfare as early as the sixth century, rams and bores were often pointed and iron-tipped for added effect, and were sometimes shaped, not surprisingly, as ram's heads. The ram or bore was suspended by chains or ropes from the ceiling inside the penthouse, so that when the besiegers arrived close enough to the castle, they would rhythmically swing the beam and pound the walls into submission.

Also known as a "cat" or "sow," the movable penthouse consisted of a lanky timber gallery covered with a pointed roof, cloaked with wet hides to prevent burning, and braced with iron plates to deflect missiles dropped by the defenders overhead. Battering rams sometimes needed scores of men to operate them. The attackers used rollers, levers, ropes, pulleys, and winches to pull the penthouse into place at the base of the castle wall. They then removed the wheels to stablize the structure.[24]

Rams were most effective against timber defenses, particularly the heavy oak doors barricading most main gates. Against stone fortifications, they worked best when battering angular corners. Antiram tactics included using hook-ended ropes to grab the ram and turn over the cat, or swinging beams on pulleys to smash the timber penthouse as it approached the castle. Popular during the Crusades, battering rams were effectively employed in 1191 to besiege Acre, a walled city with a formidable citadel. They became obsolete once the most powerful siege engine of all—the trebuchet—began to dominate European sieges.

The terrible trebuchet was the mother of all stone-throwing siege engines. A purely medieval invention, the giant machine struck fear into the hearts of many garrisons. Castle defenders were known to yield once they noticed the mighty engines rising in the besiegers' camp, especially when the attackers were led by someone with a reputation for brutality and prowess in battle. In 1304, for example, Edward I assaulted Stirling Castle using an enormous trebuchet that, when disassembled, reputedly filled thirty wagons. Even before the machine could be constructed, the sight so intimidated the Scots that they surrendered. Edward, however, decided to carry on with the siege and witness for himself the power of the masterful weapon, nicknamed "Warwolf," which accurately hurled missiles weighing as much as 300 pounds.[25]

The name, "trebuchet," probably comes from an Old French word, "trabucher," which means "to overturn or fall" and probably described the action of the timber beam that "falls over" the associated pivot. Worked with springs, powered by a counterweight mechanism, and able to accurately hit targets at a range of 500 yards with missiles exceeding 300 pounds, the trebuchet's ability to relentlessly pound a curtain wall until it broke open made the engine an invaluable siege weapon. The trebuchet was equally useful for flinging all sorts of projectiles over the curtain walls, to spread disease, break down the defenders' siege weapons, and generally create mayhem. On occasion, besiegers might strap a captive soldier, unwelcome messenger, or kinsman of one of the defenders to the throwing sling of the trebuchet and fling him—or his body parts—back into the castle.

Besiegers also used trebuchets to hurl incendiary devices, including flaming missiles, casks of burning tar, and Greek fire. Dreamt up in Constantinople in the seventh century AD, Greek fire was a particularly nasty concoction of sulfur, pitch, charcoal, tallow, salt peter, turpentine, crude antimony,[26] and other ingredients. The substance stuck like glue to almost any surface and was nearly impossible to extinguish, except with sand, salt, or urine—water only fanned the flames.[27] In twelfth-century medieval France, Count Geoffrey V of Anjou used a siege engine to hurl a heated iron jar filled with Greek fire at the castle of Montreuil-Bellay, which was promptly destroyed after a three-year siege. The exact components of Greek fire remain a mystery.

Engineers in seventh-century China may have perfected an early form of trebuchet (quite possibly, the "perrier," a traction trebuchet operated solely by men).[28] Its medieval counterpart, however, effectively applied the principle of counterpoise and replaced the manpower with a massive ballast box filled with stone and other objects, which sometimes weighed as much as 20 tons.[29] On the opposite end of the beam, a leather sling or pouch clutched whatever type of missile the besiegers had stockpiled. After mechanically hauling the counterweight into the air, the gynours allowed the box to drop. The force created by the falling weight propelled the sling-end upward and flung the missile at a specific point. The same spot could be pummeled repeatedly. Eventually, the incessant pounding breached walls, killed personnel, or crushed siege engines defending the castle.

Counterweight trebuchets probably arrived in England when Prince Louis of France besieged Dover Castle during his near-successful invasion of England. In 1216, the French army first used a variety of techniques and weapons to try to breach the resistant castle walls. However, the two sides signed a truce in October, and Louis moved most of his troops to London. After the English garrison broke the truce, killed many of the French soldiers posted outside the castle, and interfered with the movement of French troops and supplies, the prince returned to Dover to conduct another siege the following May. This time, he raised a trebuchet, which, ironically, proved ineffective. Perhaps the French army had yet to develop the skills needed to effectively use the unfamiliar siege machine.

Eight days after renewing the siege at Dover, the French suffered a massive defeat at Lincoln, well to the north, and Louis moved his trebuchet back to London. Then, in August 1217, English forces led by Hubert de Burgh, Dover Castle's constable, devastated the French fleet as they brought reinforcements to their countrymen. The defeat forced the prince to give up his ambitions for the English throne.[30] Despite the losses and his retreat back to France, Louis left an important legacy in England: new technology that not only changed how sieges were conducted but also influenced the design of castle defenses.

Described as a "master in the art of castle warfare,"[31] England's Edward I was particularly fond of the trebuchet and used it, and other siege engines, against castles in Scotland, Wales, and France during the late thirteenth and early fourteenth centuries. His siege of Caerlaverock Castle in 1300 aimed to suppress the Scottish drive to remain independent from England. Located in the Scottish Borders about 3 miles from Dumfries, the castle of the Lords Maxwell posed a formidable obstacle to the king's plans to control Scotland. According to Walter of Exeter, a Franciscan monk of the time, "Caerlaverock was so strong a castle that it feared no siege before the King came there, for it would never have had to surrender, provided that it was well supplied, when the need arose, with men, engines and provisions."[32]

To meet the challenge, Edward required all of England's noblemen who owed knights' service or held property in his name to assemble at Carlisle, in the northwestern corner of the country. He commissioned Master Richard and a variety of specialist laborers to construct a cat, battering ram, belfry, springalds, and robinets (probably trebuchets), and also stockpiled large stones, timber, bolts, animal hides, and tools. Ships hauled supplies by sea, while the siege train journeyed northward to the castle.

Once at their destination, the English army set up their camp, erected tents and huts, stabled the horses, foraged in the surrounding countryside for timber and other resources. Then, they laid siege to the Scottish castle. English and Breton soldiers toting small arms charged the castle walls while siege engines began their assault. Sappers began undermining the walls.[33] Despite the deaths of several soldiers, the garrison remained defiant and the siege continued for some twenty-four hours. Finally, the mighty siege engines breached the curtain wall. Waving a white flag, the Scots first requested a truce to discuss terms, but then surrendered when their spokesman was killed with an arrow. The English ended the siege by formally taking over the castle and flying the king's standard overhead. Incredibly, the garrison amounted to only sixty men, whose fates varied from reprieve to hanging.[34]

During the thirteenth century, cannons appeared in medieval warfare. As the new fighting machines increasingly became the weapon of choice, timber-framed siege engines became obsolete. Warfare practices changed as well. Castle-builders devised sturdier defenses to thwart the bombards, as at Craignethan Castle in South Lanarkshire, where low, thick bastion walls with cannon loops were intentionally added in 1530 to withstand cannon fire.[35] The construction of new castles waned, and Henrician gun forts, armed with heavy artillery emplacements to ease cannon positioning, began to take their place. However, until cannon technology progressed far enough to make their use more practical, medieval siege engines remained the weapons of choice and besieging armies continued to follow the conventions of warfare established centuries earlier.

COUNTERING A SIEGE

GARRISONS: THE HUMAN DEFENSES

Even though they were poised to respond to threats at a moment's notice, the majority of British medieval strongholds maintained only a limited number of soldiers. In addition to the constable, who managed the military aspects of the castle in the lord's absence, a typical peacetime garrison might consist of less than ten men, depending of course on the size and status of the castle. Even royal castles and lordship castles could capably function with between twenty and one hundred men, who might include knights, men-at-arms, crossbowmen, archers, and support ranks, such as smiths, porters, and carpenters. During the late thirteenth century, Caernarfon Castle, the king's imperial stronghold, reportedly only employed a constable, two sergeant horsemen, ten sergeant crossbowmen, one smith, one carpenter, one skilled craftsman, and twenty-five men-at-arms.[36] During wartime or when local rebellion seemed likely, garrisons would be augmented, but it was not uncommon during much of the Middle Ages for relatively small garrisons to ably thwart a besieging army.

Lords ensured the manning of their castles in wartime by imposing a feudal obligation on the local population that required tenants (holders of fiefs) to provide a specific number of men for either "castle-guard" or "knights' service" for a prescribed period of time. During the twelfth century, a quota system of sorts was used to calculate the actual number of men owed at any one time.[37] A century later, the quota system was greatly modified and then largely abandoned in the 1300s;[38] rather, a tenant's feudal obligation was often accomplished by a monetary transaction known as "scutage," the assessment of which was still based on quotas but did not involve bartering human labor. With the extra cash flow, the lord of the castle could then afford to hire professional soldiers for a permanent garrison.[39]

Also known as "castle ward" for service that often took place in the ward or bailey, castle-guard duty was normally allocated on a two-month basis so that the garrison had enough men to swiftly shift to a wartime footing and adequately defend the castle against a siege.[40] In addition to manning observation posts and gatehouses day and night, these men also took the opportunity to hone their battle skills, sparring with each other, and training for combat.

Supporting a substantial garrison cost the lord a considerable outlay of money, food, and weapons. So, members of the household, such as servants, the chaplain, and even the lady of the castle, could be called to arms when necessary. Indeed, many wives of absent lords, such as Lady Bankes of Corfe Castle and Lady Arundell of Wardour Castle, fought with their garrisons and successfully defended their homes from destruction during the English Civil War. Their husbands were elsewhere, pursuing arguably nobler vocations such as attending the king. Without the human element, whatever the gender, defense of any castle would have been futile.

THE LADY'S ROLE IN SIEGE WARFARE

In the lord's absence, responsibility for the management of the castle might fall to his wife, the lady of the castle, and to the small group of staff members who permanently occupied the stronghold. At times, the lady acted as constable (or chatelaine), shrewdly and successfully commanding her garrison and other occupants during a siege. During the English Civil War, two bold women rallied their garrisons against assaults from parliamentarian troops.

In early 1643, the English Civil War finally descended upon southern England and approached Wardour Castle in Wiltshire. For Lady Blanche Arundell, the struggle meant nothing short of sheer determination and the headstrong defense of her family's home. For two years, her husband, Thomas, 2nd Lord Arundell, had had his own troubles to contend with, thanks to his royalist affinities, and often left his wife alone to contend with the administration of the estate and castle at Wardour. Even though Parliament ordered Arundell's arrest, he managed to evade capture, organize a troop of horse soldiers, and ride to fight for the king's cause. By year's end, Arundell was at Oxford, preparing to support Charles I. Lady Blanche remained behind, to head her household, care for her children, and command her supporters against a ferocious siege.

In late April 1643, a force of 1,300 parliamentarians led by Sir Edward Hungerford besieged the castle. Despite having only twenty-five troops and a few household staff members to help defend her home, Lady Arundell refused to surrender. For eight days, the defenders withstood the onslaught. The thick fourteenth-century walls thwarted the efforts of the besiegers, and the attackers' small cannons inflicted only minor damage to some windows and a chimneypiece. Then, Hungerford ordered his men to plant gunpowder mines underneath the castle walls. They planted one mine in the service tunnel that led to the cellars under the eastern side of the main entrance, and another in the base of a latrine chute draining the private apartments. The thick-walled building actually withstood the explosions, but the garrison recognized the increasing threat and persuaded Lady Arundell to surrender on May 2.

Determined to reoccupy his ancestral home, Henry, the new 3rd Lord and heir to the Arundell estate, led a royalist assault on Wardour in December of 1643. This time, pounding by cannons broke windows and gouged the walls. The castle withstood the onslaught until mid-March 1644, when Henry Arundell ordered his men to lay gunpowder mines. This time, the royalist mines devastated the castle, much to Lord Arundell's dismay.

Apparently, one of the parliamentarian troops garrisoning the castle unwittingly tossed a match into the tunnel where a mine lay hidden. The resulting explosion ripped a gaping wound in the rear of the building and destroyed the upper floors of the castle. Asleep at the time, the parliamentary leader, General Ludlow, had to single-handedly defend what was left of his bedchamber until his men could reach him. After four days, the threat of more mining and starvation forced the defenders to admit defeat. Henry, Lord Arundell, had indeed regained control of his castle, but he had rendered it unliveable at the same time.

At Corfe Castle, Lady Mary Bankes gallantly stymied the best efforts of parliamentarian troops who readied themselves for an easy victory when the lord of the castle, Sir John Bankes, was tending to the king's business elsewhere in England. In May 1643, Lady Bankes wisely signed a treaty agreeing to turn over the castle's four cannons to the parliamentarians in exchange for her tenants' safety. Meanwhile, knowing a full-fledged attack was inevitable, she began to stock supplies and recruit aid from the king's supporters. Two months later, opposition forces began an intensive assault on Corfe Castle. For over six weeks, parliamentarian siege engines failed to breach the walls. Whereas the attacking army lost over 100 men, only two royalist soldiers died. When Lady Bankes' husband finally returned to Corfe, he espied what he interpreted as the utter devastation of his village and castle. Promptly retreating, the not-so-stout-hearted Sir John abandoned his wife, sons, and castle to the machinations of the parliamentarian forces. He died within six months.

Lady Mary, however, carried on, and brazenly again led her royalist garrison into the fray in 1645. In February 1646, one of her own soldiers betrayed his comrades and opened the doors to the besiegers, who speedily captured the castle. After withstanding seven centuries of tumult, Corfe Castle then met its demise at the hands of parliamentarian troops, who ruthlessly slighted the defiant fortress. Soon afterwards, Lady Bankes, now widowed, moved her children to safety in London.

KEEPING BESIEGERS AT BAY: THE PHYSICAL DEFENSES

Over time, builders developed increasingly sophisticated ways to defend their castles. The choice of location was always a critical decision, for castles situated in wide open spaces were naturally more vulnerable to attack than if they dominated steep-sided hilltops. Consequently, one of the first and foremost tasks would be to identify the ideal site, ideal at least in terms of what the lord deemed necessary to meet his particular needs and to fulfill his expectations for a fortified military residence. In addition to having access to a reliable water supply to replenish the well, the perfect setting might feature a vantage point from which to view the surrounding landscape (and, of course, to overawe the local populace). Indeed, scores of castles were positioned on rocky summits or parcels of land such as bluffs or promontories, where at least one side of the property possessed natural defenses, such as sheer cliffs, which would form an imposing obstacle to an advancing army. Even motte-builders often reshaped natural hillocks into castle mounds, which not only eased the laborious task of excavating and erecting the mound but also strengthened the structure. Locating a castle so that the sea or a river washed one or more sides, especially if the castle sat on its own island, was another way to make use of the land's natural defensive capacity. Whether natural or artificial, water barriers successfully kept the enemy—and their siege engines—at bay.

Contrary to the popular belief that most castles occupied hilltop positions, it is important to recognize that scores of castles were actually built on low-lying areas.[41] Castle-builders were just as likely to prize low-lying, river-ine positions, which eased the movement of supplies and soldiers to and from the castle and helped prevent them from being cut off from assistance during a siege. In fact, Edward I intentionally situated his great Welsh castles, including Conwy and Harlech, to ensure access by water. Ironically, the waters that once lapped the base of Harlech Dome, which the castle crowns, have long since receded; the modern-day vision even more dramatically reinforces the notion that the strategic value of a hilltop setting outweighed any other type of setting. Certainly locations with panoramic views and precipitously steep sides, as at Carreg Cennen, enhanced a castle's defensive capacity. Yet, completely isolating a castle on a mountain peak could also make its residents vulnerable to blockades and starvation tactics from a besieging army. The shrewd castle-builder selected a location which afforded natural defensive strength, swift communication links to distant allies, and the ability to move from place to place with relative ease.

DITCHES AND MOATS

Long before the first castles appeared in Europe, people used ditches—often in combination with substantial earthen embankments, known as ramparts—to protect themselves. During the Neolithic era and in the late Bronze and Iron Ages, enormous causewayed enclosures and hillforts such as Maiden Castle in Dorset, Old Oswestry in Shropshire, and South Cadbury in Somerset, sprang up in the countryside. Built to enclose and secure communities rather than to function as private fortifications, these distinctive forts consisted of one or more sets of earthen ramparts. Adjoining ditches traced the contours around the perimeter of the site and were topped with timber palisades for added protection.

The inhabitants of these remarkably enduring forts found themselves relatively safe from outside assault—that is, until the Romans invaded Britain and managed to breach the defenses with their superior technology. While the tribal groups who dominated Britain fought vigorously to repel the Roman advance, which began in earnest in AD 43, the invaders effectively completed their conquest within forty years, establishing a series of fortresses, erecting a 73-mile wall across northern England, and Romanizing Britain over the ensuing three centuries. Like their prehistoric predecessors, the Romans also made effective use of ditches and embankments to take command of the countryside, as at Richborough Castle in Kent, where they first established themselves in England. Now extensively decayed, Richborough (the Roman "Rutupiae") featured two distinct sets of ditches. The first, built shortly after the Romans set foot on shore in AD 43, enclosed the entire site; the second set, comprised of three ditches and adjacent banks, was added during the third century AD to enclose a smaller fort near the center of the site. The characterization of Richborough as a "castle" is misleading, for the site actually functioned as a fort.

The Romans also effectively used ditches along Hadrian's Wall to block penetration into Roman Britain from northern tribes. A ditch lined the stretches of earthworks along most of its entire length. The "vallum," a flat-bottomed ditch flanked by two earthen ramparts, paralleled the main wall on its southern side. Historians speculate that the vallum delineated the rear boundary of the military zone established by the great wall.[42]

After the Romans withdrew from Britain in the fifth century, the Saxons began to dominate the countryside. They too recognized the benefit of constructing ramparts and ditches as barricades to outside aggression. Among the most notable Saxon contributions to the British landscape is Offa's Dyke, built on the border between England and Wales by King Offa of Mercia in the eighth century. Intended to thwart Welsh incursions into Offa's territory, some 70 miles of fragments of the original bank and ditch (which faces Wales) still distinguish Saxon England from Celtic Wales.

With the Norman Conquest and the concomitant spread of castles throughout the British Isles, the creative use of ditch-building was essential to maintaining control of the kingdom. Depending upon the choice of location, castle-builders constructed ditches to enclose an entire site or to line its most vulnerable spots. For example, if the site occupied a headland, a ditch was often built only on the inland-facing sides of the castle. On the other hand, the royal builders of the Tower of London shrewdly chose to build William I's fortress immediately alongside the River Thames inside the remains of a Roman fort. The river not only allowed easy access to supplies and shipping, it also acted as a natural barrier to assault from the south. Around the inland perimeter, deep ditches defended the castle.

Even though castles are traditionally associated with water-filled ditches, commonly known as "moats," in actuality most castle ditches were dry. Nevertheless, dry ditches served the same basic function as their water-laden counterparts: to thwart a siege and prevent the enemy from capturing the castle, and, at the same time, to help perpetuate the lord's authority over the region.

Whether wet or dry, ditches formed a considerable barrier that blocked an army's approach, forced soldiers to operate siege engines at a distance too far to be effective, and made undermining of the castle walls virtually impossible. Siege engines such as the battering ram and belfry required a position immediately next to the curtain wall. In order to accomplish this, besiegers had to risk their lives filling in the ditches with bracken, rubble, and whatever else they could find to level the ground before hauling the engines into place, or they had to sail or swim across the moat, a task which could prove quite daunting at best. Wearing heavy armor and toting cumbersome crossbows hindered access to an enditched castle, especially when the attacker found himself confronted with pointed timber stakes embedded in the ditch. Even without armor, modern-day visitors will still find scaling the steep sides of a dry ditch a challenging experience.

Ditch designs differed from castle to castle. Basically, moats contained U-shaped ditches while dry ditches were V-shaped. Ditch dimensions varied considerably, widths ranging from less than ten feet to over 60 feet across,[43] and depths from as shallow as 3 feet to well over 25 feet. Many were lined (revetted) with some sort of material, such as clay or stone slabs, turf or timber, which helped prevent collapse.[44] Ditches cut into solid bedrock were effective defensive features that could easily stymie undermining. An outstanding example exists at Goodrich Castle in Herefordshire, where fossatores (the ditchers) carved a remarkable ditch (measuring 90 feet wide by 28 feet deep)[45] into the red sandstone bedrock on the castle's eastern and southern sides. The other sides sported natural defensive features. Rock hauled from the ditch, which was probably excavated in the twelfth century,

THE ROCK-CUT DITCH at Goodrich Castle. The enormous rock-cut ditch enclosing Goodrich Castle, in Herefordshire, measured 90 feet wide by 28 feet deep and acted as a formidable barrier during a siege.

was used as building material for sections of the castle itself. Other impressive rock-cut ditches can be found at Harlech Castle (Gwynedd) and at Cilgerran Castle (Pembrokeshire).

Earth and timber castles also made extensive use of ditches to extend their defensive capacity as well as to provide a convenient source of building material. The ditch enclosing the ringwork at Wooler, Northumberland, for example, measured about 3 feet deep and stretched 33 feet across.[46]

Supplying enough water to fill a moat could be a costly and complex project. Consequently, engineers relied upon nearby water sources to feed and replenish the moat. Both the impressive motte castle at Berkhamsted and the quadrangular castle at Bodiam, arguably England's best-known moated castle, were fed by springs, whereas rivers replenished the moats at Clavering in Essex and Skenfrith in Monmouthshire. Filled by the River Monnow, Skenfrith's stone-revetted moat measured 9 feet deep and 46 feet wide;[47] at Bodiam Castle, where the moat measures some 500 feet by 350 feet,[48] the broad waters came from a series of springs. Reflooded after archaeological excavations in the early twentieth century, Bodiam's enormous moat seems much more a lake than merely a water-filled ditch. At many sites, the moving waters also served as the castle's sewage system. Latrine chutes often dumped human waste into the moats at their base, and the fluctuating waters would push the remains away from the castle. In the meantime, however, sewage-filled moats made the prospect of assaulting a castle even less appealing.

The late thirteenth century experienced a surge in castle-building technology, largely thanks to the innovative minds of King Edward I and his master mason, James of St. George. Of Edward's great castles in northern Wales, all were deliberately situated to afford access to the sea for easy replenishment, the transport of troops, water defense—and the king's convenience. Edward's private entrance to Conwy Castle, for example, overlooked the confluence of the River Conwy and the Gyffin Stream and allowed him to come and go as he wished—at least in theory. The Welsh rebellion of 1295 led to Edward's self-imposed imprisonment within the castle, which lasted until reinforcements finally arrived. Fossatores situated Edward's castle at Flint so that the tidal waters of the Dee Estuary not only filled the outer ditch, which faced the medieval town, but also flowed into the inner ditch, which enclosed the great tower and lined the southern side of the inner ward, and around the northern and eastern sides of the stronghold. Today, the land remains marshy, and at times the tidal waters of the Dee still flood the site. And, concentric Beaumaris, Edward's last Welsh castle, made strategic use of the waters of Colwyn Bay to flood its enclosing moat. The sea waters once transported huge ships, some of which reportedly weighed as much as 40 tons,[49] to a well-appointed dock safeguarded by the so-called Gunner's Walk, where crewmen could unload and move cargo directly into the castle.

Technological advances in the ability to manipulate the direction of stream, river, and sea waters encouraged the construction of late medieval castles in low-lying, less naturally defended spots, such as at Bodiam, mentioned above, and at Kirby Muxloe Castle, located in Leicestershire. Begun but not completed by William, Lord Hastings, a few years before his execution in 1483, the attractive brickwork quadrangular castle featured a sophisticated system that made strategic use of dams, hollow logs, wooden plugs, sluices, and screens of oak stantions to manipulate the waters of two brooks so that they would fill the moat and also maintain a balance in the levels of the larger brook, the moat, and a vital fishpond located along the smaller brook. Despite their sophistication, neither Bodiam nor Kirby Muxloe, whose moats so visually reinforced the status of their owners, could compete with the lakelike enclosures erected by the thirteenth-century builders of Kenilworth and Caerphilly Castles, where the construction of water defenses reached their zenith.

GATEWAYS

The main entrance into a castle was also its most vulnerable spot. Whomever controlled the access point controlled the castle. Consequently, considerable attention was focused on ensuring that all gaps in the walls were as well protected as possible, so that attackers could not batter down the doorway and wreak havoc on the interior. As castle-building technology advanced, so did the defensive complexity of the main entrance. The simplest way to construct a main entrance was to cut an archway through the curtain wall and fit the opening with timber doors. However, not only were the doors subject to burning and battering, the lack of overhead vantage points meant the defenders had scant warning of an imminent attack.

In addition to simple archways cut into the curtain wall, many eleventh-century castles acquired simple square or rectangular gatetowers. Essentially redesigned mural towers, the ground floors of which were bisected by a single passage, some gatetowers projected beyond the line of the curtain wall, as at Exeter, in Devon, where one of England's earliest-known castle gatetowers still stands. Erected by William the Conqueror in about 1068, the passage itself has long since been blocked but the tower remains substantially complete. It is fronted by a barbican and a ditch, which together afforded extra protection. Other gatetowers stood flush with the curtain wall, the passageway and remainder of the structure projecting inwards into the bailey behind it.

During the late twelfth century, castle-builders increasingly experimented with the use of flanking towers to safeguard a gate passage. For example, William Marshal, Earl of Pembroke and one of Britain's most innovative castle-builders, bolstered the defensive capacity of the simple archway leading into Chepstow Castle's middle bailey by strategically placing a substantial round tower adjacent to it.

During the early thirteenth century, castle-builders like the Marshals and King Henry III took the next logical step in gateway construction. They began building twin-towered gatehouses, which were fitted not just with enormous towers that flanked elongated gate passages but also with numerous defensive mechanisms which transformed the structures into effective killing machines. A chamber over the gate passage normally contained the constable's accommodation and/or the windlass room, which held the winding mechanism used to raise and lower the drawbridge and portcullises.

LOOKING TOWARD the great keep at Chepstow Castle. A massive round tower dominates the curtain wall separating the lower and middle baileys at Chepstow Castle. Probably erected by William Marshal the Younger, the innovative round tower provided defensive support for the simple gateway alongside it. The great hall-keep looms in the background.

Internal mural passages and spiral staircases radiated from different levels of the gatehouse toward the curtain wall, where they connected to other towers and to the wall-walk and battlements, from which soldiers could fire upon the enemy. The powerful Constable's Gate added by Henry III to Dover Castle successfully organized five massive battlemented towers around a narrow passageway guarded by a single portcullis and set of double-leaved doors. Erected in the 1220s, the imposing gatehouse still serves as the deputy constable's residence.

Controlling the gate passage was the key to controlling the castle, therefore much of the goal when installing the passage was to equip the gatehouse with the most effective, state-of-the-art features. Arrowslits, narrow cross-shaped grooves also known as "arrowloops" or "crossloops," penetrated the walls at strategic locations and allowed crossbowmen to watch and shoot at an attacker while shielded by the tower walls. Sets of portcullises and heavy doors could be lowered into place in a moment's notice, barring movement through the passageway or trapping the enemy between them. Generally made from spikes of oak, covered and linked together with iron,

Portcullis. A fine example of a typical portcullis, complete with a wicket, adorns the main gateway at Caldicot Castle in Monmouthshire.

portcullises functioned as movable iron grates or grilles (known as "yetts" in Scotland), which could be lowered into place with the aid of a windlass stored in an overhead chamber. The windlass was operated by a series of ropes, chains, pulleys, and a mechanized winding drum and made use of grooved slots carved into the gate-passage walls to ensure correct placement.

A pair of heavy timber doors was normally placed close to each portcullis to manage movement along the gate passage. Consisting of thick oak timbers secured into an oak framework and reinforced with iron nails and straps, the double doors, which opened outwards, could be secured into place by sliding iron bars or bolts into slots carved into the stone doorjambs. Nowadays, even if the portcullis and doors no longer survive, the presence of grooves and drawbar holes provides reliable evidence of their medieval existence. A fine example of a medieval doorway survives at Chepstow Castle. It features a smaller wooden doorway, known as a "wicket," which could be opened to allow individual access rather than an entire entourage of people, equipment, or mounted men.

Besides the portcullis, gaping openings in the vaulted ceiling of a gate passage, called "murder holes" or "meurtrieres," allowed soldiers standing in the windlass room or constable's chamber to drop a variety of items down into the gate passage. While tradition and speculation has it that murder holes were commonly used to throw stones and other heavy missiles onto the heads of unsuspecting besiegers, they quite likely originated as devices that allowed defenders to quench the flames of an enemy's fire burning the timber defenses situated within the passage. Some historians believe that the holes functioned as slots through which timber frameworks could be moved,[50] but this seems unlikely.

One of the most characteristic yet perplexing features of many castle gatehouses, tower tops, and rooflines is the "machicolation." Said to function much like the murder hole, machicolations typically projected outward from the tops of gatetowers to create a series of openings, or crenellated parapets, which allegedly allowed defenders to safely toss missiles or water down onto enemies or fires below. Reputedly brought to Britain by soldiers returning from the Crusades, these curious devices make shrewd use of corbelling to add an ornate flair to the facades of scores of castles. Two particularly outstanding examples rim the gatehouse and towers at Raglan Castle and Caerlaverock Castle.

The constable's gatehouse at Harlech Castle, begun by Edward I in 1283, is arguably the finest example of its kind and survives virtually intact. The splendid struc-

MACHICOLATIONS. The great gatehouse at Raglan Castle, Monmouthshire, features an impressive set of machicolations, carved openings at roof level that functioned like "murder holes" and were reputedly used to pour liquids or drop missiles down on an unsuspecting enemy.

ture actually contained two gateways. The first was a squat archway, flanked by two squat cylindrical turrets that overlooked a rock-cut ditch framing the eastern, inland side of the castle (which was easier to reach than the sheer-sided western side that faced the sea). The second was an enormous multi-level twin-towered behemoth to the rear. Fitted with three portcullises, three sets of double doors equipped with drawbars and arrowslits facing into the passage from the adjoining guardrooms, the complex gate passage stretched along the lowest level of the great gatehouse and also provided access to the porter's lodge. Rising inside the two interior corner towers, the battlemented top floors of which offered panoramic views of the countryside, were spiral staircases that provided access to the upper levels, where huge, well-appointed residential chambers comfortably accommodated the constable and important guests. Residents were warmed by fireplaces and had access to the chapel and small vestries, several latrines, a great hall, and an adjoining chamber. Bed chambers filled the massive round towers. More than likely, the central story, which conveniently connected to the inner bailey via an exterior staircase, served as the constable's residence. This type of structure was also known as a "keep-gatehouse" because of its dual purpose.

Had construction been completed on Edward I's imperial castle at Caernarfon, the King's Gate would probably have surpassed Harlech's, at least in respect to its defenses. Master James of St. George intended the intimidating structure to contain at least six portcullises, five double doorways, nine murder holes, arrowslits, and spy holes.[51] However, work ceased in the 1320s, when the great gatehouse was little more than a shell.

The imposing gatehouse defending Denbigh Castle used a multitowered structure to confuse attackers and command the route taken into the stronghold. Built by Henry de Lacy, Earl of Lincoln and one of Edward I's commanders during his wars against the Welsh, Denbigh Castle is a veritable maze of features deliberately situated to thwart an enemy assault. Three 40-

THE GREAT
GATEHOUSE at
Harlech Castle.
Equipped with heavy
defenses, numerous
residential chambers,
and an unusual inner
stairway that allowed
easy access to the
upper level from
inside the castle, the
enormous main gate-
house at Harlech
Castle, in Gwynedd,
dwarfed anyone who
approached its walls.
The gatehouse still
intimidates onlookers.

foot-diameter polygonal towers guarded the exterior corners of the triangular gatehouse: two of the towers flanked the gate passage just like the standard thirteenth-century twin-towered design, whereas the third dominated the rear and projected into the inner bailey. If attackers managed to safely cross the drawbridge, they then had to tackle the two portcullises and two sets of heavy timber doors that barred their way at either end of the passage inside the gatehouse. If an enemy somehow progressed beyond the second doorway, he would find himself trapped within an octagonal chamber (reputedly a hall), from which the only escape was to confront yet another portcullis on the right, as well as five arrowslits[52] and numerous murder holes, which defended the way into the inner bailey. Guarded by postern gates, several towers, and an unusual mantlet, access to the southern side was equally daunting.

SECONDARY GATEWAYS

Generally simpler in design that the main gateway, secondary entrances known as postern gates and sally ports provided the lord and his garrison with exterior passageways through the curtain wall, which could be quickly opened and slammed shut without jeopardizing the security provided at the main gate. Using the postern gates, a besieged garrison could welcome fresh troops and supplies or launch a sudden sortie and "sally forth" against an otherwise unsuspecting attacker.

Many postern gates were strategically located so that ships could easily and surreptitiously move to and from a castle. Often known as "water gates" for their immediate access to the sea, these gateways proved essential during a siege, and in times of peace as well. Notable examples survive at Skenfrith Castle, where steps lead downward from the inner bailey to the moat, which was flooded by the River Monnow, and at the Tower of London, where the famed "Traitor's Gate" at the foot of St. Thomas' Tower opened alongside the River Thames to receive vital supplies and many of Britain's most infamous—and soon to be executed—prisoners, including the archbishop of Canterbury, Thomas More, whose name adorns the tower overhead.

Now barred, but accessible from inside the castle, one of Pembroke Castle's two water gates was actually the gaping mouth of a natural cavern gouged into the bedrock underlying the powerful fortress. Large enough to engulf large seagoing vessels, the "wogan" protected the movement of supplies and personnel between the castle and river. Today, the tidal waters of the River Pembroke have retreated from the curtain wall, but a narrow spiral staircase connects the wogan to the inner bailey above.

Not all postern gates were simple structures. Some, as at Bodiam, functioned as rear gatehouses as well as water gates. Others, like the gateways at Denbigh Castle, not only provided a passageway for moving people and supplies into the castle but also allowed defenders to stage assaults outside the castle on short notice. In fact, besides the unusual triangular gatehouse at Denbigh, the castle sported at least two postern gates, which provided access to the eastern and southern sides of the stronghold; a postern tower, which adjoined the so-called upper gate and helped defend the southern side of the inner bailey from unwanted access; and a sally port, located on the western side of the inner bailey at the base of the Bishop's Tower, an unusually complex structure that consisted of a narrow curving stair and passage equipped with a portcullis, timber doors, and murder holes in the ceiling, which led downwards and away from the castle, probably along the length of the mantlet.[53]

DRAWBRIDGES

A defensive feature commonly associated with medieval castles is the drawbridge, the movable timber bridge which spanned the moat or dry ditch and could be raised upwards to prevent unwelcome entry through the gatehouse. Almost all drawbridges were made of wood. The earliest and easiest to manipulate were "removable" bridges. When necessary, defenders could simply lift and move the timber platform away from its position, backwards into the safety of the castle. "Turning" bridges were hinged on the inner side and operated with ropes or chains and pulleys, which hoisted the timber platforms toward the gatehouse until they rested vertically alongside the wall. This not only made the ditch impossible to cross but also created

Bodiam Castle, postern gate. Used as a secondary entrance, the elaborate postern gate at Bodiam Castle, Kent, eased movement of people and goods arriving from the nearby River Rother.

an additional barrier to the interior of the castle.[54] Guards used windlasses to power the pulley system.

"Pivoting" bridges also required pulleys to haul them into place. Used increasingly from the late thirteenth century, these fairly elaborate systems effectively used counterweights, a pivot, and chains or ropes to maneuver the bridge. Depending on the exact nature of the design, drawbridge pits were often required to provide space for the weighted end of the bridge as it moved into place. Without the drawbridge to span the gap, the steep, rock-sided pits also threatened a successful assault.[55] An interesting example survives at Cilgerran Castle. Later, during the fourteenth century, a few castles adopted bascule bridges, which had "lifting gaffs" for use with the pulley system to ease the raising and lowering process. The great tower at Raglan Castle still sports the grooves for lifting gaffs.

An intriguing system of bridges and paths once forced visitors at Bodiam Castle to move at angles to finally reach the main gatehouse. Attackers unwittingly approached the site with their unshielded right sides exposed and vulnerable to retaliation from inside the castle. Before they could begin to lay siege, the invaders also had to reach the octagonal islet implanted in the moat and then cross the final drawbridge, which connected to the gatehouse. Today, the original bridges no longer exist (except for underwater pilings and the unusual islet).

BARBICANS

Even though the gatehouse developed as a way to protect the weakest spot in a castle's defenses, many builders were not merely content to rely upon the heavily defended structure to keep an enemy at bay. Rather, they preferred to compound an attacker's confusion and force them to move at unexpected angles along narrow passageways or into enclosed areas from where there was little chance of escape. Generally located just outside the main gate, the barbican was a defensive outwork, which in some cases extended a gateway already in place, as at Exeter. In other cases, the structures stood as separate buildings apart from but fronting the main gate, as at Arundel in West Sussex, which was built by Richard Fitzalan in about 1295. Numerous examples exist throughout Britain, including the D-shaped barbican that defends the King's Gate at Dover Castle. Probably erected in the late twelfth century, this barbican is one of England's oldest. In fact, barbicans served a dual defensive-offensive role, for they were intended not only to prevent or stall enemy access but were also places where the garrison could gather to stage a sortie.[56]

During the fourteenth century, John de Warenne, 8th Earl of Surrey, built the well-preserved barbican that still dominates the outer bailey at Lewes Castle (East Sussex) to strengthen the older, more weakly fortified gateway. Projecting outward from the gatehouse, the barbican contained a number of defensive mechanisms, including arrowslits, a portcullis, a drawbridge, machicolations, two projecting turrets known as "bartizans," and roof-level battlements. The compact, well-designed building prevented attackers from easily entering the grounds of the unique double-motted castle.

The twin-towered barbican at Warwick Castle is one of the finest examples of its kind. A lanky rectangular structure resembling the great gatehouse but separated from it by a drawbridge, the battlemented barbican was constructed in the late fourteenth century by Thomas de Beauchamp, Earl of Warwick. With its foundations securely embedded in the steep-sided ditch, the sturdy barbican still rises four stories. Arrowslits, a portcullis, a pair of thick timber doors, and several murder holes provided a defensive advantage. The barbican on Walmgate Bar, along York's city walls, is contemporary with, and noticeably similar to, the well-preserved barbican at Warwick.

Whereas many barbicans structurally resembled gatehouses, several were little more than curved curtain walls enclosing the open area just outside the gatehouse. One example survives at Pembroke, where the seemingly fragile barbican probably erected by William de Valence in the late thirteenth century is little more than a shell. The D-shaped outwork would have entrapped attackers before they could begin their assault on the gatehouse but after they had already passed through the flimsy archway into the barbican.

Arguably one of Britain's most interesting and clearly laid out barbicans survives at Goodrich Castle, in Herefordshire. Now standing to about half its original height, and probably constructed in the late thirteenth or early fourteenth century, the helmet-shaped structure acted as the first line of defense at the castle. Projecting eastward from the gatehouse and strategically designed with its own entrance gate, this substantial barbican could ensnare advancing besiegers when slammed shut. It was also fitted with a guard chamber, which occupied a spot near the bridgehead on the opposite side of the barbican, where a substantial bridge spanned the rock-cut ditch and allowed passage into the castle itself.

GOODRICH CASTLE, BARBICAN. The D-shaped barbican at Goodrich Castle acted as a defensive outwork that could entrap unwelcome visitors and prevent them from gaining access to the main gatehouse.

William de Valence was probably also responsible for the barbican at Goodrich, which was considerably more substantial than the one he erected at Pembroke. Quite possibly, Pembroke's barbican may have been an earlier attempt by de Valence to experiment with the design. In both cases, had attackers made it into the barbican, they would have been forced to turn and face the gatehouse (to their right at Pembroke and to the left at Goodrich), by which time, the defenders would have begun their response by lowering the bridges and arming their crossbows.

Almost 200 years after the original building period was completed in the mid–twelfth century, a D-shaped barbican was added to the substantial motte and bailey castle at Sandal, West Yorkshire. What makes Sandal Castle's barbican especially unusual is its location. Rather than being positioned to defend the main gatehouse, this massive structure—which was actually a tower rather than simply a curved wall[57]—stood between the motte and the bailey, where one would normally expect to see a bridge. Instead, bridges linked the barbican to both the motte and the bailey. When raised, the bridges would have allowed the defenders to isolate and perhaps occupy the structure during an attack, had the enemy managed to get close.

Despite its naturally defended position atop a 300-foot-high craggy hilltop in Carmarthenshire's Black Mountains, the late-thirteenth-century Edwardian builders of Carreg Cennen Castle believed it vulnerable enough to warrant not only a heavily defended gatehouse and rock-cut ditch, but also one of Britain's most creatively designed barbicans. Once an enemy managed to regain his breath after climbing the rugged slopes approaching the outer gateway, he would then be forced to breach the modest defenses and rush farther uphill, passing through the outer bailey to reach the entry point into the barbican. Modern-day visitors to the stronghold will find the slender, albeit considerably ruined, barbican a perplexing structure which routes them to the main gate.

To enter Carreg Cennen's barbican from the outer bailey, visitor and foe alike had no other choice but to make an abrupt right turn, pass through a narrow opening, and then almost immediately turn left to climb the steeply sloping, constricted 10-foot-wide rampway that led to the square, middle gatetower, an integral part of the barbican, located at its westernmost end. Strategically placed along the walled rampway, two drawbridges spanned five underlying pits and passed alongside the treacherous rock-cut ditch. They could be raised if time permitted to prevent enemy access. If an attacker managed to make it to the middle gatetower, he was then forced to make another turn, again to the left, to approach the twin-towered main gatehouse. The gatehouse possessed its own set of defensive mechanisms, including yet another drawbridge, a portcullis, timber doors, and arrowslits.

WALLS

One of the castle's most basic, yet most essential, defenses was the wall, which took many forms. Builders of both motte and ringwork castles used earthen embankments as walls to enclose the bailey. They crowned them with timber fences, or palisades, rough-hewn logs normally carved to points on one end and strapped together with either leather or iron and embedded into the earthworks. The ramparts generally ranged between 10 and 12 feet tall; some may have been crenellated.[58]

However, with timber not only in short supply but also vulnerable to rot and fire, stone became the building material of choice when it came to making castles more durable. Within a decade of the Norman Conquest, masonry curtain walls began to appear in England, as at Richmond Castle, North Yorkshire, where Alan "the Red," the son of the Count of Penthievre, began the first structure, a triangular stone wall, shortly after he obtained the castle in 1071.[59] Other early masonry curtain walls survive at Ludlow (ca. 1086), Shropshire; Rochester (ca. 1087), Kent; and Brough (ca. 1095), West-moreland (Cumbria). All enclosed and, therefore, defended, castle baileys. The term, "curtain wall," itself apparently dates to well after the last castle was erected;[60] it refers to the segments of masonry that were built to fill in the spaces between neighboring mural towers. Curtain walls surrounding an area similar to a bailey but most commonly associated with Scottish tower houses are known as "barmkins."

Castle walls basically consisted of a central rubble core, piles of unat-tractive stone, encased on either side with adeptly cut stone, known as ash-lar. The width of curtain walls ranged from 7 feet, as at Conisbrough in South Yorkshire,[61] to over 20 feet, as at Dover and Chepstow Castles. Forti-fied manors generally had thinner curtain walls, which varied from 3 to 7 feet thick. Although curtain wall heights averaged about 30 feet, some rose over 40 feet. At Framlingham Castle, which was built during the late twelfth and early thirteenth centuries, the segmented curtain wall still stands some 44 feet high and is about 8 feet wide.[62]

As a physical reminder of an area's subjugation, castles were likely tar-gets for a rebellious population or the armies of incensed rivals. A plain curtain wall was little match against an intensive assault. Without adding extra mechanisms to defend the curtain wall, the garrison inside would have been unable to respond to an imminent attack and the wall itself would have been completely exposed to siege tactics, such as battering, undermining, and escalade. Consequently, several devices were installed, largely along the tops of the walls, to enhance their defensive capacity and to provide defenders with a safety net behind which they could observe an enemy's approach, prepare their response, and retaliate against the attackers.

One of the medieval castle's most distinctive defensive features, its bat-tlements, rimmed the wall tops. The toothlike pattern, known as "crenella-tion," consisted of "merlons," squarish masonry blocks which projected upwards between two openings, known as "crenels" or "embrasures." Dur-ing an assault, soldiers could prepare their weapons while standing on the wall-walk behind the merlons and then move to either side of the masonry tooth to fire through the crenel. Some merlons were pierced with arrowslits, which served the same function as the crenel. Often equipped with wooden shutters, which could be slammed closed in the face of an attacker, crenels generally varied from 2 to 3 feet wide, whereas the intervening merlons mea-sured about 5 feet wide and rose 3 to 7 feet high (some actually stood over 9 feet tall).[63] Battlements not only topped the curtain wall but other pronounced features that the enemy typically targeted during a siege, such as the gatehouse and mural towers.

Lining the inner side of the top of the curtain wall, stone walks enabled defenders and inhabitants alike to move from place to place, to keep track of the enemy and approaching visitors, and to move to other parts of the castle, such as the gatehouse, arsenal, towers, and latrines. Also known as "allures," wall-walks were often paved with stone slabs. Some, as at Conwy, made a continuous circuit around the castle.

Even with the aid of battlements, which allowed soldiers to look out and downward over the curtain wall, blind spots and ineffective shooting angles in the overhead defenses allowed attackers to approach and assault the walls with battering weapons or by undermining. To counter these situations, garrisons constructed timber fighting platforms, known as "hoards" or "hoarding," which projected outward from the battlements and were supported by timber beams, known as "joists" or "putlogs." Gaps in the flooring of the platforms allowed defenders to observe the activities underway beneath them and to shoot crossbows or drop stone missiles onto enemy heads. Gaps in the wooden walls that protected the men from enemy fire functioned much like crenels, and provided the soldiers inside the hoard with an opening through which they defended the castle. The only lasting evidence that a castle used hoarding survives in what are known as "putlog" or "joist holes," squares positioned along the wall to hold the ends of the timber beams. Sometimes known as "brattices" or "bretaches," an interesting, albeit reconstructed, example adorns the northern curtain wall lining the inner bailey at Caerphilly Castle.

Curtain walls were also riddled with mural passages, pathways stretching within the walls themselves through which residents could roam. Their outward-facing walls often contained arrowslits and narrow windows, which met defensive needs and also allowed light inside.

Used with fortifications as early as 215 BC,[64] arrowslits consisted of narrow vertical slots cut into the curtain wall or the wall of a tower and allowed defenders to fire their crossbows from a place of cover. Rare before 1190,[65] arrowslits were often less than 2 inches on the outside and between 3 and 12 feet in length. They often featured a short horizontal slit about midway along their length. Over time, the design was modified but the purpose remained unchanged: arrowslits were used to defend the castle. During the fourteenth century, some arrowslits were widened to accommodate handguns and larger artillery. The slots then became known as "gunloops."

TIMBER HOARDING. Lining the battlements along the northern curtain wall of the inner bailey, the replica fighting platform at Caerphilly Castle provided a wider field of fire and protective shield for the defenders in the event of an assault.

TOWERS

Whether built of timber or stone, towers allowed the garrison not only to observe the comings and goings of people as they passed near the castle, but also enhanced the castle's defensive capacity. Flat, towerless curtain walls developed dead ground, or blind spots, at their foundations, which an enemy could use to their advantage to approach the stronghold without detection and begin undermining, battering, or scaling the walls. Periodically erecting mural towers along the walls dramatically extended the defender's field of fire and reduced the impact of an attacker's siege efforts.

Beginning in the late eleventh century (as at Ludlow) and continuing well into the twelfth, at sites such as Orford and Framlingham Castles, castle-builders throughout Britain began to make ample use of rectangular towers. For example, Henry II built several rectangular mural towers not only at Orford Castle but also at Dover Castle, where he erected an inner and an outer circuit of curtain towers to make the castle virtually invulnerable to an assault. Begun in about 1185, the inner curtain wall at Dover is England's earliest surviving example of its kind.[66] It features fourteen rectangular towers grouped around the formidable great keep, the focal point of the castle. Four of the towers defended the King's Gate and Palace Gate.

Even though rectangular mural towers increased a garrison's ability to defend their castle, they also had weaknesses that an attacker could exploit. Flat surfaces were relatively easy to breach by battering and corners readily collapsed with undermining. Inspired by designs they saw while fighting in the Holy Land during the Crusades, castle-builders began experimenting with new tower shapes upon their return to Britain. Chief among these designs was the round tower, which was used to great effect throughout England, Wales, and Scotland. In fact, according to John Kenyon,[67] "It is the circular or D-shaped tower which is the dominant form of the 13th century, although square, rectangular or polygonal forms were also used in later medieval castles."

Round towers were sturdier than their rectangular counterparts because they had no corners to make them susceptible to undermining. Rounded walls more effectively deflected stone missiles and thwarted battering and boring siege engines. In fact, during a siege against rebels in 1215, King John's sappers successfully undermined one of the square corner towers on Rochester Castle's great keep. Almost immediately after the end of the siege, the garrison replaced the crumbling structure with a round turret and erected a smaller round tower at approximately the same point along the adjoining curtain wall.

The early thirteenth century saw the proliferation of round towers, including at the Tower of London, where Henry III ringed the inner bailey with thirteen round mural towers and initiated the construction of an outer wall with six round mural towers. Henry's son, Edward I, completed the outer wall in the late thirteenth century. As Britain's greatest castle-building king, Edward made prolific use of round towers in England and in Wales, most notably at Conwy Castle.

Some castle-builders used the round design for self-sufficient structures, known as keeps or great towers, which stood on their own and simultaneously served as a residence and a fortified refuge. Probably erected in the early thirteenth century, William Marshal's massive round keep at Pembroke Castle remains one of Britain's most impressive round towers. The enclosing curtain wall, erected by William de Valence at the end of the century, was fitted with round mural towers. Other round keeps survive at Bronllys and Tretower castles in Powys and at Conisbrough Castle in South Yorkshire, where six enormous rectangular buttresses support the imposing cylinder.

Despite their heightened defensive capability, cylindrical towers did have their weaknesses. The difficulties of building curved walls made round tow-

GREAT KEEP, Pembroke Castle. Erected in the early thirteenth-century, William Marshal's cylindrical keep completely dominates the inner bailey at Pembroke Castle. The dungeon tower added later in the century by William de Valence stands nearby.

ers particularly vulnerable to collapse, particularly if the underlying ground subsided (as occurred at Caerphilly Castle, where one of the giant round corner towers still leans at a precarious angle). Consequently, many of the most substantial round mural towers received added support from structures known as "battered plinths" and "pyramidal spurs," which impeded undermining and helped keep the towers upright. To protect the garrison standing on the wall-walk during an attack, round towers were also often bolstered with arrowslits, battlements, timber hoarding, and machicolations.

Marten's Tower, at the southeastern corner of Chepstow Castle, is an especially impressive example. Actually D-shaped, the mammoth thirteenth-century tower built by Roger Bigod III dominates the main approach to the Welsh castle. Though originally intended as a residential tower, during the seventeenth century it served as the prison for Henry Marten, one of the signatories of Charles I's death warrant. Marten endured twenty years under house arrest in the moderately comfortable, yet well-defended, stone structure. Two powerful pyramidal spurs still rise from the foundations to the first story to interfere with undermining and, even more important, to provide greater physical support for the tower. And, to intimidate an advancing enemy, a set of fourteenth-century carved stone soldiers patrolled the battlements. From a distance, the unmoving men gave the impression that the castle had an ample garrison to defend it. The interior of Marten's Tower was fitted with arrowslits, which were later modified for use with handguns, and a portcullis defended each interior doorway. In essence, the tower functioned much like a keep; though primarily residential, Marten's Tower could also be used as a well-defended sanctuary during a siege.

Perhaps believed to be the most likely targets during a siege, the round corner towers at Goodrich Castle also relied upon enormous pyramidal spurs to buttress them. The spurs on the southeastern tower climbed from their bedrock foundations well up the sides, almost reaching the battlements. The spurs buttressing the southwestern tower, on the other hand, only rose to the first story.

GOODRICH CASTLE, corner tower. Huge pyramidal spurs climb the walls of the southeastern tower at Goodrich Castle to bolster the tower and thwart the advances of sappers mining underneath the foundations.

D-shaped, or apsidal, towers like Marten's Tower offered builders a compromise between having to deal with the complexities of erecting a completely round tower but wanting to take advantage of their defensive strength. Two basic types of D-shaped towers were built in Britain: those where the entire inward-facing wall was constructed in stone, and those only partially enclosed with timber-backing or no backing at all. Each design had its uses. "Closed" towers could serve as defensive structures, and also as domestic units, which, at the minimum, might hold the kitchen, a chapel, or bedchambers. "Open" and "open-gorged"[68] towers provided heightened security by allowing defenders to remove the timber planking and effectively isolate the spot from enemy soldiers attempting to scale the walls or to trap besiegers in an area. Interesting examples survive at Manorbier Castle and at Chepstow Castle, where the tower in the western barbican was probably open-gorged. Conwy's medieval town walls are especially noteworthy for their shrewd use of timber planking which, when removed, completely segregated sections of walling and checked an enemy's advance toward the castle, which may also have been equipped with open-gorged towers.[69]

Late twelfth and early thirteenth century Wales also saw the development of Welsh-built masonry castles, which had affinities with those built by the Anglo-Normans but also contained distinctive features, most notably elongated D-shaped towers. Several survive, albeit in ruin, at Castell y Bere and Castell Carndochan, both in Gwynedd, and at Ewloe Castle, in Flintshire. They were probably built by Llywelyn ab Iorwerth in the early thirteenth century. Only one similar tower has been identified in England, at Helmsley Castle in North Yorkshire; so, archaeologists presently speculate that the elongated D-shaped design may have been a Welsh innovation, which would have afforded a wider visual field from which to defend the castles' main approaches.[70]

Perhaps built more to impress than to serve a strictly defensive purpose, polygonal towers made their initial appearance in the early thirteenth century, as at Warkworth Castle in Northumberland, where the semioctagonal Carrickfergus Tower commands the curtain wall at the southwestern corner of the outer bailey. Grey Mare's Tail, another semioctagonal tower, which juts out from the curtain wall about midway along the eastern side, was added at the end of the thirteenth century, when construction of polygonal towers had become more common. During the latter stages of castle development in Britain, however, builders generally continued to prefer round and rectangular towers over polygonal towers, despite their stylish appearance.[71]

Not surprisingly, Edward I made ample use of the polygonal design at his mighty imperial fortress at Caernarfon. Designed to mimic the formidable walls erected at Constantinople, Edward's Welsh masterpiece featured seven polygonal mural towers and two twin-towered gatehouses fronted with polygonal towers. Of these structures, the ten-sided Eagle Tower measured internally about 35 feet across and was enclosed with 18-foot-thick walls.[72]

Two especially impressive polygonal towers guard Warwick Castle's northeastern and northwestern corners. Erected by Thomas Beauchamp, Earl of Warwick during the mid-fourteenth century, Caesar's Tower rises about 147 feet, whereas its shorter, twelve-sided counterpart, Guy's Tower, stands 128 feet high. Both structures feature machicolated battlements. The basement of the six-story-high Caesar's Tower houses the dungeon chamber.[73]

MEDIEVAL TOWN WALLS

Many medieval towns were encompassed with towered, battlemented, masonry walls, which, like castle towers and curtain walls, offered additional protection from outside attack. Oftentimes, the walls directly abutted the castle, as at Pembroke, Conwy, and Caernarfon in Wales, or enclosed the castle within them, as at York, Canterbury, and Chester in England, to create effective concentric defenses. Town wall tower designs often echoed the shape of those at the castle. They could be round, square, or polygonal.

Conwy's heavily defended walls provided the ideal complement to the hulking castle. Constructed to completely enclose the town, the triangular wall also safeguarded the northern and western sides of Edward I's castle. The ¾-mile circuit featured three twin-towered gateways and twenty-one round towers deliberately placed at 50-yard intervals which were linked by a continuous wall-walk and removable timber bridges. In the event of an attack, defenders could remove boards running across the rear of each open-backed tower and effectively isolate that tower and the adjoining length of wall. Not only did the inventive design impede enemy progress, it also gave defenders a safety zone from which to fire at attackers. The towers averaged over 5½ feet in thickness, rose almost 30 feet high to the walltops and then

CONWY TOWN WALLS. Edward I's towered, gated town walls at Conwy complement the design of his great castle. Together, the walls and castle enclosed the entire medieval town.

stood another 20 feet above the walls themselves. Today, they survive to their full extent.[74]

THE CONCENTRIC DESIGN: THE ULTIMATE DEFENSIVE STRATEGY

From outward appearances, the most successful and enduring castles are those that possess the most extensive and complex defensive structures, buildings and mechanisms deliberately devised to protect the residents living inside their thick, towered walls. The concentric plan—with its vast array of defensive mechanisms as well as walls-within-walls defensive system—offered castle-builders the perfect barrier to a successful assault. In order to penetrate the interior of the site, besiegers had to maneuver their way through a series of twists and turns while simultaneously avoiding crossbow fire and missiles hurled by defenders stationed within the walls. Soldiers defending the stronghold had an obvious advantage. Not only could they concentrate firepower onto a specific spot from several vantage points, but they could also camouflage themselves within the timber fighting platforms and behind the battlements and arrowslits that sliced the walls.

The royal builders of the Tower of London, for example, shrewdly used its natural water defenses (the River Thames) to both keep the enemy at bay and allow the passage of prisoners to and from the castle. They ensured the walls themselves were well equipped with tall battlemented towers. A series of twin-towered, heavily defended gateways fronted by drawbridges forced visitors and residents along strict pathways as they moved ever closer to the interior of the castle. The structures also afforded plenty of security for the royal occupants and their guests. In the end, ensuing monarchs and their master masons created one of England's most powerful concentric castles.

Assuming a visitor was welcome, defenders at the Tower of London, and most other castles, would lower the drawbridge, hoist the portcullises, pull open the barred timber doors, and allow passage into another defended area. The process would be repeated until the person made his or her way to the innermost part of the castle, the inner bailey, which was dominated by the White Tower, the huge multilevel keep from which the castle takes its name. Even today, as modern visitors seek to reach the inner bailey, they recreate the medieval procedure of passing through successive gateways to reach the inner ward. Nowadays, however, the likelihood of visitors finding themselves imprisoned in the Bloody Tower or their heads on the execution block in Tower Green has diminished significantly.

Poised on a steep-sided hilltop overlooking the English Channel and the famed White Cliffs, Dover Castle represents the height of castle-building in England. Originating as an Iron Age fort, the earthen ramparts of which survive in the castle's outer defenses, Dover Castle developed into the quintessential concentric fortress and has seen use throughout Britain's lengthy history, even playing a role in World War II. Over the centuries, the promontory on which the castle stands was occupied by the Romans, who established a settlement known as Dubris; the Anglo-Saxons, who built the heavily restored Church of St. Mary-in-Castro ("in the castle"), which stands next to the Roman pharos (a stone beacon that once burned with fire to warn residents of seaborne attack); and the Normans, who erected their first castle at the site, an earth and timber stronghold, almost immediately after their victory at nearby Hastings.

As at the Tower of London, successive royal owners and the army altered and expanded Dover Castle's defensive capacity. Notable structures include Henry II's enormous and virtually impenetrable great keep; two extensive towered curtain walls, one embedded within the other and defended periodically with massive twin-towered gatehouses; steeply inclined earthen embankments; and a network of underground tunnels, a portion of which was modified for use in the event of a nuclear attack during the Cold War. Still exuding power and domination, the heavily defended great keep is crowned with four corner turrets, rises some 95 feet, and has walls measuring between 17 and 21 feet in thickness. Dover Castle has served more than capably as the castle's primary strongpoint and as the monarch's residence, providing a great hall, a well, two chapels, the royal apartments, fireplaces, and garderobes.[75] During the Napoleonic Wars in the late eighteenth century, Dover's mammoth keep also functioned as a prison and housed French prisoners of war. The complex interplay of concentrically situated defensive structures and the castle's location on high ground have ensured its continued existence over the course of ten centuries.

CONCENTRIC CAERPHILLY: STONE AND WATER DEFENSES PAR EXCELLENCE

In many ways, the strength and complexity of a castle's fortifications were directly proportional to the likelihood of rebellion by the local populace or siege by rival noblemen, as perceived by the lord. In Wales, where the threat of revolt was constant, castle-builders such as Gilbert de Clare II, Earl of Gloucester and Lord of Glamorgan, and King Edward I—two of Britain's most powerful thirteenth-century leaders—erected formidable fortresses fitted with state-of-the-art, concentric defenses and massive towered walls.

Their castles represent the apogee of castle-building in Britain. The elaborate designs disclosed both men's ongoing suspicion of the Welsh and their anticipation of further revolt.

Unlike his king, who experienced an unexpected resurgence of Welsh independence despite completing a large-scale castle-building program that ringed North and Mid Wales, Gilbert de Clare endured only limited problems at the hands of the Welsh, who devastated his castle at Caerphilly in 1270 before it could be completed. Rebuilding the castle was no easy feat, but, by 1278, Caerphilly had essentially reached its full extent. Today, Caerphilly stands as a testament not only to the power and wealth of Gilbert de Clare II but also to the strength of the threat he felt from Llywelyn ap Gruffudd, the last native Prince of Wales, and his followers. Even though the Welsh attempted an assault on Caerphilly during their countrywide rebellion just before de Clare's death in 1295, they only managed to devastate portions of the town and could not breach the castle's concentric defenses.

Whereas the Tower of London and Dover Castle were the products of several building phases, Gilbert de Clare's castle at Caerphilly was Britain's first (and arguably its finest) concentric castle erected from scratch and by a single builder. The enormity of the achievement is difficult to comprehend, for de Clare not only created a unique defensive complex, he also rerouted two streams to enclose the fortress with its own water defenses. As at the Tower of London, anyone wishing progress to the interior of the Welsh castle was forced to undergo a series of maneuvers as they moved ever closer to the center of the castle. Their progress first led them across several drawbridges spanning the lakelike moats and through several twin-towered gatehouses, each of which contained a variety of defensive mechanisms. The final barrier, the great gatehouse itself, was flanked by massive round towers and a thick curtain wall. An enemy who managed to make it past the outermost defenses would find himself entrapped between the great gatehouse and the simpler gatehouse before it and exposed to arrows and missiles fired from the battlements topping the round corner towers.

Even though the present castle is a ruin, structural power radiates from every vantage point. The substantial masonry remains demonstrate what made the concentric design so valuable to castle-builders: the towers and gatehouses closer to the outside of the castle were shorter than comparable features closer to the center, where the main business of the castle was conducted. During a siege, the garrison could place themselves on both defensive rings and not worry about hitting their own men while concentrating their firepower toward the enemy. And, if an enemy managed to breach the outer ring of defenses, they would find themselves confined between lower

CAERPHILLY CASTLE, water defenses. Gilbert de Clare II modeled his great stone and water defenses at concentric Caerphilly on those of Kenilworth Castle to create the archetypal concentric fortress.

outer and higher inner defensive walls, with the defenders still firing upon them from positions of safety well over their heads.

But Caerphilly Castle was not just defended with rings of stonework. Intentionally selecting the low-lying spot, which was surrounded on three sides by high hills, de Clare astutely modeled his new castle on what he had encountered at Kenilworth Castle, the siege of which he participated in shortly after supporting Prince Edward at the Battle of Evesham in 1266. It was at Kenilworth that Gilbert encountered the formidable water defenses that he mimicked at Caerphilly. Water defenses were an essential part of de Clare's concentric plan. They acted as intervening defensive rings, which the enemy had to cross in order to assault the progressively taller gateways into the interior. No matter whether attackers used boats or attempted to swim across the lakelike moats, they would find themselves exposed to the soldiers inside the castle and unable to effectively return their fire.

To access the interior of the fortress, all visitors were forced to first cross the two bridges that spanned the outer moat and then pass through the easternmost outer gatehouse. Two massive dams flanked the gatehouse, ensuring the waters from the two diverted streams flowed properly into the artificial lakes. Twin-towered gatehouses barred unwanted access from the outer ends of the dams, the southernmost of which was once linked to the town's medieval walls.

The well-preserved main outer gatehouse was probably built at the same time as the northern dam. The bases of the twin polygonal towers were supported with angle spurs. Arrowslits and grooves for ropes to raise and lower the drawbridge penetrated the thick walls. A portcullis and six narrow murder holes defended each side of the gate passage, which was also flanked by guardrooms. During the English Civil War, this gatehouse became a prison, its heavy defenses providing more than adequate barriers to escape.

At the southernmost end of the platform of land behind the southern dam, a self-contained complex of structures guarded the approach to the castle from the town. A curious, ruined cross-wall and downward step now separate this area—the south barbican—from the rest of the dam. At the very end of the dam, a round-fronted salient, erected during the castle's initial building phase, projects outward. To its west (right), the twin-towered south gatehouse (sometimes known as Giffard's Tower or the Barbican Gate) still watches over Caerphilly town. The presence of deep pits under the main passage indicate that the gateway once linked to the "mainland" via a turning bridge.[76]

A modern footbridge now spans the inner moat at the point where its medieval counterpart would have allowed access to the middle ward, which once surrounded the entire interior of the castle. The two-story outer eastern gatehouse, with its arrowslits and portcullis, offered only modest protection from the enemy. However, if besiegers managed to pass this gateway and cross into the middle bailey, they would have found themselves face-to-face with the castle's most forbidding gatehouse and two formidable round towers.

Arguably the finest structure at Caerphilly Castle, the enormous inner eastern gatehouse not only barricaded unwanted access, it also housed the castle's constable. Probably modeled on the gatehouse at Tonbridge Castle in Kent, which was erected by Gilbert's father, Richard de Clare, the secondary stronghold functioned as a keep-gatehouse, the massive round towers and well-defended gate passageway guarding the self-sufficient structure, inside of which castle occupants could withstand a siege. Begun during the initial building phase in 1268–1271, Caerphilly's great gatehouse was reputedly the first of its kind erected in Wales. Two portcullises, heavy wooden doors, murder holes, and arrowslits defended the gate passage; inside the towers, guardrooms occupied the lowest level.[77] The placement of doorways along the passageway and the ability to barricade it from both directions made assaulting the great gatehouse a challenging, if not impossible, prospect. From the battlements, guards had clear views of all action, both inside and outside the castle. Evidence for timber hoarding and arrowslits survives.

An immense round tower defended each corner of the inner ward, and, as on the eastern side of the castle, two gatehouses defended the western front. Like the eastern gatehouses, those on the west decrease in height from the taller interior structure to the shorter outer one. Both are simpler in design than their eastern counterparts, which served as the castle's main entry points.

Today, the inner western gatehouse retains most of its original masonry. The ground floor contained two six-sided, vaulted guardrooms equipped with arrowslits. Two portcullises prevented unwanted access, one at the inner end of the passageway and the second situated midpassage. Overhead, murder holes provided defensive assistance from above. Unlike its eastern counterpart, the western gatehouse was also fitted with a pit intended to contain the workings of a drawbridge. Apparently, the medieval bridge was never finished.

Peculiarly, the two western gatehouses stand at different levels relative to each other. Possibly built this way to interfere with an assault, the outermost gateway now faces directly into the revetment of the western hornwork.[78] Often called the western island or Y Weringaer ("the people's fort"), academics theorize that the hornwork may have been the last place of refuge for local

CAERPHILLY CASTLE, great gatehouse. Inspired by his father's work at Tonbridge Castle in Kent, Gilbert de Clare's imposing great gatehouse dominates the inner bailey at Caerphilly. The hall complex refurbished by Hugh le Despenser lines the southern side of the courtyard.

townsfolk during a siege. How well the people would have been served by such an exposed, isolated area is difficult to say. The irregularly shaped earthen platform is completely encompassed by a low stone revetment wall, which was never completed; two rounded stone salients face westward. Drawbridges once linked the hornwork to the inner ward and to the northern side of the castle, and also crossed the moat.

Unlike the castles in London and Dover, both of which were held by the monarchy and poised to defend two particularly vital locations (the capital city and the portal to France), the lordship castle at Caerphilly provided Gilbert de Clare with defensive might that in some ways seems disproportionate to the seemingly small threat posed by the poorly equipped Welsh rebels or by rival lords, with the exception perhaps of Edward I, a king with an unbounded ego who had a past history of conflict with de Clare. As one of Britain's most powerful lords, the Lord of Glamorgan certainly would have wanted a castle that dramatized his status and self-importance. Caerphilly more than capably fulfilled that requirement. But, its innovative scheme of embedded defenses must have served a loftier purpose as well, for Gilbert de Clare could have easily (and probably more cheaply) showcased his superior political standing with a less complex but still substantial stronghold, something along the lines of his father's fortress at Tonbridge, elements of which he reproduced at Caerphilly.

THE BEST OFFENSE IS A STRONG DEFENSE

In theory, the best defenses provided a lord with his best offense against an assault, whether or not his perception of the threat from the local populace or an opponent's army was realistic. Throughout the Middle Ages, and later, this concept was repeatedly tested. Some castles fell; others remained strong. Some, such as Caerphilly, never really had their defenses tested. Perhaps Gilbert de Clare's masterful concentric stone and water defenses were so intimidating that the Welsh and rival lords dismissed any thought of a siege.

During its notably brief history, Caerphilly Castle never experienced a full-blown siege, nor were the Welsh successful in bringing down its walls. Their threat was minimal at best. Perhaps, the complexity of the defenses thwarted the best efforts of the Welsh against the Lord of Glamorgan; perhaps, de Clare's army was strong enough to keep the rebels away from the castle walls. Perhaps, de Clare perceived that his subjects were a greater menace than in reality they could ever possibly be. Whatever the case, Caerphilly's defenses were certainly much more complex than they apparently needed to be.

Certainly, de Clare wanted to ensure the safety and security of his stronghold, his garrison and his household against the ever-present possibility of Welsh rebellion. De Clare also recognized the need for protection against rival lords, such as Humphrey de Bohun, Lord of Brecon, with whom he had sparred for years. He may also have kept a wary eye out for the king's troops, knowing Edward I had less than positive feelings toward him. However, with Edward's attention focused elsewhere in Wales and also in Scotland, the real threat to de Clare's power base in South Wales would have been from a relatively poorly organized, weakly equipped group of Welshmen, like those who had destroyed Caerphilly Castle in the early stages of its construction.

One may conclude that the real reason behind the heavy defenses and structural complexities of the Edwardian-era castles in Wales had less to do with safeguarding its residents than it did with ensuring the Anglo-Norman lords maintained their grip over the Welsh. Certainly, such defenses would protect them during a siege. But, even more so, the structures projected a menacing posture and probably created the perception that it was not worth the effort to attempt a siege in the first place.

CONCLUSION

In effect, building a heavily defended castle was more about stressing the lord's power and control in the region than it was about protecting its residents. As such, the defensive capacity of a castle was just another aspect of its largely offensive nature. Certainly, defeat at the hands of an enemy meant death and dishonor for the lord and his garrison and was to be avoided at all costs. But even more important, defeat meant the loss of the lordship, the loss of control over a populace, and the loss of land.

The concentric design capably served a lord according to his particular needs and requirements. The Tower of London's overarching role as the capital city's royal fortress, mint, treasury, state prison, and military depot, for example, prompted its regal owners to strengthen and extend its defenses. Their goal was twofold: to prevent unwanted access to its treasures (and its prisoners) and to maintain royal authority. At Dover, the complexity of the concentric design coupled with the placement of the royal castle on a headland projecting into the sea, not only overawed and intimidated all comers, but, when called to respond, the defenses ably interfered with concerted efforts by the French dauphin, Louis, to bring down the walls in the thirteenth century. Even during the Napoleonic Wars, when the technology of warfare had advanced dramatically, the well-equipped French army avoided an assault on the reputedly unconquerable fortress, then bolstered with modern artillery bastions and heavy gun platforms.

Overall, castles were about power and control. As discussed above, lords who intended to keep control implemented creative ways to erect powerful castles, with thick walls, the latest in design technology, and a myriad of defensive features that would confuse, confine, and control the enemy.

CHAPTER 3

Castles as Residences

In all periods of the Middle Ages and not only towards the end of its history, the castle was lived in far more than it was fought in. . . .
— R. Allen Brown, *English Medieval Castles* (1954), 184

Modern-day images of medieval castles as the targets of frequent, almost incessant, battering by siege engines and knights intent on storming the gatehouse glorify the military nature of the medieval castle in Britain. But, in many ways, entertaining as they may be, they misrepresent reality. Much of a lord's year consisted of moving from place to place, to oversee the territories under his control, to administer justice, such as it was, and to attend to the monarch when summoned. Warfare became his secondary occupation. The constable or castellan managed the castle's military affairs in the lord's name and was generally a more permanent fixture in a castle than the owner himself ever intended to be. In fact, while some castles were subjected to several sieges during the course of stormy histories, the vast majority actually existed from day to day in relative peace, their residents following daily routines, completing household chores or maintaining the stronghold in a state of readiness, not only for battle but for the arrival of the lord and his retinue.

PEACETIME OCCUPATION

Under routine peacetime conditions, there was little need for a regular garrison. Large garrisons were maintained only at castles located in areas of frequent conflict or when a crisis was fomenting.[1] In fact, in the event of a sudden attack, every member of the permanent staff was expected to rise to the occasion to defend the castle and hopefully hold out long enough for reinforcements to arrive. Besides the constable, castles routinely housed the porter (also known as the "door-ward" or "durward," the person responsible for opening the doors), a gatekeeper, watchmen, a few men-at-arms, the chaplain, and craftsmen,[2] such as smiths, who prepared and repaired weapons, bowyers, who crafted bows, and fletchers, who made arrows. As the lord moved from place to place throughout the year, the attending retinue normally included his retainers, but his wife, family, her ladies-in-waiting, servants, and members of his household staff might also travel with him. In some ways, however, "castles were female preserves . . . certainly as long-stay residences and as administrative commitments."[3] Medieval noble-women could hold castles in their own right through inheritance or widowhood, but most commonly rights to the castle and any accompanying lordship passed to husbands upon marriage or remarriage. Widows often maintained control of the castle until underage sons became adults and gained their legal inheritance.

The fully occupied castle teemed with activity, much of which took place within the crowded bailey. Craftsmen worked their trades; masons, carpenters, carters, and other laborers focused on the structure itself; and, supervised by the marshal, grooms tended to the horses in their stables. Other workers included plumbers, coopers (barrel-makers), fullers (who cleaned and prepared cloth), and spencers (who dispensed bread and other foodstuffs).[4] The lord's inner household consisted of manservants to dress and attend to his needs and key advisers such as the steward (also known as the "seneschal," which derives from "styward"), who was in charge of the day-to-day management of the castle; the butler (or "bottler"), who oversaw the activities in the kitchen, buttery (the bottlery), pantry, and larder; and the chamberlain, who had responsibility for the lord's chamber.[5] Subordinates included kitcheners, cooks, bakers, brewers, tapsters, scullions, larderers, poulterers, pantlers, chandlers, washerwomen, and waterers. Gong farmers cleansed the latrine chutes. Treasurers kept the accounts. Falconers kept the hawks. Chaplains ministered not only to the lord and his family but also to the other castle residents and workers.

The lady of the castle maintained her own staff separately from the lord's household. Served by ladies-in-waiting and chambermaids, she spent much of the day overseeing their work, as well as supervising the activities of the kitchen staff. The lady also kept an eye on her large group of spinners, weavers, and embroiderers, who had the enormous responsibility of keeping everyone clothed and offering the lady companionship. In addition, the ladies of the castles were responsible for educating the young pages, who, at the age of 7, came to the castle to learn religion, music, dance, hunting, reading, and writing before moving into knights' service as squires. The lady of the castle also had charge of it in her husband's absence.

LIVING WITHIN THE LORDLY RESIDENCE

The sheer number of people (along with their own families) who might occupy the castle when the lord and his family were in residence necessitated the construction of special facilities, which became increasingly elaborate over time. Regardless of the size, complexity, and building materials used to construct Britain's medieval castles, most contained a fairly consistent set of domestic structures, which provided life's necessities and as much comfort as possible given the temperament of the times, the castle's location, and the lord's personal requirements and preferences. The hall, kitchen block, and residential chambers might be located on the upper stories of the great tower, or keep, or occupy their own designated towers; but just as often they rimmed the interior of the curtain wall enclosing the bailey, or stood freely within the bailey, as just one of the variety of buildings that filled the castle.

THE HALL

Though often described as the focal point of the castle, for much of the day the hall stood empty, and the other structures in the bailey bustled with activity. However, when it came time to dine—and, for some castle occupants, when it came time to sleep—residents headed to the hall. Logically, it made complete sense to locate the kitchen and its associated service rooms, the buttery and pantry, adjacent to the hall. The proximity of the structures, which were often secreted behind timber screens, allowed servants to prepare and serve meals while they were still hot. The lord and higher-status diners normally sat at the opposite end of the hall, where their table and chairs rested on top of a dais, a raised platform which emphasized their elevated status over the other diners in the room. The lord's private chambers generally occupied the area immediately behind the dais wall, a matter of convenience that not only allowed the lord to retreat discreetly and reiterated his overall importance, but also afforded him and his family the ability to keep an eye on the activities in the hall, as many of the walls were equipped with spy holes.

A fine example of a hall complex dominates the entire western range of buildings at Manorbier Castle. Said to be the oldest stone building surviving in any castle in West Wales, the twelfth-century three-story hall block at Manorbier measures over 65 feet in length and about 33 feet wide. As the castle's primary residential building, the ornate great hall erected by William or Philip de Barri centered the first floor and was accessed from the inner bailey via an impressive stone porchway, added at a later date, which is now extensively ruined. A huge fireplace dominated the wall near the doorway leading into the great hall. Placed alongside the fireplace, a large window overlooked the inner ward. Domestic chambers would have occupied the level above the great hall, while underneath, three barrel-vaulted, windowless chambers probably provided ground-level storage space. The buttery and pantry filled the western end of the hall block and serviced the lord and his guests dining in the adjoining chamber; a small chamber fitted with a fireplace and latrine, which emptied outside the castle wall, occupied the area above the two service rooms. During the late thirteenth century, the solar and an elaborate chapel building were added either by David de Barri I (d. 1262) or by his son, David de Barri II, who served as lord justiciar of Ireland in the 1260s. The complex of new buildings also included a latrine tower and a water gate or postern tower.

Most earth and timber castles and many stone castles contained at least one timber hall. Sadly, virtually nothing survives of these structures, which have decayed over time or were replaced with hardier masonry. However, archaeological excavations have revealed the remains of postholes and other evidence of the presence of timber halls at sites such as Hen Domen (Montgomeryshire) and Rhymney (Glamorgan), where the halls stood on their own in the bailey and at some distance from the main tower. The dimensions of timber halls which have been excavated vary noticeably: the hall at Castle Bromwich (Warwickshire) measured 69 feet by 16⅖ feet, whereas Hen Domen's largest hall (only partly excavated) ranged about 46 feet by 23 feet. Some timber halls stood more than one story high and were fitted with one or two roofed aisles, which created additional living space within the building.[6]

Stone halls suited men of higher social status. Often lavishly furnished with fine carvings, painted plasterwork, and decorative glass, and dominated by huge windows with side seats and enormous fireplaces, the stone hall formed the architectural centerpiece of the lord's castle. Inside, special festivals and banquets were staged for important guests. The chambers also formed the ideal setting for the lord to conduct his business affairs, for the flamboyance of the great hall vividly displayed his political and social stature and reminded guests of his supremacy within his own lordship.

Erected in the 1070s, one of England's earliest stone halls still occupies the southeast corner of the triangular bailey overlooking the River Swale at Richmond Castle, in North Yorkshire. Named for the steward to Alan the Red, the first earl to hold the Honour of Richmond, the rectangular Scolland's Hall stood two stories, the ground floor of which was used for storage and as cellars, while the upper level held the hall itself. Windows lined the exterior wall and offered fine views of the rushing river below and the lush green countryside beyond. From the hall, a doorway led into the great chamber, to where the lord would retreat after an evening's festivities. The kitchen block stood on the western side of the hall, but originally servants did not have direct access from the food preparation areas into the hall. Eventually, however, a window was enlarged to form a doorway.

Scolland's Hall is just one example of many castle halls that were built around the outside perimeter of the bailey. Another example can be found at Conisbrough Castle, where, in about 1180, a rectangular aisled hall was constructed on the northwestern angle of the bailey some 60 feet away from the great cylindrical keep. Between the two structures—and making use of the same length of curtain wall—stood the kitchen block, at its regular position at one end of the hall, and the servants' quarters. At right angles on the opposite end of the hall, the great chamber connected to the hall, and a series of other buildings lined the western and southern sides of the bailey. The now extensively ruined hall once stretched approximately 70 feet by 30 feet. It was heated by a substantial central hearth, which was probably replaced by the fireplace built into the curtain wall.

Hugh le Despenser the Younger, Lord of Glamorgan and Edward II's hated chamberlain, revamped Gilbert de Clare's great hall at Caerphilly Castle, which lined the southern side of the inner bailey. Transforming it into an eye-catching fourteenth-century spectacle, Despenser added elaborate carved corbels, which bore the likenesses of King Edward II, Queen Isabella, and Hugh himself, and also a giant fireplace, flanked by huge, skillfully carved windows, which commanded the center of the north-facing wall. As at other castles, the Lord of Glamorgan's private apartments were easily accessible on the western side of the great hall. To the east, the buttery and pantry attached to the kitchen tower. Restored by the 3rd Marquess of Bute in the 1870s, Despenser's great hall is now adorned with an impressive timber-beamed ceiling similar to the one that the Lord of Glamorgan would have enjoyed when entertaining his king in 1326.

OAKHAM CASTLE great hall. Arguably the finest surviving example of its kind in England, the freestanding great hall at Oakham Castle, in Leicestershire, commands a place of attention inside the motte and bailey castle.

One of the most complete and impressive examples of a freestanding castle hall dominates the western side of the otherwise vacant bailey at Oakham Castle, in Leicestershire, which possibly replaced an earlier timber hall erected by William I shortly after his victory over the Saxons in 1066. Still displaying its original Norman architecture, the double-aisled hall features exquisite carvings and sturdy arcades that date to the late twelfth century. At one time, a kitchen block and stables stood along the eastern side the hall, and the solar block projected from the western side. A chapel may once have stood here as well. Today, an extensive collection of historical horseshoes tend to distract visitors' attention away from the fine medieval interiors and the remains of the motte castle and earthworks that still enclose the site.

Another outstanding example of a freestanding castle hall survives in the remains of Winchester Castle, in Hampshire. Built from 1222 to 1235 by Henry III, Winchester Hall stretches some 110 feet in length,[7] occupies more than twice the area of Oakham's hall,[8] and is best known for its curious wall hanging, which has long been touted as King Arthur's Round Table.

Castle halls also served an administrative function, as the chamber where the lord conducted business, handed out justice, and collected rent.

THE KITCHEN BLOCK

Like the halls with which they are so intimately associated, castle kitchens were constructed either in the bailey or inside a tower. More often than not, they stood adjacent to or on the level beneath the hall, intentionally positioned to allow rapid and efficient movement of meals between the two chambers. The buttery and pantry, the two primary service rooms, were often positioned between the kitchen and the hall, from which they were separated by screens or a screen passage. Inside, final preparations were made before the food and drink were carried into the hall. By the late thirteenth century, construction intentionally joining the kitchen and service rooms had become common practice. At many castles, such as Pembroke and Chepstow, the arrangement is identified by the presence of a trio of doorways, a central service door flanked by two others, which led to and from the buttery and pantry. Together with the kitchen, the three facilities formed the kitchen block.

Many early medieval castles had timber kitchens, but the fire hazard they created necessitated a quick switch to stone construction, which was less susceptible to burning. Early kitchens relied upon central hearths, open fires based in the floor in the room's center that vented smoke through openings in the ceiling. In time, the hearths were replaced by fireplaces, which were built into the curtain wall or into an inner wall, as at Conisbrough, and located closer to the halls which they served.

Even at ruined castles, kitchens are most easily identified by the presence of a fireplace and ovens, many of which (as at Montgomery Castle) were actually installed inside the hearth and used to bake bread, a staple of the medieval diet. One should keep in mind when visiting a castle, however, that the presence of fireplaces and ovens does not necessarily prove the original structure that held them was a kitchen. For example, powerful fireplaces dominate both sides of the inner bailey at Manorbier Castle. While the set on the northern side may indeed have equipped the castle kitchen, considerable evidence suggests that at least one served as an iron forge during the sixteenth century. In fact, many castles maintained separate bakehouses. They also had mills for grinding the grain used to make bread. Mills were sometimes also in the brewhouses, which were often located in the bailey. Kitchen blocks occasionally contained kilns for drying corn. Scotland's Urquhart Castle, in Highland, features a rare example of a kiln combined with a mill within one of the gatehouse towers. Kilns were also used to burn lime, a critical ingredient for making the mortar that held the masonry together. Fine examples survive at Carreg Cennen Castle and at Weobley Castle, on the Gower Peninsula, both of which were located outside the castle

BIGOD'S APARTMENTS at Chepstow. Roger Bigod III expanded the domestic facilities at Chepstow Castle to include a complex apartment range, which overlooked the River Dee and featured the great hall and accommodation not only for the lord or his guests but also for resident military officers.

walls but close enough so that workers could haul the lime to the building site when needed.

A CLOSER LOOK

Forming the entire northern side of the lower bailey at Chepstow Castle, Roger Bigod III's late-thirteenth-century impressive residential range was created not only to comfortably house the lord and his family, it was also carefully designed to function efficiently and effectively. The service rooms (the buttery and pantry), a service passage, and the kitchen separate the two-story hall from the smaller chamber block. Interestingly, Bigod located the main set of private chambers, which were heated with a large fireplace, on the story above the buttery and pantry, rather than placing them at their normal location at the end of the hall opposite the service rooms.

Fronted by a battlemented, two-story painted porch, which allowed access through the screen passage, Bigod's great hall measured 85 feet by 29 feet and featured tall windows with decorative carvings and painted designs that opened into the lower bailey and also overlooked the River Wye. The basement level beneath the great hall contained a vaulted cellar and two service rooms equipped with cupboards, and a stairway to the upper level, where the pantry and buttery were located. The cellar may have also stored wine.[9]

Situated at a slight angle to the hall block, the kitchen and the eastern chamber block comprised a two-story building that probably accommodated special guests or higher-ranking officers in Bigod's retinue, who might require quick access to the adjoining prison tower. The quarters were lit with finely carved windows, fitted with latrines, and probably heated with fireplaces.

Kitchens often occupied more than one level in a mural tower, as at Raglan Castle, where the massive hexagonal kitchen tower dominates the northern corner of the pitched stone court. Erected during the 1460s by Sir William Herbert, Earl of Pembroke, the upper stories of the battlemented tower contained two large fireplaces with ovens, one of which was elaborately decorated, drains, and windows with seats. Steps led downward into the dank and cool "wet larder," where food items such as fish, meat, and dairy products were probably stored. Adjacent to the kitchen tower, the pantry filled the entire northwestern side of the courtyard. The basement level contained a cellar for storage, while the upper levels not only provided the normal services expected from the pantry but also held accommodations for members of the household.[10] A passageway runs from the pantry into the adjoining buttery, which stood on the northern side of the great hall and contained a hatch through which food could be passed into the great hall. The upper stories held additional living quarters for staff.

James of St. George, Edward I's inventive master mason, creatively situated Conwy Castle's residential structures around the two baileys and also within specifically designated towers. The inner bailey solely served the king and queen. In addition to the chapel tower and king's own tower, the enclosed area apparently provided a private kitchen, the solar and great chamber, and the privy and presence chambers required by the king when conducting official duties. The outer bailey contained many key residential facilities, including the great hall, kitchen, and chapel. Even though the outer bailey provided accommodation for the garrison, household staff, and other residents, it could also be used by the king to entertain important guests.

Interestingly, the kitchen block and stables at Conwy Castle occupied a portion of the outer bailey immediately in front of the kitchen tower and provided access into the tower, which took its name from its location. The kitchen tower contained a basement-level storage area, possibly used as a larder. Two upper-story chambers overlooked the ditch on the northern side of the castle and gave views to the town and the estuary beyond. The massive bakehouse tower, at the southern end of the curtain wall separating the outer and inner baileys, rose three stories and was topped by a narrow observation turret; the basement level contained a baking oven, hence, the tower's name, bakehouse tower.

GREAT HALL, Conwy Castle. When viewed from the battlements, the enormity of the great hall at Conwy Castle dramatically reveals itself. About midway along the southern wall, the prison tower provided facilities of a different sort.

Across the courtyard from the kitchen tower, Conwy's magnificent great hall took up the entire southwestern wall. An anteroom and lesser hall occupied its western side, and the chapel filled much of the eastern side of the structure, which, strangely, also gave access to the prison tower located on its southern wall.

THE LIVING QUARTERS

Every castle had some form of living space set aside for the lord and his family when in residence. In the lord's absence, the constable might use the chambers. While the rest of his household and staff might bed down in the hall or in their specific workspaces, the lord routinely stayed in his own chamber. Early castles generally offered very basic accommodation, and the lord often shared quarters with his men, bunking down in the hall. Yet, even the most rudimentary motte castle also provided a private chamber for the lord inside the timber tower or stone shell keep that stood atop the motte.

As previously mentioned, the solar, or withdrawing room, was an essential feature of the hall complex. Often situated behind the dais-end of the hall or on the level immediately above, the solar served as the lord's private parlor and allowed him and his lady, and, perhaps other family members, the luxury of retreating from the activities taking place in the hall. Inside the solar, which probably acquired its name from its well-lit, south-facing position, the lord and lady could relax while also keeping an eye on what was happening in the neighboring chamber.

The specific location of the solar, and also the lord's private apartments, was often determined by the amount of available space. At many castles, the amount of free space was restricted by the presence of other buildings and by the dimensions of the site itself. Consequently, in order to make do with the space they had, castle-builders developed creative ways to provide themselves with adequate accommodation. They might occupy the upper stories of mural towers, the great tower (keep), or the gatehouse, erect residential chambers around the bailey (as at Haverfordwest and Conisbrough), or expand the castle's perimeter to provide additional living space.

One of thirteenth-century England's finest residential structures is now little more than a jumble of ruins crowning the highest point of Corfe Castle. Completed in 1204 by King John, the Gloriette was a lavishly decorated royal residence that stood in the inner bailey to the east of the great keep. In its heyday, the Gloriette consisted of courtyard, enclosed by an extensive hall range and kitchen block, the great chamber and the king's presence chamber. On the northern side, royal residents could stroll through the open garden and admire King John's prized castle.[11]

The wealthiest castle-owners, such as the Dukes of Norfolk and the Earls of Warwick, constructed state apartment blocks, which essentially transformed their properly fortified military residences at Arundel and Warwick into palatial fortresses. Both castles have retained their powerful defensive structures and also contained the finest furnishings that money could provide. The transformation of the royal castle at Windsor into a fortified palace began in earnest during the reign of Henry III, after his marriage to Eleanor of Provence in 1236.[12] Intent on impressing his new queen, Henry ordered the construction of a lavish set of apartments and a new block of royal apartments in the lower bailey. Several residential towers, including the Salisbury Tower, Garter Tower, Curfew Tower, and King Henry III Tower, also date to the thirteenth century. Succeeding monarchs left their own architectural marks on Windsor Castle. Most recently, Queen Elizabeth II directed the reconstruction of eight of the main state rooms, the private chapel, and scores of smaller rooms that been destroyed during a devastating fire in 1992.

Arguably a castle's two most important residential features were fireplaces, which provided warmth, and latrines, which offered personal relief. Yet, many castle living spaces lacked these facilities; instead, occupants used portable braziers for heat and chamber pots for overnight toilet needs. Unlike most kitchen fireplaces, those that heated living chambers were often quite ornate. Chimneypieces, adorned with heraldic emblems, stone carvings, and painted designs, not only enhanced the character of the room but also highlighted the status of the occupant. Other fireplaces were quite mundane for they were used more for their original purpose than to impress.

No other structure inside a castle has the uncanny ability to connect modern-day visitors with the castle residents of the Middle Ages than the latrine. Even in ruined castles, the latrine has a curious way of surviving and bringing a strong feeling of humanness to the site. Also known as the "garderobe" or "privy chamber," latrines afforded a moderate degree of comfort and privacy that many castles otherwise lacked. Commonly positioned at the end of a narrow, angled mural passage, the latrine might provide facilities for a lone occupant or accommodate two or more users. Discreetly placed doorways often linked the solar, great hall, or guardrooms to the latrine. Some latrines were strategically located at points along the curtain wall or the wall-walk. Wooden or stone seats rimmed the opening in the latrine.

Human waste dropped down a masonry chute, the exit to which dumped into a cesspit at the latrine tower's base, as at Weobley Castle; into the ditch or moat outside the curtain wall where the waters might periodically flush away the waste, as at Caerphilly Castle; or, rarely, into the bailey itself, as at Orford and Middleham Castles. One of Beaumaris Castle's more peculiar, albeit innovative, features was a series of back-to-back latrine units. Accessed periodically along the wall-walk, the units had individual doors for privacy and wooden seats for convenience. Fitted with ventilation shafts rising from basement-level pits that allowed air to circulate and also opened into channels underneath the outer bailey, the latrines offered considerable comfort in the otherwise hostile environment.

THE CASTLE WITHIN THE CASTLE

Early castles, whether of stone or timber, generally consisted of a single tower and an enclosing circuit of walling. Originally, these towers were called the "turris magnus," a term which, along with "keepe," appeared in medieval documents.[13] Then, the word associated the tower with its military role as a defensive stronghold. Only relatively recently has "keep" come into common usage. Evidently, the French word, "donjon," was the earliest label used for these self-sufficient, fortified residences. Over time, the French word evolved into the now very familiar "dungeon." Interestingly, the two structures had very different uses. One served as a prison; the other functioned as a castle in miniature. "Donjon" is rarely used to identify keeps in Britain; the great cylindrical tower at Flint, erected by Edward I, is known as a "donjon."

Most keeps were freestanding, self-sufficient structures. They often dominated the inner bailey or stood on top of the motte. On most days, the great tower housed the lord of the castle and his family. But, during times of attack, it became a refuge for the lord, his household, and the garrison of soldiers. Great towers were heavily defended and also contained a store-house of supplies and weaponry. If the outer defenses were breached by the enemy, the castle's inhabitants could flee to the keep and continue fighting.

Keeps were designed in a variety of sizes and shapes. Types include the shell keep, the rectangular keep, the round or cylindrical keep, and the polygonal keep. Some, like the keeps at Manorbier and Chepstow castles, were blocklike hall-keeps. Each new design gave the owners hope that their keep would be stronger—and more impressive—than its older counterparts, would accommodate more people and a wider range of activities, and would not collapse when bombarded by siege engines.

The first-floor level above the basement and upper-level rooms generally contained the hall, kitchen, and living quarters for the lord and his family. The strategically placed main entrance opened at first-floor level, forcing both inhabitants and visitors to use wooden ladders or a stone stair fitted with a detachable bridge (similar to a drawbridge) to reach the doorway. When the ladder and drawbridge were removed or lifted, the resulting gap

HALL-KEEP, Chepstow Castle. Probably begun by William FitzOsbern, Earl of Herefordshire, in 1081, Chepstow Castle's massive hall-keep is believed to be the oldest surviving secular stone structure in Wales.

prevented intruders from entering the hub of the castle. As building techniques evolved, some keeps were built as taller, sideways versions of the hall-
keep. The extra stories allowed for privacy and more breathing space and
also allowed guards to see farther into the distance and watch for any suspicious activity.

SHELL KEEPS

The logical replacement for the timber tower, the shell keep consisted
of a stone wall that encircled the top of a motte. Inside the hollow
shell stood the main buildings, which used the keep's walls for support.
The ring wall distributed the weight of the masonry around the top of the
motte, so that it could support the keep without buckling under the
weighty mass. Well-preserved examples survive at Restormel, Cardiff,
Rothesay, and Windsor, where the existing shell keep probably resembles
the original keep even though it has been greatly altered over the course of
time.

Despite the effects of time and neglect, Restormel Castle in Cornwall remains an outstanding—and unique—example of its kind, an earthen
mound crowned with an almost perfectly round shell keep. Protected on
three sides by natural slopes and entirely encircled by a 50-foot-wide ditch,
the deceptively squat site is surely the West Country's most impressive castle.
Planting the castle in the midst of an enormous deer park, Restormel Castle's Norman builders may have originally intended the compact earth and
timber stronghold to serve as a hunting lodge. By the late thirteenth century,
after its acquisition by the Earls of Cornwall, the site developed from a modest stronghold with timber defenses into a moderately secure two-story stone
castle. Its battlemented walls rose 26 feet and measured over 8 feet thick.
Windows were installed only on the upper story. A substantial gatetower and
drawbridge defended the main entry point.

Inside, the formidable slate shell stretched 109 feet in diameter. It
supported the standard buildings expected of any noble castle—domestic
quarters, latrines, the great hall, kitchen, and service chambers—and surrounded an open courtyard, which offered wandering and work space to the
inhabitants. Beyond the solar, the chapel tower projected outward into the
ditch.

Restormel's shell keep is particularly noteworthy for its physical relationship to the earthen mound at its base, which has been characterized as a motte
but was more than likely a ringwork. Rather than constructing the wall around
the summit, as typically occurred when timber keeps were refortified with
stone, workers sank the foundations of the shell keep 6 feet down into the

earth, cutting away a portion of the mound that had originally risen higher. The modifications created the castle's deceptive low-lying appearance.

Originating as a motte and bailey fortress, Gloucestershire's Berkeley Castle developed into a substantial stone enclosure castle dominated by a masonry-wrapped motte and a circular courtyard surrounded by the main residential chambers built within the curtain wall. The enormous great hall measures 62 feet long by 32 feet wide by 32 ½ feet high and retains some of its medieval fabric. The kitchen, buttery, and beer cellar display their medieval origins and reveal the working side of castle life. An unusual subterranean passage beneath the buttery leads to the well and once funneled water to the entire town.

Dating to the twelfth century, Berkeley's massive shell keep has stalwartly withstood the test of time and looks much as it did in its heyday. Built around the base of the motte, the keep actually engulfs the earthen mound. The castle's oldest surviving structure, the motte, provided the scene of one of England's most grisly executions (see chapter 2). Peering into King Edward's Room, with its stone-cold walls, iron-barred windows, and adjoining pit-prison, visitors will easily envision the circumstances of the king's last days.

BERKELEY CASTLE, KEEP. Hubbing the inner bailey at Berkeley Castle, Gloucestershire, the unusual shell keep completely engulfs the Norman motte. Inside, Edward II met a grisly fate in 1327.

Cardiff Castle forms the core of the Welsh capital city. A conglomeration of building periods perhaps best known for the lavish interiors recreated by the Marquess of Bute in the late nineteenth and early twentieth century, the stronghold also enclosed one of Britain's finest shell keeps. Erected in the twelfth century by Robert "the Consul," Henry I's natural son, the twelve-sided keep remains in solid condition. Modern-day visitors must climb the steep set of stairs, once covered by a forebuilding, to enter the castle via the imposing gatetower, which was added by the de Clares, Lords of Glamorgan, before the early fourteenth century. The seven-sided gatetower rises three stories and was defended by a series of arrowslits and drawbars, which barricaded timber doors. The first floor held the hall and a garderobe; the second story still contains well-preserved Tudor window frames. Today, the shell keep no longer shields the timber buildings that once stood along the walls, but a large fireplace and corbels indicate the rooms' original locations.

York's two castles, Clifford's Tower and Baile Hill, flank opposite sides of the River Ouse in North Yorkshire. Both were motte castles built in 1068–1069, soon after the Norman Conquest. Once topped with a timber keep, only Baile Hill's earthen motte remains. Recent excavation confirmed that steps led up the side of the motte to a timber building (probably the original keep), which was enclosed by a wooden palisade.

Situated not too far from Baile Hill, Clifford's Tower is a superb example of a motte castle. Presently topped with an unusual quatrefoil (four-lobed) shell keep, the 60-foot-high motte originally supported a series of timber keeps and palisades, which the unique stone shell keep replaced in the thirteenth century. The Normans erected the first timber tower in 1069, shortly after the locals rebelled against the despised king. Almost immediately thereafter, Vikings also assaulted York. Trying to flush out the rebels, Norman soldiers promptly set fire to the city's houses. However, much to their dismay, not only did the Normans lose control of the fire, but they also destroyed their two timber castles, Baile Hill and Clifford's Tower, which burned to the ground.

After the Danes routed the Normans at York, William I wreaked havoc in the area, implementing the "Harrying of the North" and devastating Yorkshire villages in order to quash any other rebellions. The Normans then rebuilt the castle's keep in timber. The tower remained secure until the anti-Jewish riots of the late twelfth century. Religious intolerance came to a head during the coronation of Richard the Lionheart in 1189. Mobs attacked the Jewish community who had come to honor their new king. Similar assaults spread throughout the realm, but, in York, Jewish residents were offered sanctuary inside the castle. Unfortunately, the timber refuge became the Jews' prison after they refused to allow the sheriff to enter the tower.

CLIFFORD'S TOWER.
Crowning the
substantial motte
castle at York,
Clifford's Tower is a
well-preserved
multilobed shell keep
that still dominates
the site close to the
River Ouse, where a
Norman-built second
motte, Baile Hill, also
survives.

During the ensuing assault on the castle, several Jewish leaders killed themselves and their families, and attackers burned the timber keep to the ground. Again rebuilt in wood, the timber keep continued to overlook York until 1228, when a powerful gale leveled the tower.

In 1245, Henry III ordered the complete rebuilding of York's timber castle. During the next twenty-five years, the bailey received a towered curtain wall and two gateways and the keep was finally refortified in stone. The king consulted Masters Simon of Northampton and Henry of Reynes, both of whom had major roles in the construction of Windsor Castle. Known as the King's Tower until the late sixteenth century, York's unique shell keep consisted of four interlocking lobes. In all, Henry invested about £2,600 in the construction of the unique shell keep.

Today, a modern set of stone steps probably marks the site of the original stairway that led into Clifford's Tower. What survives mainly dates to the late 1600s after Charles II's Restoration, when the original forebuilding (slighted during the Civil War) was rebuilt. Visitors now enter the keep through a three-story forebuilding located where two of the "foils" (lobes) intersect. The chapel, with its decorative arcading, sits just above the entrance. On the floor above, a small chamber once housed the portcullis mechanism, the chains of which extended through the chapel to raise or lower the massive iron grille.

Constructed with limestone and ashlar blocks, the exterior of the marvelous shell keep remains in excellent condition. A slightly projecting plinth supported the base and prevented the walls from collapsing under their own weight. Where two lobes intersected, the castle builders placed a small turret at the second-floor level. Each turret had a defensive arrowslit to compensate for any blind spots unintentionally created by the keep's lobate shape. The two turrets nearest the forebuilding contained spiral staircases, and the third served as a latrine chute. Originally, the ramparts and a wall-walk rimmed the top of the tower. A third story may have been planned but was never completed.

Once surprisingly elaborate, the north and west lobes probably housed a garrison or residents of status, for each contained chambers with fireplaces and latrines. Four sets of spiral stairways eased passage around the keep. The eastern lobe just right of the forebuilding also held the well, which plunged 50 feet down into the water table. Notably, unlike most shell keeps, an octagonal pier once supported the roof of the shell keep; its foundations were only recently uncovered.

One of Scotland's few medieval shell keeps rings the mound at Rothesay Castle, which is located on the Isle of Bute. Also known as a castle of "enceinte," Rothesay features a circular shell wall, erected in about 1150, which traced the shape of the supporting mound and enclosed a courtyard stretching about 150 feet in diameter. The shell keep surrounded several domestic structures and a chapel. Equipped with arrowslits and defended by four strategically placed towers, the 10-foot-thick battlemented walls offered tremendous protection to castle inhabitants.

THE RECTANGULAR KEEP

Emphasizing verticality, rectangular keeps ranged from three to five stories; some rose as high as 120 feet. The massive bulk of the rectangular keep, which could sport 20-foot-thick walls, necessitated a move away from the motte. The tall towers were generally erected in the bailey. Only a few mottes, such as Clun in Shropshire, supported fairly compact rectangular keeps, which were embedded into the earthen mounds to prevent the walls from collapsing.[14]

Many rectangular keeps were freestanding structures, clearly intended to be self-sufficient, into which the garrison and other castle residents could flee to safety during a siege. Outstanding examples survive at Dover, Rochester, and Canterbury Castles, in Kent; Goodrich Castle in Herefordshire; Bamburgh and Norham Castles in Northumberland; and Richmond Castle, in North Yorkshire, where the keep actually forms part of the enclosing wall rather standing on its own. Britain's best-known rectangular keep centers the Tower of London. Known as the White Tower, the impressive structure dates to the reign of William the Conqueror. The massive four-story structure stood about 90 feet high, its corner turrets rising an additional 15 to 20 feet above the main battlements. The White Tower measured approximately 151 feet long by 110 feet wide. Interestingly, builders used brickwork and decorative stone quarried from a nearby Roman-era site to enhance the look of the keep. The two uppermost levels were demolished in the late seventeenth century.[15] William I also erected the powerful rectangular keep at Colchester Castle in Essex shortly after the Norman Conquest. Like the Tower of London, Colchester Castle is well preserved and open to the public. As Europe's largest stone keep, Colchester measures 152 feet by 112 feet.

Virtually every domestic convenience a lord and his household could want was incorporated into these fortified residential structures, which appeared throughout the Norman-controlled countryside during the twelfth and early thirteenth centuries. The basement or ground level inside a rectangular keep was normally used for storage, while the next floor up housed the hall and, perhaps, main living areas. For defensive purposes, and perhaps as well for privacy, access was located at this level and not on the ground floor, as occurs at later and modern-day buildings. Removable timber ladders and stone forebuildings typically offered access into the hall. During an assault or at nighttime, the ladders would be pulled into the great tower for safekeeping. The keep's uppermost stories contained additional living space, a chapel, observation decks, and sometimes, an arsenal. Spiral staircases connected the levels and often provided a pathway to latrines positioned within the adjoining mural passages. Lower-level windows tended to be narrow at best, little more than a slit in the masonry that prevented unwanted access, whereas larger, often ornately decorated windows lit upper stories. On occasion, a corner turret contained the all-important well.

A massive 50-foot-high keep dominates the ringwork stronghold at Castle Rising (Norfolk), as it would have in its heyday when it served as the stylish home of the lord of Rising and his lady. Entered at the northeastern corner through one of England's finest forebuildings, the rectangular keep stands essentially intact, its well-preserved ornamentation still displaying the status of the d'Albini family. Containing two wide flights of stairs, the first of which stopped at the middle doorway and acted as a stopgap measure, the elegant forebuilding provided formal access at the first-floor level. From inside the forebuilding, visitors passed through an entrance vestibule into the exquisitely decorated great hall. Discreetly placed latrines and servants working in the adjoining kitchen and service rooms capably met the needs of the lord and his guests in the great hall. Beyond a cross-wall, the lord's private chamber and chapel filled the southern side of the keep. Clearly the highlight of the first-floor level, the lovely chapel features skillfully carved Norman arches, ornate diamond and chevron patterns, and decorative columns. Traces of medieval paintings also survive.

DOLWYDDELAN CASTLE. Llywelyn ab Iorwerth's rectangular stone keep at Dolwyddelan dominates a pass in the Snowdonia Mountains. Now largely restored, it is a fine example of a Welsh-built stone castle.

Few Welsh castles featured rectangular keeps. Of those, one of the most noteworthy—Dolwyddelan Castle—is located along a mountain pass in Snowdonia National Park. Although cited by many historians as Llywelyn ab Iorwerth's birthplace, the native Prince of Gwynedd also known as Llywelyn the Great probably built the masonry castle early in the thirteenth century. Llywelyn's stronghold featured a single rectangular keep accessed by a forebuilding, enclosed by a stone curtain wall and a simple gateway, and defended on two sides by a deep ditch. Restored in the nineteenth century, the stone keep originally rose two levels; the great chamber, equipped with fireplace and latrine, occupied the first story and provided access to the basement via a trapdoor in the floor.

Another Welsh castle with a rectangular keep was erected by the Normans in Glamorgan in the early twelfth century. Known as Ogwr in Welsh, the ringwork castle at Ogmore was begun by William de Londres possibly as early as 1106. Its oval-shaped, steeply banked earthworks enclosed an area measuring 164 feet by 115 feet. A deep, rock-cut ditch also surrounded the site; it was dry, except during high tide, when the waters of the River Ewenny flooded the spot. The flat inner ward at Ogmore Castle would have contained a variety of timber structures, and timber ramparts would have provided defensive strength.

Shortly after completing the ringwork, the Norman lords began transforming Ogmore Castle into stone. The castle's first masonry building was the simple square keep. Probably built by Maurice de Londres in the 1120s, the ruined keep is the castle's tallest surviving building, and one of the oldest in South Wales. Situated to the left (north) of the decrepit main gateway, the keep still rises two stories. Even though only three of its four original walls survive, they are substantial enough to indicate how the keep originally looked. Built with irregularly shaped field stones and glacial pebbles interspersed with Lias limestone slabs, the structure was held together with brown mortar. Notable features include round-headed windows dressed in fine Sutton stone ashlar and an ornate fireplace, which would have heated the first-floor great hall. Initially, the keep only rose one level, but in the early thirteenth century another story was added to hold private apartments. A two-story latrine tower was also fitted onto the exterior. Accessed from inside the keep, the well-preserved tower provided garderobes on both levels.

Rectangular keeps had one serious flaw: the square corners which joined the walls were vulnerable to undermining and bombardment. Miners known as sappers would dig a tunnel under a corner tower, propping it up with a timber frame. Then they would set the framework afire, and the stone tower would usually collapse. As mentioned above, the mighty rectangular keep at Rochester was successfully undermined in 1215. When rebuilt, the angle tower was replaced with a round tower.

THE ROUND KEEP

To strengthen the keep against siege weapons and thwart undermining, castle-builders began erecting cylindrical keeps during the late twelfth and early thirteenth centuries. Unlike their rectangular counterparts, round towers were better able to withstand undermining (there were no corners to collapse) and bombardment (missiles generally bounced off the curved walls). Like shell keeps, their rounded design dispersed the weighty masonry load, and motte castles now began to support round keeps, which were smaller in area than rectangular keeps but contained extra living space.[16] Round keeps also afforded an all-around view that enhanced the garrison's ability to defend the castle.

Arguably England's finest round keep, Conisbrough Castle dominates a hilltop in South Yorkshire. The unique keep dates to the late twelfth century, making it the oldest and most impressive example of its type in England. Refortifying the original earth and timber castle in stone, Hamelin Plantagenet, the 5th Earl of Warenne, designed the five-story tower as a grand fortified residence. The walls rose 90 feet, had an average width of 15 feet, and encompassed a 62-foot basal diameter. To ensure the keep's stability, the earl erected six semihexagonal stone buttresses, five of which were completely solid, while the sixth contained a small chapel.

Access into the great tower at Conisbrough was on the first-floor level. A trapdoor in the floor provided the only way into the basement, which held the well. Each story contained a single, large chamber. The lord occupied the first floor. Heated by an ornate fireplace, his chamber featured a washbasin,

CONISBROUGH CASTLE, KEEP. England's largest circular keep stands in the inner bailey at Conisbrough Castle, South Yorkshire. Six enormous buttresses distinguish the great tower, which may have been inspired by Henry II's castle at Orford, in Suffolk.

a window with stone benches, and access to a latrine, which emptied outside the curtain wall. Accommodation on the second story mirrored that on the first floor below, but the upper level also contained a lavishly decorated hexagonal chapel built within the adjoining buttress. A spiral staircase led to the battlements and rooftop wall-walk. Curiously, even the tops of the buttresses had their own roles supporting a dovecote, an oven, and water tanks.

One of the Middle Ages' greatest knights and most innovative castle-builders was William Marshal, whose incredible hulking keep at Pembroke ranks as Wales' greatest round tower. Rising over 80 feet and measuring about 53 feet in diameter, the great cylinder still dominates the inner ward. Constructed from carboniferous limestone, the walls of the keep remain intact, measuring some 13 feet thick. Originally, the main doorway to the keep was on the first floor and accessed via an external stone stairway, but the entrance was later moved to the basement. A restored spiral staircase rises within the thickness of the walls from ground level to the roof of the now floorless keep. On top of the dome-capped tower, modern-day visitors, like the medieval guards before them, will discover expansive views of the walled town and surrounding countryside. Notable features include a battered foundation, string courses, putlog holes, beam holes for timber hoarding, fireplaces on the first and second floors, an ornate window with seats on the second story, and arrowslits. The third level evidently served as a fighting platform, while the domed vault that covers the rooftop completely enclosed the fourth floor. The keep is noticeably lacking in sanitary facilities, which were provided in several other buildings and along the wall-walk.

Interestingly, the majority of Britain's round keeps were built in South Wales and the Welsh Marches. Many historians speculate that round design was transitional in nature. Yet, their frequency in the border region between England and Wales implies a different rationale. Perhaps their builders preferred the design for its ease of construction. Perhaps, round keeps, with their unprecedented layout, were considered status symbols. Perhaps, they reflected a regional preference or a psychological connection with France, where round towers were common. Fine examples, all erected by Anglo-Norman lords, survive at Bronllys (Breconshire), at Skenfrith, and also at Longtown, on the English side of the Marches in Herefordshire. One of Wales' most substantial round keeps commands the southeastern corner of Edward I's castle at Flint. Begun in 1277, the unique great tower known as the "donjon" was heavily defended, surrounded by its own moat, and contained a variety of residential structures, including the well, latrine chutes, a spiral staircase, and a chapel.[17] Welsh-built round keeps still stand at Dolbadarn Castle, in Caernarfonshire, and at Dinefwr Castle, in Carmarthenshire. The round keep at Dryslwyn, also in Carmarthenshire, was recently excavated.

Architectural progression from earth and timber motte castle to stone stronghold to residential comfort is vividly but strangely displayed at Tretower Castle and adjoining Tretower Court in Breconshire. The castle at Tretower consists primarily of a tall, foreboding round keep, which the Picard family built in the early thirteenth century to fortify an older shell keep. The round keep actually sits inside the polygonal shell keep built in about 1150, which replaced the original timber keep. Today, the shell ruins

TRETOWER CASTLE. The curious embedded towers at Tretower Castle in Powys date to two separate building periods. The taller round tower was deliberately constructed within the walls of the earlier shell keep.

gird the taller tower. Though much of the original Norman shell keep was demolished to make room for the taller round tower, remains of some of its domestic buildings have survived, including the outlines of windows and the fireplace. When it stood alone in the twelfth century, the shell keep also contained a kitchen, the hall, and a range of apartments. Why the thirteenth-century owners saved the shell keep is unclear, for at best after the completion of the taller keep, the site must have become stifling and claustrophobic. Perhaps they believed it afforded added defensive might.

Probably erected by James, Lord Berkeley, Tretower's cylindrical keep dominates the spot. Once rising three stories, the round tower contained fine apartments furnished with fireplaces and windows with seats and also incorporated structures from the earlier shell keep as well. The uppermost level supported a timber hoard, or fighting platform, which projected out from the rooftop over the ground below. Today, the castle is little more than a shell within a shell, but it still dramatically displays the cramped living quarters that must have prompted the construction of Tretower Court, a residential courtyard complex, in the early fourteenth century. Even though the castle remained operational until the sixteenth century, the Berkeleys, who owned the estates until Sir William ap Thomas, Lord of Raglan, purchased the site in the 1420s, made increasing use of Tretower Court as their primary residence.[18] During the fifteenth century, when Sir Roger Vaughan acquired the property from his half brother, Sir William Herbert (Lord Raglan's son), he extensively remodeled Tretower Court, adding a series of residential ranges that essentially enclosed the entire courtyard and created a comfortable house befitting a family of status. Today, the two sites—one a true castle, the other purely residential—occupy opposite sides of an aging farm; the ruins of the bailey wall are visible as well.

Taking its inspiration from the great French donjon at Coucy, which was destroyed in 1916, ruined Bothwell Castle remains Scotland's greatest thirteenth-century stone enclosure castle. Dominated by the massive 90-foot-high cylindrical keep, one of the few built in medieval Scotland, the polygonal red sandstone fortress also featured a twin-towered gatehouse and massive round towers. Enclosed with 15-foot-thick walls and protected with a 15-foot-deep ditch spanned by a drawbridge, Scotland's tallest round keep rose 90 feet high. Built to serve not just as the castle's strongpoint but also as its grandest residence, the great keep featured a vaulted basement primarily used for storage; a 20-foot-deep well; a first-floor hall; second-story quarters for soldiers or retainers; and an upper level fitted with the lord's private apartments, a latrine, and access to the wall-walk. A turnpike staircase connected the levels, while a well-preserved expanse of curtain wall linked the keep first to a smaller postern tower, which allowed escape during a siege, and then to the battlemented prison tower.

ORFORD CASTLE: HENRY II'S TWELFTH-CENTURY ANOMALY

Like his half brother's castle at Conisbrough, Henry II's stronghold at Orford introduced a new concept to British castle-building. Predating the keep at Conisbrough by a mere ten years, Orford Castle's great keep combined a cylindrical core with three rectangular buttress towers to produce an imposing six-story-high, twenty-one-sided stronghold, which the king believed would easily control two rival lords, William de Blois and Hugh Bigod, both of whom held castles in East Anglia. The power of the royal castle is reflected in its present condition, which remains strong even though the accompanying defensive structures have long since disappeared.

Rising about 90 feet and having an interior diameter of 49 feet, Orford Castle's great keep foreshadowed the appearance of other freestanding cylindrical keeps, which arose throughout Britain just a few decades later. What makes Orford's keep particularly unusual is the shrewd use of the three evenly spaced buttresses, which contained additional living space, including two kitchens, the chapel, and at least two solars or small living chambers. Orford's great keep may have served as the model for Hamelin Plantagenet when he constructed his own imposing keep at Conisbrough.

LATE MEDIEVAL KEEPS

During the thirteenth century, the trend in castle design shifted away from the keep toward the gatehouse. New castles were often keepless, or contained what some historians have mislabeled as "keep-gatehouses." Several of Edward I's castles in Wales, such as Harlech, feature outstanding examples of this kind of structure. Nevertheless, keeps never truly went out of fashion. Constructing late-medieval keeps was an expensive undertaking and normally only the wealthiest families could afford to build them. Men such as Lord Cromwell in Lincolnshire, Lord Hastings in Leicestershire, Lord Percy in Northumberland, and Lord Raglan in Wales all qualified.

Two substantial rectangular keeps made their appearance during the fifteenth century. Built by Ralph, Lord Cromwell, high treasurer of England from about 1434 to 1446, Tattershall's 100-foot-tall keep is virtually all that remains of the original enclosure castle located in Lincolnshire. The attractive red-brick keep was a strong structure with polygonal turrets at each of its four corners, machicolations, and a fighting platform, but Lord Cromwell ensured his five-story-tall fortress was comfortable and stylish as well. The first story contained the hall, the second probably housed Cromwell's presence chamber, and the solar apparently occupied the next level. Ornate windows also highlighted the owner's prestige.

Even in ruin, the great keep at Ashby de la Zouch in Leicestershire completely dominates the site. Also known as the Hastings Tower, the five-story spectacle extended the medieval manor house that had occupied the property since the Norman Conquest and transformed it into a well-defended fortified residence. Built in the late fifteenth century, the 90-foot-tall rectangle measured a narrow 47 feet by 41 feet and had walls over 8 feet thick, an entrance protected by a portcullis, machicolations, polygonal corner turrets, and a well.[19] An even taller extension occupied the northeastern side and contained seven stories. The intimidating structure was decorated with elaborate carvings, including heraldic lions, and contained several living chambers and latrines, a kitchen, the hall, and a solar. An underground passage, which still survives, connected the basement of the great tower to a separate kitchen block situated to the northwest of the keep, which was part of the earlier manor house and dates to the late fourteenth century.[20]

ASHBY DE LA ZOUCH. Although now extensively ruined, the late medieval keep at Ashby de la Zouch, in Leicestershire, contained a five-story core and a seven-story corner tower, and displayed the wealth and status of its builder, William, Lord Hastings, who also began construction at Kirby Muxloe Castle.

Because they were more difficult to erect and needed heavy buttressing to prevent the walls from falling outward, relatively few castle-builders experimented with polygonal keeps. Those polygonal keeps that were attempted were mostly the architectural fancies of their creators rather than effective improvements over the rectangular and round designs. It is not surprising that this design was never fully embraced. Arguably England's most impressive example stands tall, albeit in ruin, at Warkworth Castle, in Northumberland.

From above, the 4th Lord Percy's one-of-a-kind keep looks like a cross superimposed on a square. Riddled with passageways leading to spiral staircases and a myriad of chambers, including the great hall, kitchen block, solar, bedchambers, chapel, chancel, and sacristy, the keep rose three stories. The mazelike building also had room for beer and wine cellars. Adorned throughout with the Percy lion, the late-fourteenth-century great tower vividly dramatized the family's status.

Stokesay Castle near Craven Arms, in Shropshire, contained both defensive and domestic facilities, including a polygonal great tower. Largely dating to Lawrence de Ludlow's occupation in the late thirteenth century, the attractive site possessed several features typically associated with medieval castles: it was surrounded with a water-filled moat; the curtain wall that once rose over 30 feet (the last remaining portion stands alongside the south tower); a gatehouse offered access; and two formidable towers offered defensive protection. At the same time, the structure contained elaborately decorated domestic chambers, including the great hall and kitchen block, and the lord's private chamber.

The five-sided north tower at Stokesay Castle consisted of two upper stories, one of which supported timber hoarding, and a basement level that probably served as the castle's storeroom. The basement still contains traces of medieval painting and a deep drain that emptied into the moat. The well-preserved hall block occupies the gap between the north and south towers. Well-lit, the great hall stands 35 feet high and stretches over 50 feet in length. It still displays the original timber-beamed ceiling and remains of the timber staircase, which once allowed access to the north tower. Traces of a central hearth also survive.

Located between the hall and the south tower, Stokesay Castle's elaborate solar was decorated with Elizabethan oak panelling and a magnificent fireplace. The ornately carved Flemish mantlepiece retains remnants of its original medieval paint. Squint (or spy) holes allowed the castle owner to watch the action in the neighboring great hall.

Adjacent to the solar, Stokesay's battlemented south tower capably served Lawrence de Ludlow's defensive needs, and in several ways may rightly be classified as a polygonal keep. The sturdy tower rises over 65 feet and has 5-foot-thick walls supported by two heavy buttresses. Although the main entrance is now at ground level, the tower was originally accessed via a drawbridge, which linked the fortified structure to the solar. It also contained latrines, which dumped into the moat, fireplaces, and tall lancet-headed windows with side seats.

ANCILLARY STRUCTURES WITHIN THE CASTLE WALLS

Scattered in and around the inner and outer bailey, several less-substantial structures contained the castle's primary support facilities, such as the stables and mills and the ever-essential well.

THE STABLE BLOCK

Other than their foundations, few intact stable blocks survive at any of Britain's castles. These important buildings housed the lord's horses and readied them for the journey to their next stop on the annual itinerary, for the hunt, or to do battle. Some castles had more than one stable block. Arguably the finest example of a castle stable is situated along the line of the curtain wall in the outer bailey at Kenilworth Castle. Flanked on either side by now-ruinous thirteenth-century medieval towers, the stable block added by Robert Dudley, Earl of Leicester, during the sixteenth century, stretches just over 164 feet and stands two stories tall, the upper level timber-framed and the lower level completed in brick. The building presently serves as the castle café and exhibit area.

THE CASTLE MILL

Whether powered by human strength, waterwheels, or horses, the mill played a key role in the daily life of the castle. As with stables, most castle mills are ruined; few survive to any extent at all. Examples can be seen at Caerphilly, where the remains of a water mill occupy a space about midway along the southern side of the central platform, the bailey-like open area that stood on the eastern side of the concentric fortress. The sixteenth-century mill at Middleham Castle, in North Yorkshire, on the other hand, occupied the ground-floor level of a building in the southern range, which lined the inner bailey. Inside, horses walked in circles to drive the wheel to grind grain, which was then used in the nearby bakehouse or brewhouse. Many, perhaps the majority, of mills actually stood at some distance from the castle they supported. For example, at Manorbier, the mill's empty shell is accessible to the public in the low-lying area just west of the hilltop castle.

WELLS AND CISTERNS

No facility was more important to the survival of the castle and its residents than its well, which provided a constant source of fresh drinking water. Commonly located in the inner bailey near the keep or kitchen block, wells were generally lined with stone and protected by a stone well-house. They could be well over several hundred feet deep, as at Dover Castle, where the well plunges 350 feet, and at Beeston Castle, Cheshire, where the well drops at least 400 feet. Some wells were actually situated inside the keep or in one of the mural towers, where the walls prevented an enemy from poisoning the water supply. Notable examples can be found at Flint Castle, where the well occupies an unusual position along the vaulted gallery (passageway) that rings the first floor of the circular donjon, or great tower, and at Bodiam Castle, where the castle well occupied the basement level of the southwest tower alongside the kitchen block. Measuring about 8 feet in diameter and 11 feet deep, the stone-lined well was fed by the same springs that filled the moat.

Placing the well outside the curtain wall was one of the poorest decisions a castle-designer could make. If attackers seized or poisoned the well, defenders would find themselves without access to fresh water, and thirst would give way to surrender. Curiously though, some castles, such as Carreg Cennen and Weobley, lacked wells. To compensate, builders constructed cisterns, stone-lined containers that collected and stored rainwater. Whereas wells penetrated the water table or were constantly fed by springs and could be relied upon as a water source, except perhaps in years of severe drought, cisterns were undependable at best, dependent on frequent rains for renewal, and vulnerable to evaporation. Nonetheless, they were the reasonable alternative at castles where the water table could not be broached, largely due to impenetrable bedrock. Weobley Castle featured a cistern turret, so-named for the large pit that fills most of the lowest level. Presumably, the pit was used to collect rainwater as it flowed downwards from the rooftops of adjoining structures.[21]

Rarely, a castle might feature both wells and cisterns. Caernarfon, for example, was amply equipped with well, cisterns, and a well tower, and also had a cistern tower. The basement entrance into the well tower, which was located in the lower-lying western bailey, actually allowed supplies brought by ship to be carried directly into the castle. An adjoining lead-lined 50-foot-deep cistern provided ground-level access to the castle's water supply. Across the castle at the southeastern end of the upper bailey, the cistern tower featured a stone-lined tank that gathered rainwater and then piped it into the adjacent Queen's Gate.[22]

Castles that presently appear not to have had a well would either have relied upon cisterns, traces of which no longer survive, or the occupants had their water piped into the stronghold, as at Pembroke Castle. On the other hand, some castles had several wells, as at Ashby de la Zouch, fitted with four wells over the course of its history,[23] and Caernarfon, which reputedly had at least seven.

ANCILLARY STRUCTURES OUTSIDE THE WALLS

The castle food supply was almost as necessary as a reliable water source to survival during a siege, and certainly was just as important to the residents' daily standard of living. In order to ensure a constant and plentiful supply of both meat and produce, the castle and its surrounding countryside formed what amounted to a symbiotic relationship. The local peasantry was the essential link that kept the lord and his household well supplied with food. The lord, at least in theory if not necessarily in practice, maintained order and provided the locals with security in times of strife. Life inside the castle could not be sustained without the efforts of the populace living outside its walls, who tilled the fields and managed the orchards and vineyards.

In order to maintain a supply of fresh meat throughout the year, castle dwellers bred fish, rabbits, pigeons, and deer, in fishponds, warrens, dovecotes, and parkland. In most cases, these facilities were located outside the castle walls but close enough that they could be administered and farmed as necessary. Normally under the supervision of the castle constable, fishponds were relatively easy to manage. Long since drained of water, in most cases only the rectangular earthwork retaining walls survive. An interesting, but fairly late example, can be viewed at Ashby de la Zouch Castle, where earthworks in an open garden, known as the "Wilderness," mark the site of several ornamental ponds, which the Earl of Huntingdon probably added in the early seventeenth century during the castle's transformation into a palatial showcase. Traces of Manorbier Castle's fishponds can be identified in the grounds near the ruined mill, and remnants of those at Kenilworth survive just south of Forest Road, which leads to the castle car park. Keen-eyed visitors should be able to locate the earthwork remains of these, and other, castle fishponds.

Even though the lord and his guests might entertain themselves with a hunt in the castle deer-park, the scenic lands, which were enclosed by earthworks and timber or stone walls, primarily functioned as deer farms, which provided fresh venison throughout the year. Today, most castle deer-parks are little more than forested areas just outside the castle walls, but many stately homes still pride themselves on the extent and quality of their deer-parks. During the Middle Ages, as now, the presence of a deer-park emphasized the status of the property owner, who was required to obtain a royal license to establish the park.[24] Whereas the bishops of Winchester's deer-park at Farnham now serves as a public park, Raby Castle's deer-park still features a fine herd of deer. Windsor Great Park once served the monarchy as a venue for hunting deer and wild boar.

In order to breed pigeons, which were considered a medieval delicacy, castle-builders often erected dovecotes, curious structures containing a series of roosting holes where the birds lived and raised their young. Reputedly introduced by the Normans, many of these freestanding buildings normally stood just outside the castle walls; however, some interior walls also sported pigeonholes. Accessible to the public, a fine conical dovecote stands near the fishpond and ruined mill just west of the castle at Manorbier. The domed building contained at least 250 rectangular boxlike holes. Inside the castle, another dovecote occupied a section of the wall of the great hall. Speculation exists that, whereas those doves bred outside the castle were used for food, these birds were used as carrier pigeons. The placement of the dovecote in the southwest tower at Bodiam Castle, on the other hand, reveals that the birds must have been used as a source of food. Located at the

OXWICH CASTLE, dovecote. Now largely exposed to the elements, the remains of an enormous dovecote reveal scores of pigeon holes that once provided meat for the food supply at adjoining Oxwich Castle, on the Gower Peninsula in Wales.

top of the tower, which stood immediately alongside the kitchen block and also contained the well, the dovecote provided some 300 roosting spaces.[25] A fine, albeit partly ruined, example also survives at Oxwich Castle, on the Gower Peninsula.

The lands outside the castle walls were not just used to produce food or venues for hunting deer and game. They often featured lavish gardens, which offered the lord and his lady an enjoyable place to spend time and a pleasant place for entertaining and impressing guests. The earliest-known castle garden was added by Henry II at Arundel Castle during the 1170s and 1180s. By the fourteenth century, most castles had a garden of some sort, often walled or enclosed with hedges, which displayed a spectacular mix of flower beds and lush lawns.[26] Some castles, such as Conwy, maintained herb gardens. Kenilworth Castle not only had extensive sixteenth-century knot gardens inside the curtain wall, which have been recreated in recent years, but the palatial fortress also featured an unusual pleasure garden known as a "pleasaunce," which could only be reached by boat. Constructed in 1414 by Henry V just west of the castle, the pleasaunce consisted of a platform of land, enclosed by earthworks and moats, which supported a timber banqueting house and a walled courtyard with small towers. Today,

the house no longer survives, but visitors may wander the square earthworks and try to visualize the grand sight enjoyed by Queen Elizabeth I when Robert Dudley entertained her at the castle 400 years ago.

KENILWORTH CASTLE GARDENS. Occupying the grounds just north of the great keep at Kenilworth Castle, in Warwickshire, the Tudor gardens have been restored to their original splendor.

TOWER HOUSES

Primarily distributed throughout the border region separating England and Scotland, tower houses seemed a particularly reasonable response to the sociopolitical conditions peculiar to the region, such as clan rivalries, reiver raids, disputes over land ownership, and brief incursions into territory owned or occupied by a rival nation. Structurally quite similar to the rectangular keep, tower houses simultaneously served military and residential functions, albeit on a scale much less dramatic than displayed at the more complex stone fortresses previously discussed. Tower houses were privately fortified residences, sometimes known as "castles of enceinte," and in many ways meet the criteria for classification as true castles.

Like rectangular keeps, tower houses were freestanding structures generally encompassed by a masonry wall, the "barmkin." Many were enclosed with ditches or moats filled from the waters of neighboring streams. They stood between 40 and 80 feet tall, contained at least three stories, and had walls averaging between 6 and 7 feet in thickness. Like rectangular keeps, access was often at the first-floor level via a removable exterior ladder. The main entrance was also defended with an iron grate, known as a "yett." Each level had a single function. Consequently, space became a priority. The ground floor was used for storage. The first floor held the hall or the kitchen and contained a trapdoor to access the basement. Residential chambers filled the uppermost levels. Tower houses appeared in Scotland in the fourteenth century. They represent the one castle design that had direct associations with medieval Scotland.

Located in Dumfries and Galloway, Threave Castle is the archetypal Scottish tower house. Serving the Black Douglases as a springboard against their rivals, the Stewarts, during the fourteenth and fifteenth centuries, Threave Castle stood five stories high and had 8-foot-thick walls. Used for storage, the vaulted basement contained the well, a sink, and a drain—and the dungeon. It may also have housed the servants' quarters. The kitchen level above had a large fireplace, a stone sink, a deeply recessed window, and a latrine. Besides its role as the lord's kitchen, the chamber probably also provided dining space for the servants. A spiral staircase eased the transfer of meals between the kitchen and the great hall located on the floor above. The great hall contained an ornate fireplace, three windows with seats, a latrine, and a doorway leading to the boat docks on the River Dee, which surrounded the site. Private apartments occupied the level above the great hall, and sparse accommodation filled the top story.

By the end of the fourteenth century, the need for additional living space prompted the construction of L-plan tower houses, which featured a smaller, square wing situated at a right angle to the main tower. Dunnotar Castle in Aberdeenshire was just one Scottish castle that featured an L-plan tower house. William Keith, hereditary Great Marischal of Scotland, erected the tower house on the site of an earlier medieval earth and timber castle at the end of the fourteenth century. Also during the late fourteenth century, King David II of Scotland erected an L-plan tower house at Edinburgh Castle to replace the royal residence destroyed during the Wars of Independence earlier in the century.

H-plan and Z-plan tower houses also made their appearance in Scotland during this time. Fine examples include Hermitage Castle, in the Scottish Borders, and Claypotts Castle, in Dundee. The Z-plan had offsetting wings jutting out from opposite ends of the main rectangular tower that not only provided additional living quarters but also improved the castle's defensive capabilities.

Serving the same basic function as Scottish tower houses, "pele towers" proliferated in northern England. Generally slighter than their northern counterparts, pele towers stood two to four stories tall. Tower walls averaged from 3 to 4 feet thick and were normally enclosed by a barmkin. At one time, Northumberland featured 200 pele towers, while Cumbria and Westmoreland had ninety.[27] The Vicar's Pele at Corbridge is one of Northumberland's finest examples.

Irish tower houses developed in the early fifteenth century. Ranging from three to six stories high, their most distinctive features include stepped battlements and double-gabled roofs, which held the attic. Those with an extra corner turret resembled Scottish L-plan tower houses, and those having turrets at opposite ends resembled the Z-plan. One of the Republic of Ireland's most impressive examples is Bunratty Castle, in Shannon. The tower house consists of a rectangular core fronted on the northern and southern sides with bulky facades. Each facade is flanked by two enormous corner towers linked together with arches that span the void between them. Measuring 62 feet by 41 feet, the central tower rises four stories, each of which contains a single large chamber. The first-floor entrance leads directly into a vaulted hall, which once serviced the garrison. On the level above, the Earl of Thomond held court in the lavish great hall, which was, interestingly enough, heated by a brazier. Each five-story-high corner tower at Bunratty Castle measured over 23 feet square and contained residential facilities, including private apartments and the solar, chambers for the captain of the guard, the kitchen, rooms for the castle priest, and two chapels.

Harkening more to Irish or Scottish origins, Angle Tower in Pembrokeshire is the only structure of its kind left in Wales. Although no garrison guarded the structure, the site was a stronghold in which the builders, the Shirburns, could feel at least a moderate sense of safety if an enemy approached. Rising over 34 feet and constructed with walls 3 feet thick, Angle's machicolated tower house provided single living chambers on each of the upper three floors. The ground level had a vaulted ceiling and was probably used for storage. The main entrance was at first-floor level, and apparently a movable drawbridge allowed visitors to gain access. Movement from floor to floor was accomplished by using the corner spiral staircase—the rounded turret holding the stairs is noticeable from the outside at the tower's

TOWER HOUSE, ANGLE. The well-preserved tower house at Angle, in Pembrokeshire, is one of the finest of its kind. Its resemblance to the classic Irish tower house may not be mere coincidence, as Angle is located just across the Irish Sea from Ireland.

northeastern corner. Each chamber had its own fireplace, small unglazed windows and arrow loops, but only the first floor was equipped with a garderobe. Corbels still rim the roofline. Not too far from the tower house, a decrepit medieval dovecote survives behind a row of modern structures, providing evidence that the Shirburns occasionally harvested meat for their meals from the pigeon house.

Quite possibly, Irish construction styles influenced the design of Angle's tower house and, perhaps also, the medieval building behind the post office, which bears a close resemblance to the standard Irish hall-house. Located on the Irish Sea, Angle was a convenient landing point for seafarers. With Ireland so close, it seems reasonable to assert that the Irish landed here and that the locals sailed to Ireland and back. If the Shirburns had traveled to Ireland, they would have had ample opportunity to see tower houses and bring the design concept back to Wales.

FORTIFIED RESIDENCES: BRIDGING THE GAP

During the fourteenth and fifteenth centuries in Britain, the trend in the construction of privately fortified military residences began moving away from a heavy reliance on strong defensive protection and toward a preference for domestic space and comfort. New castles appeared. Older ones were remodeled. Both reflected the social attitudes, changing politics, and developing warfare practices of the times. Nonetheless, men of stature and wealth continued to value ownership of private fortifications, "even though they had reduced capacities for military involvement when compared with many of their predecessors."[28] Furthermore, as battle strategies moved away from concentrated castle sieges to open battlefields, owners were able to lavish more money on the residential nature of their fortified homes.

Late in the Middle Ages, a new category of fortified house, the "castellated residence," appeared in the British landscape. These structures might physically resemble earlier castles with battlements and defended gateways, machicolations, portcullises, and moats spanned with drawbridges. Yet, increasingly, heavy defenses gave way to weaker fortifications that were intended largely as adornment and display. Consequently, some late-medieval privately fortified residences, such as Bodiam, Kirby Muxloe, and Wardour, featured seemingly heavy defenses and carefully laid out residential ranges, whereas other late-medieval fortified houses, such as Nunney in Somerset, and Weobley and Oxwich on the Gower Peninsula, were lightly defended at best and mainly fulfilled a residential role for their owners. These less substantially fortified buildings are more accurately characterized as "castellated residences."

It is, however, important to remember that, even though new castellated residences were being erected throughout Britain, many older, more power-fully constructed castles coexisted with them. All castles were expensive to maintain and to occupy, and over time they decayed if their owners could not afford their upkeep. However, even in decay, Britain's medieval castles continued to function as privately fortified military residences, which were garrisoned if and when necessary. While some owners abandoned their cas-tles and migrated to more comfortable quarters elsewhere in the kingdom, many castles were recalled into action, most notably during the English Civil War in the 1640s, which pitted King Charles I's royalist supporters against Oliver Cromwell's parliamentarian opponents.

LATE MEDIEVAL FORTIFIED RESIDENCES: MORE CASTLE THAN HOUSE

In 1393, John, the 5th Lord Lovel, acquired a license to crenellate and began construction of his new castle at Wardour. Taking its inspiration from contemporary French design currently in vogue, Lovel's master architect, probably William of Wynford, created a splendid hexagonal castle that com-bined beauty and comfort and resembled a polygonal keep more than a house. Fronted by a drawbridge and enclosed by a dry ditch, Wardour Castle would have posed a considerable threat to attackers in the fourteenth and fifteenth centuries. Among its defensive features were a series of portcullises, massive walls, and corner turrets crowned with battlements. Around the perime-ter, a substantial curtain wall provided enhanced security for the castle.

Wardour Castle's four stories surrounded a central courtyard, where the well was located. Doorways led from the courtyard to the upper levels and the keeplike structure focused almost entirely on accommodating the lord and his household. An enormous kitchen block filled the ground floor and much of the first floor with several huge fireplaces, bread ovens, walk-in cupboards, sinks, and drains leading to storage cisterns in the basement. The pantry and buttery stood nearby, poised to serve the guests in the ornate great hall, which spanned the area immediately above the main entrance-way. Spiral staircases allowed access to the uppermost levels, which held the private apartments and, possibly, the chapel, before their destruction in the Civil War.

When Sir Matthew Arundell altered the castle into a more comfortable yet still fortified home in 1570, he weakened the structure's defensive capa-bilities by removing the towers that flanked the main entrance. In their place, however, he added one of the castle's finest features, the curious set of decorated shell-headed seats, and adorned the facade with a bust of Christ

and the family's coat of arms. Above the entryway, Sir Matthew embedded an inscription to emphasize his role in the reconstruction of the castle and his hereditary ties to the Arundells at Lanherne. In addition, Arundell remodeled the great hall, built a new minstrel's gallery, realigned the doorways, added more fireplaces, and replaced most of the windows. Clearly, he concentrated on the appearance of his castle, the impression it would have presented to guests, and the comfort it gave the Arundells. Even so, Wardour Castle retained its defensive capacity as well.

Kirby Muxloe Castle in Leicestershire now primarily consists of its main gatehouse and the three-story west tower. Designed by master mason, John Cowper, the quadrangular castle replaced an earlier manor house. Constructed with 100,000 bricks fired on site, Kirby Muxloe featured four corner towers. The curtain wall linked the towers to the gatehouse and to other towers placed midway along each length of wall. Around the entire complex, a moat provided defense against intrusion. A timber drawbridge originally spanned the water-filled ditch and gave access to the gatehouse, which in turn allowed entry into the inner ward via a single passageway.

Facing northwest, the rectangular gatehouse at Kirby Muxloe now only rises a single story over the gate passage. On the outside, the red-and-black brickwork diamond pattern and heraldic carvings showcased the prestige of

the castle's fifteenth-century owner and builder, William, Lord Hastings. The two octagonal corner turrets that projected outward into the moat contained single chambers on both levels. One was used as a guardroom, while the opposite held the porter's lodge. Each contained fine fireplaces, windows facing into the castle, and private latrines, which emptied into vaulted cesspits. The upper level of the gatehouse contained a large central room, brick fireplaces at two corners, and six windows, which overlooked the inner ward and also outside the castle. From this chamber, the single portcullis and drawbridge were raised and lowered as needed. The only other defensive features in the gatehouse (which are repeated in the west tower) are a series of low-lying gunports. Overlooking the inner ward, two octagonal stair turrets allowed movement between the two levels of the gatehouse. Quite possibly, Lord Hastings intended the gatehouse to rise at least another level, but he met his demise before he could enjoy the finished product.

Almost perfectly preserved, the rectangular west tower dominates Kirby Muxloe Castle. It was probably the one structure that Hastings managed to complete before his execution on Tower Green at the Tower of London in 1483. Like the gatehouse, the battlemented tower was built in brick and decorated with red-and-black patterns. On the north and east sides, two turrets

KIRBY MUXLOE CASTLE. Lord Hastings' castle at Kirby Muxloe, Leicestershire, sharply contrasts with his great tower at Ashby de la Zouch. Only rising to its first story, the gatehouse at Kirby Muxloe features brick-work patterns and large upper-story windows. Rerouting the waters of two nearby brooks created the enclosing moat.

rose another level; the northern one contained a newel staircase and the eastern one held latrines. Gunports defended the castle from the tower's lowest level; chambers overhead provided accommodation for overnight guests and household staff. It remains speculative whether Kirby Muxloe, never completed due to Lord Hastings' untimely demise, can be classified as a true castle. Perhaps the builder intended for the defenses to impress and forewarn, rather than withstand an onslaught.

The compact "castle" at Nunney in Somerset is an anomaly that harkens more to its French origins than to England, where John de la Mere began its construction after receiving a license to crenellate from King Edward III in 1373. The walls of the quadrangular structure are flanked on the north and south sides by twin round towers situated so close together that hardly any walling separates them. Access was through a simple gateway, which would never have kept out a determined enemy. The ground floor of de la Mere's weakly fortified residence contained the kitchen with its large fireplace, storage areas, and the well. The pantry, buttery, and servants' quarters probably occupied the next story, and the hall and private apartments filled the two uppermost levels. Each of the machicolated corner towers played a key role within the castle. The northwest tower contained the castle's only staircase, which linked the upper and lower levels, the southeast tower held the chapel, and the two remaining towers contained additional accommodation.

Castellated residences, more often known as fortified manor houses, are rare in Wales. Weobley Castle is one of the finest examples of its type. There, the castle-builders seem to have been more concerned with personal conveniences than defensive might. Superficially, the structure seems to have been built with a randomness that reflects the flimsy construction of its defenses. The earliest buildings include the hall block, which lines the northern face of the castle, the large southwest tower, and portions of the eastern range. The de la Beres added the gatehouse, almost as an afterthought, to fill in a gap between the hall and solar and the southwest tower. The gatehouse contained a simple archway defended by wooden gates, which were placed on the outermost side of the gateway. Significantly, the castellated "strongpoint" lacked both a portcullis and arrowslits, which would certainly have bolstered its defensive capabilities. The upper story provided accommodation and shared a latrine with the solar.

Across the courtyard from the extensively ruined chapel stand the fourteenth-century hall block and great porch. Initially, the hall and kitchen block both occupied the ground floor, but, during the second phase of building, when the great hall moved to the upper story, the kitchen took over the entire lower level. The porchway was added to the interior wall at that time. Features emphasizing the residential focus of this fortified house include a drain in the central splayed window, a small round-backed fireplace and another, much larger fireplace. The windows had seats and could be barricaded with iron grilles and shutters. A doorway offered access to the solar, which had a fireplace, mullioned windows with side seats, and a private garderobe. A covered wall-walk linked the hall block with the eastern range, which provided three very essential garderobes and access to a latrine turret at the northeastern corner of the site.

Characterized as a "mock–fortified manor house,"[29] Oxwich Castle, located on the opposite end of the Gower Peninsula from Weobley Castle, seems small, its modest gatehouse stunted and fragile. Almost all of what survives dates to the massive rebuilding program undertaken by Sir Rice Mansel and his son, Edward, in the mid- to late sixteenth century. Only the recently discovered cross-wall in the east range predates this era and may actually be medieval. Oxwich Castle consisted of two adjacent ranges of buildings surrounding a cobbled courtyard. The gatehouse and south range reflect the stylistic taste of their builder, Sir Rice Mansel, who not only served as chamberlain of Chester and as a member of the Council of the Marches, but was also a vice-admiral in charge of ten ships. Originally flanked on either side by solid round towers, the gatehouse is hallmarked by a fine heraldic emblem, which dominates the archway overhead.

Upon stepping through the main gate, visitors immediately encounter a cobbled courtyard and, beyond the open area, a flat, off-putting wall pitted with several windows, which seems more like a barrier than a residential feature. However, a porchway once projected into the courtyard from this side of the wall; now only foundations survive. The western half of the castellated residence was constructed by Sir Rice during the first building phase at Oxwich; the eastern range was added later in the century by Sir Edward Mansel. The south range of buildings once held Sir Rice's two-story residence, with the great hall, kitchen block and, perhaps, servants' quarters. At one time, the courtyard may have also contained gardens.

Of particular note just outside the walls, Rice Mansel's ruined dovecote now lacks its dome and a large portion of its exterior wall. The gaping hole now allows visitors to see the symmetrical arrangement of the 300 pigeon holes that once bred meat for the castle food supply.

Edward Mansel was responsible for the extensive residential block well hidden from view behind the huge eastern wall. Shaped like a sideways "E," Mansel's "great house" once featured three enormous towerlike wings. Each projected outward from the high wall that formed the eastern side of the cobbled courtyard. Today, only the southeast wing stands to its full six stories. Sadly, the middle wing has been leveled to foundations; the northeast wing rises only partially but manages to preserve an impressive oven. Scattered within the ruins of the residential block are fragments of the first-floor hall and fireplace; the long gallery that ran along the third story; remnants of a pillar staircase; windows with flanking seats; and vaulted basements. The southeast tower is arguably Oxwich Castle's most imposing structure. The six-story-high walls are riddled with windows of varying height. Each single-chamber level held at least one fireplace. Quite possibly, this building housed the Mansels' huge entourage of retainers and other workers. Certainly, the lack of substantial fortifications and the predominance of residential structures support the implication that Oxwich "Castle" is a misnomer, as was the case with so many later castellated structures.

CHAPTER 4

Castles as Status Symbols

Castles . . . are the perfect architectural expression of feudal lordship of which they were the conscious symbol as well as much of the substance.

R. Allen Brown, *Castles: A History and Guide* (1980), 14

Not only was medieval Britain a contentious time, it was a time when ambitious men strove to achieve social status and maintain power as wealthy landowners and influential politicians who wielded authority much like the monarch they represented. Success and admiration were overriding goals. Men of royal birth or noble status strove to retain their power bases. Men of lesser status strove to reach the upper classes. One of the most obvious marks of achievement, a badge of honor and accomplishment, was the construction and possession of a castle.

DISPLAYS OF POWER, RANK, AND WEALTH

Possession of a castle, no matter its complexity, was a symbol of success and character that distinguished men from each other. During the Middle Ages, however, size did matter. The more powerful the lord, the larger his castle, or, at least, the larger or more innovative certain structures within the castle would be. Even though the military nature of the castle was always a lord's priority, the appearance of the castle, the complexity of its layout, the location of specific structures, and the skill and ornamentation displayed by the final product were all intentionally planned to display his status. Only monarchs and men with "the right stuff" could afford to build castles. The effort required an enormous investment of money to pay laborers, purchase and transport building materials, and then to maintain the complex structure in working order. Having a castle signaled to all comers that the lord had indeed "arrived" and was a man to be respected—perhaps even awed.

Edward I took this concept to an extreme. Intent on demonstrating to the Welsh that he had conquered them once and for all, Edward set about establishing a network of massive castles, the likes of which had never been seen in Britain before the thirteenth century nor afterwards. Now known as his iron ring of castles, Edward I's mammoth strongholds were deliberately placed at strategic points around North Wales and in Mid Wales, at Flint, Rhuddlan, Aberystwyth, Builth, Conwy, Caernarfon, Harlech, and Beaumaris. The state-of-the-art strongholds physically dominated their surroundings. Visually demonstrating the subjugation of the Welsh at the hands of the English king, the fortresses were intended to intimidate Edward's rebellious subjects into complete compliance.

In order to accomplish his grandiose scheme, Edward hired the most talented master mason of the times, James of St. George, and spent about £80,000 virtually bankrupting himself in his rush to squash the Welsh.[1] Impressive lordship castles were also erected in support of the king at Denbigh, Ruthin, Chirk, Holt, and Hawarden to enforce the conquest of Wales. Edward also replaced several key Welsh-built castles (Criccieth, Dolwyddelan, Castell y Bere, and Carreg Cennen) with English-built structures and garrisons, which reiterated his dominion over the Welsh. Ironically, Edward's first series of castles, built in or shortly after his initial success in Wales in 1277, proved incapable of preventing further Welsh rebellion. So, in order to avoid another debacle like the second foray into Wales in 1282, Edward commanded the construction of four huge, heavily defended royal castles and also enclosed two of the four adjoining towns (Caernarfon and Conwy) with towered curtain walls.

Edward I's castle at Caernarfon stands out from among the rest, not only for its fine state of preservation and its historic role as the venue for the investiture of the Prince of Wales, but also for its symbolic value to the thirteenth-century king. As indicated earlier, the great warrior-king believed Caernarfon was the only place where he could erect his imperial fortress, a structure he imagined would prove beyond all doubt that he was as great a ruler as the Byzantine emperors. And, the omens seemed to support his belief. Not only had Caernarfon served as a Roman outpost during Constantine's reign, but when Edward prepared to establish his new castle, reports circulated widely that a tomb belonging to the Roman emperor himself had been discovered in Caernarfon. Certain his destiny paralleled that of the Holy Roman Emperors, Edward ordered the castle built on the shores of the River Seiont, close to the aging Roman fort, and designed it to mirror the walls of Constantinople.

Caernarfon Castle and its circuit of medieval walls embodied Edward's vision of himself as a warrior-king who stood head-and-shoulders above the common man and whose accomplishments rivaled those of Constantine, who had ruled some 700 years earlier. Unlike his other great fortresses in North Wales, the imperial stronghold at Caernarfon featured giant polygonal towers crowned with battlements, the walls banded with stone of contrasting color, and clearly resembled the walls of fifth-century Constantinople. The Eagle Tower was the largest and most complex of the eleven polygonal towers that commanded strategic points around the castle walls. Topped with sculpted stone eagles, the tower symbolically linked Edward to the Romans (who used the eagle as their imperial symbol). Certainly, anyone approaching Edward's castle would appreciate its singular importance as a king's palace and fortress, and cower in its presence. When Edward pronounced his son, Edward, as the "Prince of Wales," English by blood but Welsh by birthplace and spoken language, his Welsh subjects could no longer claim the Prince of Wales as their own. Thenceforth, the Princes of Wales were heirs to the English throne, the eldest son of the reigning monarch, rather than the heirs of the native Welsh princes. Many modern-day Welsh believe that the persistence of the investiture ceremony at Caernarfon Castle, Prince Edward's birthplace, symbolically restates their subjugation.

LICENSES TO CRENELLATE

Obtaining a license to crenellate was almost as much a mark of status for a man as building the castle itself. Although never mandated by the monarchy nor a common practice until after 1200, applying for royal permission to erect a castle or to fortify an already extant residence indicated not only that the applicant had the self-confidence to approach the king, but also demonstrated that he possessed the financial and personal status that came with the ability to build a castle. For many lords, receiving the license to crenellate was accomplishment enough, so they felt no urgency to complete the process with an outlandish expenditure of money that could result in bankruptcy. Just having the royal license proved they were qualified to move in the circles of the rich and famous and that the monarch recognized their social status. The first license to crenellate was possibly issued for Bishopton Castle in 1143, though earlier licenses gave permission to strengthen an existing castle. The last license was granted to Sir William Fitzwilliam for Cowdray in Sussex in 1533.[2] A license issued in 1281 by Edward I to Stephen of Penchester and Margaret his wife authorized them to "fortify and crenellate their house at Allington in the County of Kent with a wall of stone and lime, and that they and their heirs may hold it, thus fortified and crenellated, in perpetuity." The resulting house, now a fortified residence, was Allington Castle.[3]

Overall, Edward III issued 181 licenses; Richard II issued 60; Henry IV, 8; Henry V, 1; Henry VI, 5; and Edward IV, 3. Indeed, of the 500 or so licenses that were granted between 1200 and 1500, only about 13 percent were ever fully acted upon; in other words, only about forty licenses resulted in the construction of true castles. Late-fourteenth-century examples include Bodiam and Wardour castles. The remaining licenses were either never acted upon or led to the construction of weakly fortified residences, crenellated for show rather than to thwart a serious attack.[4]

As time progressed, kings became more reluctant to grant licenses to crenellate. In fact, the license to crenellate was more often than not a ceremonial document that acknowledged the relationship between subordinate and monarch. Applicants generally sought out the honor that came with the license, and the right to build a castle, or fortify an already existing structure. It should be noted as well that many castle-builders never bothered to obtain a license to crenellate, feeling confident that they had achieved enough political and social clout that the king would not interfere with the project. And, some licenses were granted well after the fact, long after the castle was in operation.[5] However, even today, centuries after the last castle was constructed, possession of a license to crenellate remains a source of pride. A few castles, such as Chillingham in Northumberland, have placed their medieval license on public display.

THE EVER-CHANGING FABRIC

Displaying heraldic emblems above the main gateway into the castle, as at Warwick, Wardour, and Arundel, embedded in the interior and exterior walls, as at Caerlaverock, Warkworth, and Alnwick, or adorning the massive chimneypieces and walls in so many great halls and private apartments also symbolically and visually emphasized the historical and social importance of the lord. Heraldic emblems not only highlighted a lord's personal achievements but also reaffirmed the lengthy and prestigious pedigree of his ancestors. Indeed, even where the bulk of a castle lay in ruin, quite often the heraldic carvings survive, albeit worn by exposure to the elements (rains, winds, and fluctuating temperatures), as perpetual evidence of the lingering relationship between the present and the historic. From the Percy lion to Dudley's initials on Leicester's Gatehouse to the many coats of arms and inscriptions displayed to grand effect on the walls of Caerlaverock's Nithsdale Apartments, the intricate carvings continue to project the self-importance of the lords they symbolized.

As castles passed through the generations of a single family or were relinquished to a different series of owners, successive lords made sure to leave their mark by altering the structure itself. Some added new chambers or remodeled what already existed; others tore down earlier structures and rebuilt the castle according to their own ambitions and needs. Such projects often involved the addition of heavier and more complex defensive structures, larger or more ornate facilities and palatial features that demonstrated beyond any doubt (at least in their minds) that they were men of substance, stature, and financial independence who deserved the social position they held.

Royal castles physically document the changing times and changing preferences of reigning monarchs. In 1496 at Stirling Castle, for example, Scotland's James IV began the castle's first extensive building program. His achievements include Scotland's largest great hall, which measured 138 feet by 47 feet. Heated by five huge fireplaces, lit by two giant bay windows and several smaller lights, equipped with four turnpike staircases, and adorned with conical turrets and ornate carvings, the stunning building provided the setting not only for kings to confer with Parliament, but also for feasting and celebrations. Then, in 1594, James VI decided to renovate the Chapel Royal in honor of his son's christening and to vividly display the magnificence of the Scottish monarchy. After the ceremony, the king staged a sensational banquet in the great hall, where he had his men construct an 18-foot-long wooden ship with 40-foot-high masts which fired thirty-six brass cannons in celebration and carried the fish course to his guests.

Begun only twenty years after the great hall, James V's palace at Stirling Castle was intended to impress his second wife, Mary of Guise, whom he had married in 1538. Bedecked with an array of sculpted creatures, gods and goddesses, and even a carved portrait of the king, the Renaissance facade is the palace's most impressive feature, and one of the first of its kind to appear in Britain. Besides the bedchamber, the king's lodgings contained two public rooms for receiving guests and conducting the affairs of state. For his queen, James V added a similar set of chambers, which included a guardroom, the queen's presence chamber, and her bedchamber.

As the monarch's primary residence, Windsor Castle is known for the grandeur of its State Apartments, which, along with the Private Apartments, enclose the upper bailey. Over the centuries, reigning monarchs have periodically demolished and replaced the royal apartments, recreating them to new specifications that displayed his or her tastes and ambitions. In the late seventeenth century, Charles II embarked on a major building project at Windsor, hiring architect Sir Hugh May, painter Antonio Verrio, and wood-carver Grinling Gibbons to transform the fortress into a Baroque palace, the interiors of which rivaled France's Palace of Versailles. While only three of Charles II's rooms now survive (the King's Dining Room, Queen's Presence Chamber, and Queen's Audience Chamber), their painted ceilings, wood carvings, and gilt ornamentation resplendently reflect the grandiosity of the times. They remain a remarkable tribute to their builders.[6]

In the late twentieth century, Queen Elizabeth II transformed Windsor Castle's State Apartments, employing modern craftsmen to restore the northeastern corner of the castle after a devastating fire in 1992. While some areas, like the Green and Crimson Drawing Rooms and the Grand Reception Room have been restored to their earlier glory, the Octagon Dining Room, Lantern Lobby, and St. George's Hall were rebuilt using new designs. Undoubtedly, these rooms reflect the queen's preferences and will be her lasting legacy to the ever-evolving castle.

Lordship castles likewise evolved over time as new owners added new structures, revamped the furnishings, and modernized their homes. Castles such as Warwick, Arundel, and Alnwick, the fortified residences of the most important lords in the realm—the Earls of Warwick, the Dukes of Norfolk, and the Dukes of Northumberland—bridged the status divide between royal castles and those of lesser lords. Developing and expanding with the times, all three castles retain their regal stature and their medieval essence, and powerfully dramatize the splendor that came with the attainment of political and social rank. Like the monarch's residence at Windsor, these three lordship castles feature state apartments, which display their owners' station in life as well as their wealth and accomplishments.

Throughout Britain, lords of varying rank used their castles to showcase their continuing importance within a region and to the nation's history. The promontory site dominated by the sprawling ruins of Carew Castle in Pembrokeshire has supported a fortified stronghold of some type at least since the twelfth century, when Gerald de Windsor, the Norman constable of Pembroke Castle, acquired the site upon his marriage to Nest, the daughter of Rhys ap Tewdwr, Prince of Deheubarth. Some historians speculate that the first Norman castle at Carew was a motte castle, while others believe it would have been a ringwork. The oldest surviving masonry structure at the castle is the so-called Old Tower, which dates to the twelfth century and may have been built by de Windsor or his heir. Originally fronted with a large outer bailey on the eastern side and protected with four corner towers, the stone castle was essentially rectangular in plan. Over time, modifications were made to the plan, new towers erected along the eastern and southern walls and a new facade added on the northern side. Ultimately, Carew Castle combined standard military and trendy decorative features into a strong yet very attractive fortified residence, which served as the scene of the last great tournament in Wales, which honored King Henry VII and the selection of Sir Rhys ap Thomas as a Knight of the Garter in 1505.

During the Wars of the Roses, Rhys ap Thomas initially sided with Yorkist Richard III, agreeing never to allow the king's rival, Harri Tudor, into Pembrokeshire. However, when Tudor landed in West Wales, Rhys actually joined the Lancastrian cause and fought at Bosworth Field. Upon Tudor's victory at Bosworth, the new king knighted Rhys ap Thomas and also created him chamberlain and justiciar of Wales. Even though Sir Rhys became an active member of King Henry VII's English court, his Welsh castle at Carew remained a favorite stronghold.

Sometime before the death of Arthur, the Prince of Wales, in 1502, Rhys revamped Carew Castle, adding the ornamentation that emphasized his ties to the monarchy, a residential level over the lesser hall, an oriel window in the great hall, and a plain two-story outer gatehouse. Sir Rhys' most noteworthy contribution was the grand porchway opposite the main entrance into the inner bailey. Over the entryway, he placed three skillfully carved heraldic emblems: the arms of King Henry VII flanked by the arms of his first son, Arthur, and his son's wife, Catherine of Aragon. Quite possibly, the crests were added to honor the marriage of Prince Arthur and Catherine of Aragon in 1501. The attractive emblems have survived the ravages of the damp Welsh weather in remarkably fine condition.

TUDOR EMBLEMS, Carew Castle. Erected by Sir Rhys ap Thomas to pay tribute to Henry VII and the Tudor Dynasty, three eroding but attractive heraldic emblems adorn the great porchway at Carew Castle, in Pembrokeshire.

In 1506, Sir Rhys held the grandest tournament he could muster to honor his king. For five days, the participants, numbering well over 600 knights, their ladies and other nobility, retainers, and servants gathered for what turned out to be an enormously successful celebration.[7] Bedecked in the finest gilded armor, Rhys umpired the events. At his side were heralds and trumpeters, who announced each event and readied the knights. Contests included the joust, wrestling, tossing the pike, and swordplay. The tournament day was probably chaotic, with many events occurring simultaneously, but, despite the unavoidable drunkenness, no blood was shed. The expensive yet dignified production, and the attendant overhaul of his castle, demonstrated Sir Rhys' strong ties to the Tudor dynasty and proved his worthiness to be a member of the Order of the Garter.

Even in ruin, Warwickshire's Kenilworth Castle exudes an air of splendor befitting the lords who transformed it from a heavily military stronghold into one of Elizabethan England's grandest structures. Originating in the late eleventh or early twelfth century, Kenilworth's massive stone enclosure castle features elements from essentially every era of castle-building in British history. The basic shape of the site and the presence of the massive rectangular keep still reflect the castle's medieval origins, while the skillfully carved mullioned windows and the showy Leicester Gatehouse demonstrate the flamboyance of the Elizabethan era. The marshy grassland now enclosing the ruins once functioned as a scenic lake and a giant moat known as the "great mere." Created in the early thirteenth century by damming the waters of the neighboring Finham and Inchford Brooks to flood the open area, the great mere was a key part of the castle's defensive system.

In the late fourteenth century, John of Gaunt, Duke of Lancaster and father to King Henry IV, began the castle's conversion into a palatial dwelling that melded grandeur and comfort—in the form of a splendid new great hall—with its powerful defenses. In 1553, Edward VI granted the castle to John Dudley, Duke of Northumberland and Earl of Warwick. After the king's untimely death the same year, Dudley unwisely supported Lady Jane Grey as queen of England (for a brief nine days), but lost his head when the rightful queen, Bloody Mary Tudor, seized the throne and reclaimed Kenilworth Castle for the monarchy. Ten years later, Mary's sister, Queen Elizabeth I, sought to put things right and awarded the grand fortress to her favorite courtier, Robert Dudley, John's heir and Earl of Leicester. Dudley assumed responsibility for the castle and completed its transition into one of England's greatest palatial fortresses, adding stylish Leicester's Building and the grand gatehouse adorned with his initials.

Besides more than capably fulfilling its military role, Kenilworth Castle acted as the stunning backdrop from which Robert Dudley displayed his passion for and loyalty to his queen with one of the most widely acclaimed events of his day. For nineteen days in 1575, he wined, dined, and feted his queen and her entourage of thirty-one barons, numerous ladies-in-waiting, and 400 servants. Housing Elizabeth in Leicester's Building, Dudley ensured she had the most stylish accommodation. He also organized a wondrous water pageant, masques, fireworks, hunting and bear baiting, music, dancing, minstrel shows, mystery plays, and, of course, feasting. In all, the

Earl of Leicester spent £1,000 a day bankrupting himself for his queen's amusement, as any loyal lord would endeavor to do to prove his mettle.[8]

During the early fifteenth century, Henry, the 4th Lord Percy and 1st Earl of Northumberland, began Alnwick Castle's transformation into the splendid ducal residence still occupied by his descendants to this day. Erected in about 1350, Percy's most impressive addition, the great keep, dominates the site. Although heavily refurbished during the eighteenth and nineteenth centuries, Alnwick Castle retains its original medieval plan, which consisted of a low mound (possibly a Norman motte), a circular keep, two baileys, and a multitowered, irregular curtain wall. In 1755, the 1st Duke of Northumberland hired the incomparable architect, Robert Adam, to recreate his ancestral castle. However, almost 100 years later, the 4th Duke turned to architect Anthony Salvin to complete the castle's rebirth. Salvin demolished most of Adam's work and restored the residence to its original, battlemented glory.

Fronted by Percy's octagonal towers and defended with seven semicircular towers enclosing an inner courtyard, the four-story-tall, polygonal keep commands a place of pride atop the grass-laden medieval mound at Alnwick. Patrolling the battlements, life-sized stone soldiers steadfastly guard the grounds below. Visible from quite a distance, the finely carved sentinels

LEICESTER APARTMENTS and John of Gaunt's Oriel, Kenilworth Castle. John of Gaunt's fifteenth-century construction of an elaborate hall complex fitted with an unusual oriel (right) and the addition of an enormous block of apartments by Robert Dudley in the sixteenth century, ensured Kenilworth Castle's transformation into a palatial fortress.

CAERLAVEROCK CASTLE, Nithsdale Apartments. The lavishly decorated windows of the Nithsdale Apartments display heraldic emblems and classical designs that probably took their inspiration from similar work at Linlithgow Palace, the birthplace of Mary, Queen of Scots. The Earls of Nithsdale added the Renaissance style to the Edwardian-era castle at Caerlaverock.

would have presented a distant enemy with the impression that a formidable garrison of living soldiers awaited their approach. Even today, the stone men exude a quiet but steadfast presence, and rank high amongst Alnwick's alluring treasures. Now more palace than fortress, Alnwick Castle is one of England's finest stately homes.

Erected in the late thirteenth century, Caerlaverock Castle's triangular shape is distinctive; no other medieval castle in Scotland was built with this design. Surrounded by two water-filled ditches (moats) and acres of rolling green grass, the rust-colored fortress seems to float on the water's surface. At two corners, massive round towers once rose several stories; now, only the westernmost tower rises to its full height. Adorned with heraldic emblems, the castle's machicolated twin-towered gatehouse still dominates the spot, symbolizing the power of the Lords Maxwell during the Middle Ages, who first occupied the site in the 1220s.

During the seventeenth century, Robert, 1st Earl of Nithsdale, transformed Caerlaverock Castle into a grand palace. The fancy Nithsdale Apartments make a dramatic contrast with the simpler medieval parts of the castle. Each window is framed with a triangular-shaped design called a "tympanum," which is decorated with scenes from mythology and heraldry. The lovely carvings only hint at the grandeur that once made Caerlaverock Castle one of Scotland's most splendid sites. Even today, it is easy to imagine how the charming castle would have impressed the guests of the Earls of Nithsdale.

THE CASTLES OF ECCLESIASTICAL LORDS

The Norman Invasion not only brought castle-building to Britain, but powerful ecclesiastical figures arrived as well. Having tremendous influence over their secular counterparts and the ability to curtail a lord's aspirations, these religious leaders accumulated great wealth while pursuing their own very worldly ambitions. Like a secular lord, a bishop traveled frequently throughout his domain, accompanied by a large entourage of people, including individuals of lesser religious status, servants—and even a garrison. In order to house the bishop and his company, great stone residences (palaces and smaller houses) were put up at each spot regularly visited. The most prosperous bishops controlled several of these imposing structures. In the twelfth century, for example, the bishops of Winchester maintained six castles and two palaces, while the archbishops of Canterbury kept as many as twenty-one palaces.

By the end of the fourteenth century, the fortified residence of the bishops of St. Davids at Llawhaden in Pembrokeshire possessed all the essential features one normally associates with a medieval castle. Much more than a palatial residence, Llawhaden was a true castle in every sense of the word: its twin-towered gatehouse overlooked a deep ditch, not only augmenting the castle's defensive strength but also providing quarters for the garrison, while the lanky great hall, flanked on the east by private apartments and on the west by the kitchen and a bakehouse, filled the opposite side of the inner bailey. Nearby, the well dropped over 98 feet into the ground. A second range of residential chambers—added during the final building phase— occupied the southeastern side of the castle, the northern end of which held the chapel and the unusual porch.

Built on lands owned by the bishops of St. Davids in the early twelfth century, the earliest castle at Llawhaden was a formidable ringwork with a steep-sided circular embankment and deep ditch. The substantial earth and timber stronghold dominated the site for about twenty years before the clerics decided to strengthen it in stone. The earthen embankments and deep ditch that presently encompass the castle date to this time. When Gerald of Wales visited Llawhaden in 1175 to meet with his uncle, Bishop David FitzGerald, the earthwork castle was still defended by a timber palisade and drawbridge.

In the early thirteenth century, the bishops regained control of the castle site from the Welsh who had destroyed the timber defenses in 1192. They promptly began a major rebuilding program at Llawhaden, which involved the construction of a stone curtain wall and at least two substantial round mural towers. Measuring about 26 feet across, the larger tower may have served as the keep. The smaller semicircular tower had a diameter of approximately 18 feet. At one time, the two towers were linked by a faceted curtain wall, a configuration often used when fortifying ringworks with masonry defenses (other examples include Coity and Newcastle Bridgend, in Glamorgan).

Like other thirteenth-century lords, Thomas Bek, who served as Bishop of St. Davids from 1280 to 1293, began the castle's transformation into a comfortable, yet still fortified, residence. His chief contribution was the two-story great hall. Together with the kitchen and solar, which extended from either side of the upper level, the great hall measured over 78 feet in length by 23 feet in width. Underneath, the bishops used the vaulted undercroft to store food and other supplies. For a time, the great hall was accessed up a set of timber steps from the inner ward, but the ladder was eventually replaced with a stone stairway and forebuilding, remnants of which survive. The forebuilding itself was later removed to make way for a bakehouse.

Late in the fourteenth century, Bishop Adam de Houghton hired master mason, John Fawle, to begin the southeastern range of residential buildings, which eventually contained an undercroft and two apartments, which were fitted with fireplaces, lit with crossloops and separated by an octagonal latrine tower, the shaft of which ran down the wall between the two apartments. These rooms presumably accommodated guests of some standing or members of the bishop's retinue.

Rising from the ditch outside its walls, the castle chapel occupied the eastern end of the range. A five-story porch fronted the chapel, providing access from the inner ward and outstanding views of the surrounding countryside and also emphasizing the important role played by the bishops, not only as clerics, but also as lords in their own right. Interestingly, the series of small chambers on the upper floors of the porch, which are linked by a spiral staircase, may have housed the bishop's exchequer. A finely carved lintel and stone heads resembling a crowned male and a female wearing what appears to be a wimple adorn the doorway; some scholars speculate that the figures may represent the king and queen of England. The polygonal tower at the chapel's eastern corner contained another latrine and also held the dungeon, just like any secular castle.

Bishop Houghton's most impressive legacy at Llawhaden is the great gatehouse, its two semicircular towers supported by spurred buttresses, which still reach into the ditch. Arrowslits open from the guardrooms that once stood alongside the gateway. Murder holes and a portcullis slot are visible in the ceiling above the gate passage, which was reached by a movable drawbridge. The better-preserved eastern tower retains interior walls, floors, fireplaces, and window seats. These rooms accommodated the castle constable and his household, or other members of the garrison.

Scattered throughout England, bishops' castles were located in distant areas such as Sherborne in Dorset, Rochester in Kent, Farnham in Surrey, and Durham in County Durham, where the clerics had the proud distinction of

being designated as Prince Bishops of the palatinate of Durham, a "state within a state," which they ruled as kings subordinate only to the King of England (at least according to the law) until the nineteenth century, when the motte and bailey castle became home to the University of Durham. At Durham, the Prince Bishops could hold their own parliament, raise armies, administer justice, levy taxes and collect other revenue, and mint their own coins. The layout of the Norman castle is still obvious, despite the addition of modern structures during the course of its lengthy history. Like Llawhaden, Durham Castle features all of the structures normally associated with a true medieval castle, including a shell keep and motte, a large bailey, a gatehouse, the great hall, a chapel, and private apartments for the bishops. Standing close to Durham Cathedral, one of Europe's greatest example of Norman architectural achievement and now a designated World Heritage Site, the castle not only documents the history of the Prince Bishops but also displays the intimate relationship between church and castle that spanned the Middle Ages.

Bishops in Scotland also maintained fortified residences, most notably at St. Andrews in Fife, where the ruined castle remains one of the finest examples of its kind.

LLAWHADEN CASTLE, GATEHOUSE. The twin-towered gatehouse at Llawhaden Castle, in Pembrokeshire, still commands attention from all comers, even though it is now little more than a façade. The Bishops of St. David's ensured that their fortified residence had all the militarized features expected of a substantial medieval castle.

REFLECTING THE SOCIAL ORDER OF THE TIMES

The location and design of specific parts of the castle not only served a functional purpose, they also symbolically reflected the status of the people who resided within or had access to different areas.[9]

THE GREAT HALL

Generally recognized as the castle's social and administrative center, the great hall was usually the most ornate room in the castle, with the exception, perhaps, of the chapel. Everything about the great hall displayed the status of the lord, from the ornate carved windows, giant fireplace hoods, and timber-beamed ceilings to the sheer size of the chamber, the presence of heraldic emblems, and the position of the lord's table on a raised dais at the end of the hall. The elaborate great hall added during John of Gaunt's transformation of Kenilworth Castle into a palatial fortress remains one of the castle's most impressive features. Even in ruin, the late-fourteenth-century chamber dominates the western side of the inner bailey and is clearly identifiable from both inside and outside. Replacing an earlier range of domestic facilities, the great hall was particularly notable for its undercroft, bays flanked with finely carved columns, and the four tall lancet-headed windows. The unusual three-sided oriel commands attention in the inner bailey. Comparable to a dais, the oriel was actually a separate room still located within the great hall. Inside, the lord and visiting dignitaries ate their meals and watched the activities in the courtyard as well as in the hall itself.[10]

Another impressive medieval great hall survives at Berkeley Castle in Gloucestershire, its furniture and furnishings poised to entertain stately visitors. Measuring over 32 feet high, 62 feet long, and 32 feet wide, the fourteenth-century chamber features a timber-beamed ceiling, wall tapestries, stained glass windows, and the original sixteenth-century painted screen which displays an eye-catching array of heraldic shields and a carved arcade.[11] Behind the raised dais, a skillfully carved yet modest chimneypiece adorned the fireplace that warmed the lord and his guests.

CHAPELS

Many medieval castle-builders portrayed themselves as devout Christians who served as patrons for local religious establishments, such as abbeys or priories, many of which were built at the behest of the lord. Indeed, it is not surprising to find a parish church standing fairly close, within walking distance of the local Norman castle, for example, at Rochester, Durham,

Castle Rising, and Castle Acre, all of which are located in England. At Manorbier in Wales, the parish church was located across the narrow valley from the castle but close enough that a young Gerald de Barri sought refuge there when Welsh rebels stormed nearby Tenby. Not only did the church provide sanctuary to the lad, it also played a key role in Gerald's future, preparing him for ordination as a priest, his position as chaplain to royal princes and his selection as Archdeacon of Brecon.[12] Nonetheless, despite the proliferation of churches throughout the British countryside, most castles had at least one chapel where the lord and his family could attend mass on a regular basis. At Manorbier, the de Barris added a separate chapel tower onto the eastern end of the hall block during the mid–thirteenth century. Among its finery, the chapel had a tiled floor and ornate lancet-headed windows. Many castles also maintained a smaller, secondary chapel which offered services to the household and other residents.

Just as a grandiose great hall displayed the lord's status, so did an ornate chapel. Arguably England's best-known castle chapel fills the second story of the White Tower, the great keep at the Tower of London. Dedicated to St. John the Evangelist, the chapel royal is an excellent example of Norman architecture, its circular limestone columns now lacking their original medieval paintwork but still crowned with stylishly carved capitals and a triforium on the uppermost level. In its heyday, the chapel featured lavish stained glass windows, a painted rood screen, and other furnishings and could be entered from the great chamber. The White Tower also contained a chapel for the constable. The Chapel of St. Peter ad Vincula ("in chains"), a separate structure on Tower Green, once stood outside the castle walls. During the expansion of the castle in the late thirteenth century, Henry III enclosed the building, which had been the local parish church, inside the new curtain wall. He then refurbished the church so that the castle's numerous residents would have a place to worship.[13] Remodeled more than once, St. Peter's contains memorials to former residents and also the tombs of several people who lost their heads on Tower Green, including Queens Anne Boleyn and Katherine Howard, Lady Jane Grey, and Sir Thomas More.

Often identifiable by their fine windows or the presence of a piscina, aumbry, and sedile, individual chapel towers graced many medieval castles. Some chapels occupied an entire mural tower. At Kidwelly, in Carmarthenshire, the late-thirteenth-century chapel tower projects outward from the eastern face of the castle. Its base supported with pyramidal spurs that prevented collapse into the river below, the chapel tower is the only structure of this type at the castle. The chapel itself occupies the uppermost story and features a series of windows adorned with special white stone, a double piscina (a stone basin where the priest washed the communion vessels), and a sedile, a special seat used exclusively by the priest. Adorned with a cruciform roof, a slender turret known as the sacristy rises along the chapel tower's southern side. Inside the sacristy, the priest stored the containers, cups, and candelabra used during mass. He lived in the chamber on the level below.

The Chapel of St. Mary Magdalene, Ludlow Castle's unique stone chapel, stands on its own in the inner bailey, one of two chapels at the great Marcher castle. The other, dedicated to St. Peter, stands at the southeastern corner of the outer bailey. Now little more than a shell of its former self, the rectangular structure was added in about 1328 by Roger Mortimer, who had been freed from the Tower of London five years earlier and reputedly built the chapel to celebrate the event. Before its ultimate decay, the Chapel of St. Peter was also used as a courthouse and records office.[14]

Erected two centuries earlier than the Chapel of St. Peter, Ludlow's splendid round chapel remains an impressive example of Norman-era architecture. Dedicated to St. Mary Magdalene and possibly built by Hugh de Lacy, the unusual battlemented cylinder functioned as the chapel's nave; it was possibly inspired by the Church of the Holy Sepulchre in Jerusalem. Originally, the chapel would also have featured a 26-foot-long rectangular

LUDLOW CASTLE, chapel. One of the few medieval round chapels erected in England, the charming chapel at Ludlow Castle, in Shropshire, is adorned with classic Norman designs, including a fine Norman archway. At one time, the now demolished chancel linked the round structure to the curtain wall.

chancel that stretched to the curtain wall. During late seventeenth century, Sir Henry Sidney ordered the demolition of the chancel and made several alterations to the round nave, including the insertion of a window alongside the entrance, the transformation of a Norman window into a doorway, and the construction of an upper story.[15] Nevertheless, much of the original Norman fabric still graces the chapel. The western door retains its Norman archway, which is highlighted with a distinctive chevron pattern and interior arcading.

Even more impressive than having one or two castle chapels (Edward I reputedly had made plans for four chapels at Caernarfon), building an entire church within the castle walls proved not only the lord's piety but also dramatized his extreme wealth. After all, how many men, even those who had achieved a large degree of success, could afford to erect and furnish such as a special church, let alone one inside the castle walls. At Farleigh Hungerford in Somerset, Sir Walter Hungerford deliberately enclosed the local parish Church of St. Leonard within the walls of the outer bailey when he expanded the site in the 1420s. Today, the building, now known as the Chapel of St. Leonard, is the best-preserved structure at the otherwise heavily ruined castle, which was begun in the late fourteenth century by Sir Thomas Hungerford, Britain's first Speaker of the House of Commons.

FARLEIGH HUNGERFORD CASTLE, chapel. Originally serving as the parish church, the well-preserved Chapel of St. Leonard inside the walls of Farleigh Hungerford Castle, Somerset, contains the colorfully decorated tombs of members of the Hungerford family, as well as impressive wall paintings. The crypt below contains several plain lead coffins that still wear the funeral masks of the individuals buried within.

Vividly displaying a number of well-preserved medieval wall paintings and the Hungerford arms, the fine chapel contains the elaborate tombs of several generations of Hungerford, including Sir Thomas and his wife, Joan Hussey. Beneath the chapel, a vaulted crypt still protects the lead coffins of other members of the Hungerford family, which are still adorned with lifelike lead masks. To compensate for the annexation of the original parish church, Sir Walter built a new church, likewise dedicated to St. Leonard, which serves the parish about ½ mile south of the castle.[16]

Undoubtedly, St. George's Chapel inside the royal castle at Windsor is the best-known example of its kind. Remodeled by Edward IV in the late fifteenth century (Edward III had established the College of St. George in 1348 in the earlier chapel on the site), extended by Henry VII, and completed by Henry VIII in time for his own burial, the magnificent Gothic structure remains the castle's crowning glory. One cannot help but be amazed by the vision of flying buttresses rising to pinnacles topped with carved figures, drawing one's eyes to the heavens to memorialize the royals who rest within. Inside, meticulously carved fan-vaulting pulls attention toward the fabulous choir, where intricate carvings honor the Knights of the Garter, whose banners fly overhead. The resting place of kings, queens, and other royals, the chapel dominates the lower bailey and is the first structure visitors see when entering the castle through the King Henry VIII Gate. In reality, the new chapel was a collegiate church managed by sixteen vicars, a deacon gospeller, thirteen lay clerks, two clerks epistoler, and thirteen choristers.[17] Like the castle in which it stands, the great chapel has been modified over time to accommodate the stylistic tastes of reigning monarchs.

One of the few lords who could afford to construct entire churches within his castle was Henry, 4th Lord Percy, whose collegiate church at Warkworth Castle (initially planned by his grandfather, the 3rd Lord Percy) now lays extensively ruined midway between the great polygonal keep and the outer bailey, where the shell of a substantial chapel stands just west of the main gatehouse. This outer chapel was probably used by the members of the castle staff, retainers, and other residents. By building an entire church in the center of the inner bailey, the Percys undoubtedly intended to symbolically reconfirm their supreme importance to England—and probably to God as well. Curiously, Percy's church was apparently never completed. Now represented by its cruciform foundations, the collegiate church would have housed a group of priests who sang masses and prayed for their benefactor.

Indeed, everything about Warkworth Castle displays the power, wealth, self-confidence, and self-importance of the Percys, lords of Alnwick, who acquired the castle and other lands in Northumberland in 1332 by a grant from Edward III. A castle already stood at Warkworth, and the Percys set about strengthening and expanding the structure into an architectural masterpiece like no other, adorned throughout with the Percy heraldic lion and dominated by the unique keep, which Percy erected on top of what is believed to be the original motte at the site. Inside the keep, the Percys had their own private chapel, where they could attend services in style and maintain a sense of social separation from the rest of the castle.

COMMUNAL LIVING ARRANGEMENTS

The nature of one's position and the type of labor he or she performed often determined where individuals slept within the castle. For example, cooks often slept in or near the kitchen, the chaplain slept in a chamber adjoining the chapel, and grooms slept with the horses.[18] At some sites, the castle-guard and resident knights occupied small houses in the bailey, as at Cardiff Castle, where the Lord of Glamorgan owned the houses but required the occupants to repair and maintain them. One "domus" still stood in the outer bailey when Rice Merrick visited Cardiff in the sixteenth century; archaeologists unearthed foundations during excavations from 1974 to 1981.[19] On the other hand, higher status members of the household might have their own sleeping chambers, and guests might sleep in the lord's own bedchamber. Alternatively, the lord and his family often occupied a specially designated tower, a keep, or a block of private apartments.

Royal castles, not surprisingly, were fitted with apartments specifically designated for the king, queen, and their retinue. King Edward I ensured he and his queen, Eleanor, had comfortable, private accommodation at Conwy Castle, where the four-story King's Tower contained royal bedchambers and adjoining buildings housed the great chamber, the presence chamber, and the privy chamber. Traditionally believed to have been favored by Queen Eleanor, the chapel tower stood on the opposite side of the inner bailey. The king's garrison and key members of the household staff lived on the western side of the castle, which was physically separated from the king's residence by a cross-wall.

In 1533, King Henry VIII added the lavish half-timber and brick Queen's House to the Tower of London to impress and accommodate his second wife, Anne Boleyn, whom he had only recently wed. Three years later, however, the unfortunate woman would find herself imprisoned by her vengeful husband inside the castle, accused of adultery and beheaded on Tower

Green within sight of her former residence and adjacent to the Chapel of St. Peter ad Vincula, where she was laid to rest.

WHEN PRIVACY BECOMES PARAMOUNT

Beginning in about 1200, the trend shifted away from the lord sleeping together with his men in the hall. Increasingly, lords preferred to have private accommodation and began building separate series of residential units that not only enhanced the quality of life for the occupants but also socially distanced higher-status castle residents from the rest of the occupants.[20] Not only did this practice emphasize the supremacy of the lord within his own castle, it also symbolically—and quite visually—reiterated to the other residents exactly where they fit within the "chain of command." Visitors and residents alike recognized that the largest suites and most elaborate structures housed the most important members of the castle family. They then maintained the appropriate social distance.

Throughout the medieval period, living in the keep or the dominant mural tower at a castle was a mark of status normally reserved for the lord and his family. From the earliest motte castles, with their timber towers or shell keeps, to the finest stone castles of the Middle Ages, the great tower most visibly distinguished its occupants from other castle dwellers. Even though they now exist only as hulking shells of their original selves, the great keeps at lordship castles such as Pembroke, Conisbrough, and Warkworth clearly demonstrate the powerful effect created by self-reliant, freestanding keeps, especially when they were so obviously unlike the castle's other structures. Those lords who implemented the latest, state-of-the-art construction techniques, for example, erecting round mural towers or keeps, not only demonstrated their creativity and forward thinking, they also displayed their superiority over those men whose castles did not possess such innovative features. Medieval visitors—and their modern-day counterparts—would have immediately identified the imposing structures as being of central importance to the castle and also reflecting the special status of the lord.

This perception persisted throughout the Middle Ages,[21] even when the construction of new keeps waned and great gatehouses, with their heavy defenses and more spacious interiors, were preferred for their extra living space and elaborate defenses. Making a comeback of sorts late in the Middle Ages, the great keep hallmarked palatial fortresses like Raglan Castle, where the moated Yellow Tower of Gwent erected by Sir William ap Thomas in the early fifteenth century still commands attention alongside machicolated gatetowers and lavish residential facilities built by his son and later owners. Now largely in ruins, the five-story-high, hexagonal great tower once contained a basement-level kitchen, the great chamber on the next story above, and living quarters with latrines and fireplaces on the uppermost levels. The topmost story was battlemented. The unique great tower reflected the social achievements and personal pride of its builder, a Welshman by birth also touted as "the Blue Knight of Gwent."

At nearby Chepstow Castle, not only did Roger Bigod III construct separate apartments for himself and for his in-house military officers during the last decades of the thirteenth century, but he also erected a massive mural tower to fortify and dominate the easternmost corner of the outer curtain wall. Crowned with its very own stone security force, a set of carved figures, the four-story tower featured elegant paintings, windows with seats, fireplaces, latrines, a private chapel, and portcullises to barricade the doorways into the tower; the self-contained unit held all the domestic conveniences and security the lord of the castle, Roger Bigod III, required.[22]

ACCOMMODATING DIFFERENT SOCIAL STRATA

As social expectations changed, the lord and his family began to favor living at a distance from the great hall—and from the rest of the castle's inhabitants. They constructed new apartment blocks, consisting of several chambers, the existence of which reiterated their social separation from their subjects and from their guests. Accommodations for members of the household were increasingly based on their social status. Those residents whose chambers were placed nearest the lord's apartments had the highest status and, perhaps, the lord's ear as well. The social hierarchy within the castle was directly reflected in the overall layout and decoration on both the inner and exterior walls of the rooms.

For many castle-builders, display of status, power, wealth, and self-assurance was a major priority. In some cases, it was an obsession. Careful thought went into the design of new castles and into the expansion of those castles already occupied. The need to house the families of permanent staff members (such as the steward or the constable) prompted some owners to build separate residential suites, as at Goodrich, Bolton, and Bodiam castles, which were essentially smaller versions of the lord's private apartments and thereby reflected the lesser status of their occupants. During the late thirteenth or early fourteenth century, the Earl of Pembroke, William de Valence, and his son and heir, Aymer, completed several substantial construction projects. At Pembroke, the men erected the towered curtain wall, elaborate great gatehouse, and the circuit of walls that linked the adjacent town to the castle. They also extended their fortress, Goodrich Castle, which safeguarded the Forest of Dean on the English side of the Welsh border. Already a substantial stronghold centered by a tall rectangular keep, the Goodrich Castle of the de Valences acquired two substantial residential ranges, which lined the inner courtyard. Today, the structures are extensively ruined, but enough survives to reveal their place within the fourteenth-century castle.

Whereas the exterior emphasized heavy defenses, with its massive corner towers, barbican, and deep rock-cut ditch, the interior of Goodrich Castle focused on meeting the lord's residential requirements. In addition to the great rectangular keep, which was built during the mid-twelfth century and still dominates the stronghold, the inner courtyard was encompassed by several residential ranges, which not only served the needs of the lord but also accommodated his household, resident soldiers, and guests. Situated at right angles to the great hall and lord's private solar, the so-called north hall featured a ground-floor hall or great chamber and also a basement-level hall, believed to have been used by the servants. The northwestern tower which stood at the angle between the northern and western ranges contained at least two stories of living quarters and was well-appointed to house the lord and his family. Running eastward from the north hall, a timber-framed set of chambers provided additional living space and access to the chapel.[23] Another series of residential chambers and an associated hall filled the eastern range, which connected to and ran due south from the chapel tower. This block probably accommodated the castle's constable, other military occupants, and members of the permanent staff; the imposing tower at its southernmost end would have serviced guests of more noteworthy status.[24]

One of the most dramatic examples of a lord consciously planning and building a series of residential suites to accommodate residents in accordance with their social rank was Richard, Lord Scrope's quadrangular castle at Bolton, in North Yorkshire. Begun in the 1370s, Bolton Castle is dominated by four enormous rectangular towers, each of which rose five levels. Three-story-tall residential ranges occupied

BOLTON CASTLE INTERIOR. Bolton Castle's shrewdly planned interior both physically and symbolically assigned staff members of differing status to different parts of the castle. Lord Scrope erected self-contained suites of chambers to accommodate not only his own family but also those of his workers.

the walls linking the corner towers to each other. Lord Scrope constructed eight completely self-contained residential suites, each focused on its own hall, and an additional set of twelve individual lodgings.[25] Around the central courtyard (the inner bailey), ground-level rooms contained storage space, the stables, bakery, brewhouse, and lodgings for lower-status workers, and the main living chambers filled the first and second stories. Senior members of the household occupied private apartments fitted into the northwest and southwest towers and the western range between them, and the eastern range housed military personnel.[26]

Bolton Castle's southeastern tower and adjoining south range contained structures whose functions were already provided elsewhere in the castle. An entirely separate section that could function without relying on the other facilities inside the castle, the southern range contained ground-floor guardrooms, storage, and a bakehouse; a hall and kitchen block on the floor above; more private accommodation on the second story; and access to the southeastern tower, which held additional lodgings.[27] More than likely, this group of buildings served the lord, who could effectively distance himself and live separately from his staff members. Lord Scrope's castle both physically and symbolically put people in their place.

Sir Edward Dalyngrigge's quadrangular masterpiece, Bodiam Castle, also separated its residents by social status. As at both Goodrich and Bolton Castles, the inner courtyard at Bodiam was enclosed by residential structures. At Bodiam, however, the great gatehouse also contained a number of living chambers and was connected to the northeast tower, another residential building fitted with two halls and living quarters. Each of the four main residential suites contained a hall, living chambers, service rooms, and bedrooms and could access the adjoining corner tower. They were allotted to the lord and his family, important visitors, higher-status members of the household, and the lord's retainers. Sir Edward occupied the eastern range, which contained the great chamber, lord's hall, the chapel, a secondary hall, and two other chambers, and the east tower, which held two more living chambers, garderobes, fireplaces, and access to the wall-walk. Dalyngrigge also provided modest accommodation for the servants,[28] and the retainers' quarters filled the opposite side of the courtyard from his own domestic range.

This type of layout not only emphasized the social distinction between the castle's different residents, but also served a practical purpose; after all, in an age where wealth and status were measured by the appearance of one's castle, it only made sense that the lord would provide special accommodation for his household and military employees. Extra accommodation showed that the lord could both afford the expense and was himself of such

BODIAM CASTLE INTERIOR. Sir Edward Dalyngrigge apportioned out the inner chambers of his great castle at Bodiam to accommodate his own household in style and also to ensure that his retainers were well provided with their own facilities.

importance that he required a large, varied, and expensive staff.

STATUS IN THE LANDSCAPE

As mentioned in chapter 1, medieval lords deliberately planned their new castles to emphasize their control over the local populace. They placed their castles on sites for maximum visual impact as constant reminders of the power and dominion of the outsiders who controlled the region. The stronghold itself was built for the same purpose: to intimidate, repel rebellion, and maintain the lordship. Yet, many lords did not stop at the physical structure when it came to symbolically reiterating their position. They also sought to impress and command respect from their guests and rivals. An effective way to accomplish this goal was to also design the surrounding landscape and the approach to the castle to instill awe and at the same time to subtly remind oncomers of their place within the social hierarchy. Choreographed pathways to the castle, water-filled landscapes, and lush terraced gardens not only enhanced the appearance of the grounds, they also created an image of a man with substantial wealth and political clout who was worthy of admiration, deference, and at least a smidgen of fear. On occasion, however, some guests might experience the reverse of what Sir Edward intended with such dramatic vistas. Jealousy often led to simmering resentment, which could prompt betrayal or an attack, given the right circumstances.

Sir Edward Dalyngrigge recognized the power of symbolism and went out of his way to incorporate it into Bodiam Castle. In addition to ensuring the structure had the basic elements that made it a castle—battlements, towers, defended gatehouses, and a wide moat—Dalyngrigge arranged the interior to reflect the social status of its residents. Yet, he did not stop at the design of the castle when it came to dramatizing his self-importance. He also laid out the encompassing landscape so that visitors were forced to follow a pathway that weaved and turned as it neared the castle, pointing guests—and potential attackers—toward specific vantage points.

Even today, the approach to the castle prompts emotional responses from visitors. For much of the way, the castle seems invisible, hidden from view behind the sloping ground. Suddenly, it springs into existence, mystically floating atop the expansive waters of the moat. During the Middle Ages, the effect would have been much the same. Almost at once, the route shifted to the right, moving visitors along the southern side, where the great postern gateway acted as the secondary entrance into the castle. Movement was then guided around the eastern side of the castle to the low hill overlooking the main gatehouse. From there, visitors would not only appreciate the majesty of the castle itself but had views beyond the castle to the River Rother, which it reputedly commanded. The pathway to the castle then took another sharp turn away from the main facade and forced visitors to proceed around to the western side, cross a drawbridge, and turn again to face the castle. At this point, they were greeted with Dalyngrigge's heraldic emblems and again reminded of their own social status relative to their host's.[29] Attackers who followed the same route, on the other hand, found themselves exposed to the defenders on the battlements, who had a clear view of their approach.

As at Bodiam Castle, Kenilworth Castle was laid out for maximum effect. Not only did the great mere act as a defensive strategy to keep attackers at bay, it also created visual drama that must have stunned the senses. Walking across the drawbridge to the main entry point at Kenilworth Castle would have encouraged visitors to take in the panoramic, water-filled scene, and, perhaps, cause them to wonder how the lord of the castle managed to create such a spectacle. Then, once across the bridge and past the gatehouse, they would then proceed onward to the central hub of the great castle, the pathway to which forced them to turn to their left. Facing the inner bailey full on, guests would suddenly feel dwarfed by the hulking red structures that stood on the hill and towered overhead. The experience still occurs for modern-day visitors. Clearly, Robert Dudley understood how to manipulate the vistas to their advantage, as when he staged gala events at the castle in 1575. So did his predecessor, Roger de Mortimer, who held a raucous medieval tournament at the castle in 1279, treating the water defenses as the star attraction and making special use of the tiltyard. While their ladies watched, 100 knights competed for three days in the traditional joust and in a new type of contest called "the Round Table," during which the group of jousting knights would treat each other as equals, no matter their status, and sit at a circular table while dining and participating in other activities.

The splendor of Raglan Castle was only recently put into context with archaeological confirmation that a series of spectacular terraced gardens and huge artificial lakes were added by the Somersets, Earls of Worcester, between 1550 and 1646.[30] The gardens were in essence an extension of what had existed at the site during the fourteenth century, before its acquisition by William ap Thomas, who began its transformation into one of Britain's greatest palatial fortresses, as will be discussed in the next chapter.

THE SHAMS

A special type of folly exists throughout Britain, one that displays the grandiosity and narcissism of the rich and famous. More aptly called "sham castles," these structures were not constructed for military purposes, as were true castles. Instead, these modern strongholds showcased their owners' wealth and proclaimed the establishment of a new form of feudalism. With their battlements and towers, they seemed like true castles but in reality they were merely fantasies incapable of withstanding a siege. The pride of the rich, who displayed their wealth as the lords of the Middle Ages did, by spending it on grandiose homes, structures such as Eastnor Castle in Herefordshire and Lulworth Castle in Devon may look like castles but they are not, nor were they ever intended to be, properly fortified military residences.

Sadly, by 1650, the majority of Britain's great castles were rendered useless. Those that managed to escape Cromwell's demolition teams at the end of the English Civil War battled other daunting foes. The natural effects of time and aging caused the stone structures to crumble. Without routine maintenance, castles quickly decayed, due to rain, wind, erosion, the intrusion of vines and shrubbery, and animals. And, local people used castles as convenient quarries, pilfering stone and lead for other building projects.

Repairing stonework broken down during sieges or from neglect has always been a tremendously costly endeavor. Some noblemen even bankrupted themselves to keep their castles in good condition. Most castles needed almost constant attention to ensure they would not decay. The price for that attention was staggering. So, when faced with repairing a castle or building another one somewhere else, many post-medieval owners moved elsewhere and started over, building homes that were more cost-effective. Nonetheless, Britain's medieval castles had firmly entrenched themselves in the national mind-set.

In the eighteenth and nineteenth centuries, a new attitude of romanticism spawned organized efforts to preserve medieval castles and other historic sites in Britain. Early in the twentieth century, the British government intervened and many castles were placed in state care. Most of Britain's great castles are now in the care of a state agency such as English Heritage, Historic Scotland, or Cadw. Private organizations such as the National Trust care for many of the better-preserved sites, thanks to legal agreements between the Trust and owners, whereby the owner continues to live in the castle but agrees to open at least part of it to the public. The Trust relieves the financial burden but respects the history and rights of the owner. If such agreements were not possible, too many castles and stately homes would have disappeared long ago. Other castles are privately owned and remain closed to the public. Some have been converted into stylish castle hotels.

THE WELSH EXAMPLES

Wales has several notable sham castles, most of which were built in the nineteenth century by men who accumulated their wealth exploiting their fellow humans while ravaging the countryside. Like the Normans, who established a feudal order over 900 years ago, the nineteenth-century industrialists imposed a new social system on the Welsh. Some historians describe the system as "industrial feudalism," a process that, like the Norman Conquest, greatly changed the face of Wales. Like the Normans, the industrialists often proclaimed their potency by constructing what in reality were imitation castles. And, as in the Middle Ages, the general population labored and suffered in the service of their lord. Yet, to confuse them with true castles is a mistake. These follies never withstood the hardships of siege warfare; indeed, the worst they endured was the temperamental Welsh weather. The average citizens, the men and women, old and young, who labored inside the mines in exchange for a mere pittance, were the ones under siege.

Among the Welsh shams are Penrhyn Castle (near Bangor), Bryn Bras Castle (about four miles east of Caernarfon), Ruperra Castle (near Cardiff), and Cyfarthfa Castle (at Merthyr Tydfil). Fanciful Castell Coch, built by the Marquess of Bute close to his Cardiff-based empire, differs in one respect: Lord Bute and his architect, William Burges, made a serious effort to reconstruct the ruined castle according to its medieval plan and incorporated as much as they could of its original foundations.

At first glance, each of these shams looks like a castle. However, their histories and actual purpose identify them as stately homes, the splendid modern residences of the industrial lords of Wales. Certainly, each memorializes its medieval predecessors with richly battlemented towers, Norman arches, and antiquated features. Even now, they manage to inspire awe. With some imagination, we can envision that, in earlier times, these shams would have

RUPERRA CASTLE. One of several sham castles that dot the Welsh countryside, Ruperra Castle in Glamorgan was built to resemble a medieval stone castle. The original Norman motte still graces a ridgetop within walking distance of the sham.

intimidated even the most self-assured visitor. Nonetheless, they remain nothing more than skillful copies, recalling idealized days when life seemed so much more gallant and feudal lords controlled the land and people of Wales.

Considered Britain's foremost example of neo-Norman architecture, mighty Penrhyn Castle in Caernarfonshire was founded on slate mining, as was its close copy, Bryn Bras, also in Caernarfonshire. Built in 1820 by George Hay Dawkins Pennant, Lord Penrhyn, the sham castle is one of Wales' most pretentious structures. Its walls topped with perfectly balanced battlements and fine rectangular towers, Penrhyn's grandest architectural feature is a classic Norman keep. The slate bed, upon which Queen Victoria refused to sleep, makes the ideal symbol for a family who prospered from the vast slate-mining industry that still characterizes North Wales.

At the opposite end of Wales sits Cyfarthfa Castle, overshadowed for decades by the waste heaps that dominated the valleys of South Wales. Constructed to overlook the Cyfarthfa Ironworks, the sham castle not only glorified the accomplishments of the Crawshay family (the patriarch, Richard Crawshay, who died in 1810, was one of Britain's first millionaires), but also accentuated the chasm that separated the haves and the have nots, just as authentic castles did during the Middle Ages.

As their workers endured deplorable working conditions, poverty, disease, and squalid living arrangements, ironmasters such as the Crawshays became wealthy enough to live in a newly constructed castle. Adding salt to his laborers' wounds, in 1825, William Crawshay (the "Iron King of Merthyr Tydfil") built his mock castle within walking distance of the Cyfarthfa Ironworks. Not a day passed without this blatant reminder of the social distance between master and employee looming in the background as the workers passed to and from the Ironworks.

Perhaps, Cyfarthfa Castle was more of a true castle than we realize. Neo-Gothic in design, Cyfarthfa Castle is adorned with battlemented towers and sham arrowslits and looks ready for a royal visit. Surely, the presence of Cyfarthfa Castle did not endear William Crawshay to his workers. Perhaps, its sham fortifications were more than symbolic of the owner's power and prestige. Perhaps, the Crawshays unconsciously realized the need for a strong fortress to sequester themselves, a place to take refuge in the event of a rebellion. Perhaps, the Iron King anticipated the events of 1831 and fled to his castle after announcing his ill-timed decision to lower his workers' wages. Crawshay's announcement reportedly provoked the Merthyr Rising, when government troops shot to death at least twenty people who were among the thousands of rioting laborers.

Today, the Crawshay's baronial home houses a museum and gallery. The Ironworks was closed in 1921 after over 150 years of industrial activity. Interestingly, the last Iron King of Merthyr Tydfil is buried underneath a stone slab which states, Robert Thompson Crawshay 1817–1879 GOD FORGIVE ME.

SCOTLAND'S BARONIAL CASTLES

Whereas the sham castles of Wales were built from scratch to dramatize the power and prestige of their owners, the castellated residences that distinguish the Scottish countryside frequently incorporate remnants from their medieval past, many of which have been disguised to the point that they are no longer recognizable. Whether one can rightly classify such structures as true castles rather than as shams is doubtful, but that many replaced earlier strongholds is undeniable. Hallmarked by pointed turrets, mock battlements, crow-stepped gables, and corner bartizans, Scotland's so-called baronial castles powerfully link past and present and provide their owners with proof of their ancient and historical pedigree.

The Scottish baronial style of architecture had its origins in the late sixteenth century, when the Stewart monarchs and the upper-class landowners began transforming their heavily militarized castles into palatial fortresses.

DRYBURGH ABBEY HOTEL. Located within view of ruined Dryburgh Abbey in the Borders, stunning Dryburgh Abbey Hotel displays characteristics of the Scottish baronial style.

They modeled their details on the Renaissance chateaux typically associated with France, but combined them with a romanticism that harkened back to the Middle Ages. During the early nineteenth century, a revival of interest in the Scottish Renaissance style led to the widespread adoption of the Scottish baronial design for the homes of the rich and stylish, which had modern conveniences but also displayed castellated features, such as turrets and bartizans.

One of the earliest proponents of the Scottish baronial style was Sir Walter Scott, who advocated the conservation of Scotland's medieval past at sites such as Smailholm Tower in the Borders. Notably, Scott also championed the resurgence of Scottish nationalism with the construction of his own baronial masterpiece, Abbotsford, near Melrose, also in the Borders, which he built in 1816. A forerunner of later, more flamboyant baronial castles, Abbotsford featured battlemented gateways, crow-stepped gables, pointed turrets, and machicolations, elements inspired by medieval architecture that created—for Scott—a personal link to his nation's past. In addition, his work prompted a new wave of architectural expression, exemplified by the works of David Bryce and his mentor, William Burn, which can be found throughout Scotland. Among the best-known examples of the Scottish baronial style are Glamis and Balmoral castles, both associated with the late Queen Mother; Blair and Blairquhan castles; Crathes and Thirlestane castles; Inverarary and Dunvegan castles; and Culzean, Dunrobin, and Fyvie castles, considered by many architectural historians to be the most impressive of Scotland's baronial castles. Many of these castellated residences—this is the most accurate description of these baronial castles—have long served as clan seats and the ostentatious country homes of Scottish noble families, including the Dukes of Argyll, the Dukes of Atholl, and the Lords of the Isles.

Originating in the fourteenth century as a simple royal hunting lodge, the first Glamis Castle, in Angus, probably consisted of a small building, a few ancillary structures, and a courtyard enclosed with a timber palisade and moat. Over time, the site quickly developed into a substantial tower house, its eight-foot-thick walls absorbing the earlier structure. During the early fifteenth century, the Lords Glamis, members of the Lyons family, replaced the timber defenses with a barmkin and improved the outbuildings. By the 1440s, the addition of the main tower gave the castle its L-shaped plan.

During the seventeenth century, Patrick Lyon, 9th Lord Glamis and 1st Earl of Kinghorne, transformed the site into a baronial marvel by adding conical turrets and bartizans, three vaulted stories to the central tower, and round towers at either end of the wings. He also erected the unusual stair tower in the angle of the "L" formed at the junction of the two main wings. The stair tower rises 143 steps from the basement up to the battlements. Late in the same century, the 3rd Earl of Kinghorne, another Patrick Lyon, tore down much of his namesake's work and transformed the red castle into the turreted palatial marvel that presently dominates the grand estate. Inside, Glamis Castle is adorned with memorabilia, fine artwork, tapestries and furnishings, ornate plasterwork ceilings, heraldic emblems, and lavish chimneypieces that display the status and wealth of its famous residents, including Lady Elizabeth Bowes Lyons, the late Queen Mother.

Inveraray Castle, the seat of Clan Campbell, is located in Strathclyde on the edge of Loch Fyne and impressively combines neoclassical Greek and Roman features while remaining essentially a baronial castle. Begun in 1743 by Archibald, the 3rd Duke of Argyll, to replace the less-than-adequate stronghold on a neighboring island, the massive building is blocky and rectangular in plan and dominated with long, conical corner turrets. These "pepper-pot" domes give the castle the illusion of great height, when in reality it stands just three stories tall. Its beauty comes from the well-balanced mix of châteauxlike turrets, the boldly colored blue-green chlorite masonry, the rows of lance-headed windows, and the lovely, lush surrounding parkland. The imposing, solidly majestic structure is well suited to carry out its role as the headquarters of the Dukes of Argyll, Chiefs of Clan Campbell.

Inveraray Castle hallmarks the completion of the stylistic transition in Scotland from defensive to residential construction. Its castellated exterior was designed by Roger Morris with inspiration from Vanbrugh and features battlements, drum towers at the corners, and thick walls. It was completed in 1770 by the famous architects, the Adams, under the scrutiny of the 5th Duke. In the late 1800s a fire led to a major rebuilding effort, during which the attic-level dormer windows and pepper-pot domes were added along with the tower in the central courtyard. The tall central tower resembles a keep and barely peaks over the chlorite battlements, which survive from the eighteenth century. In 1975, Inveraray Castle was again ravaged by fire, but Iain, the 11th Duke of Argyll and the 25th MacCailean Mhor, faithfully restored it to its original splendor.

While the castle's exterior gives the impression of power and status, the exquisite interior exhibits the glories of the Campbells at Inveraray. Designed by Robert Mylne, the lavish rooms date from 1772 to 1782. Spectacular plasterwork and gilded ceilings, outstanding wood carvings and painted paneled walls, Beauvais tapestries, ornate French furniture, an extensive collection of armor and Scottish weaponry, portraits, and porcelain embellish this grandiose home. Each item provides insight into Clan Campbell's momentous impact on Scottish history.

Complementing the architectural magnificence of the castle are the spectacular gardens, which span some sixteen acres and include formal lawns, brilliant floral combinations, woodlands, and parklands. Initiated by the 3rd Duke of Argyll in 1744, they were redesigned in 1848 by the 8th Duke. The crowning glory of the gardens lines the main drive to the castle. Known as the "Flag Borders," the unique pattern is based upon Scotland's national flag, the saltire, and is planted to resemble the St. Andrew's Cross.

COMBINING MEDIEVAL REALITY AND MODERN WHIMSY

Two of the nineteenth century's most fascinating and eccentric medievalists, John Patrick Crichton Stuart, the 3rd Marquess of Bute, and his architect companion, William Burges, yearned to live in the Middle Ages. Twenty years older than Bute, Burges was an expert on medieval architecture and a true medievalist at heart who actually wore medieval attire at home. Their two most famous creations, Castell Coch and the nineteenth-century interiors at Cardiff Castle, were bold products of their fanciful mind-set.

Originally hailing from the Isle of Bute in Scotland, the Bute family courted the privileges of the upper class. Marrying wealthy heiresses, the 3rd Earl of Bute (who served as prime minister under King George III) and his heirs acquired enormous estates throughout Britain. John Crichton Stuart, the 2nd Marquess, is best known as "the Father of Modern Cardiff" for his involvement in the industrialization of the area, the development of the coal fields in neighboring valleys, and the construction of the docks in what became known as Butetown. He also began the restoration of Cardiff Castle. Dying in 1848, he left his enormous fortune to his infant son, John Patrick Crichton Stuart.

Having acquired Castell Coch as part of his inheritance, the 3rd Marquess of Bute eventually decided to explore the site on the south-facing hillside overlooking the River Taff. There, he excitedly discovered a jumble of ruined structures covered by undergrowth, the moat infilled with rubble and earth. In 1871, Bute decided to restore Castell Coch (the Red Castle) and called upon his friend, William Burges, to spearhead the project. Together, Bute and Burges created a castle like no other in Wales, reputedly as faithful to the original medieval structure as possible, while also creating wildly flamboyant interiors, which never would have graced the medieval castle.

Incorporating the surviving portions of the medieval castle, Burges rebuilt the kitchen and keep towers with nine-foot-thick-walls and sturdy spurred buttresses at their bases. He also added arrowslits, putlog holes and drainage holes, and constructed rectangular latrine turrets on both towers — their chutes still dump into the moat. The well tower, on the other hand, lacks a spurred base but does contain a dungeon, which is reached by stepping downwards from the wellhead inside the tower. A nine-foot-thick battlemented curtain wall links the well tower with the kitchen tower, as the shell wall would have done in the thirteenth century. A wall-walk and embrasures with arrowslits complete the "authentic" appearance of the castellated Victorian wall.

Inside the castle, a set of covered stairs leads to the great banqueting hall, the first of Burges' Castellan Rooms. This enormous chamber spans the entire length of the curtain wall between the keep and kitchen towers. Below, the servants' quarters stand on the site of the medieval hall. When compared to the other interior chambers, the banqueting hall is surprisingly mundane, but every bit as inventive. Supported by two long timber beams, the hall's dramatic ceiling was decorated with stenciled wooden panels. Fine murals adorn wall tops and display the violent deaths of several Christian martyrs; these are accentuated with painted arcading and portraits. The banqueting hall's most impressive attribute is the ornate fireplace hood crowned by a figure of St. Lucius, who perpetually watches over the rather dull, utilitarian furniture.

Certainly, Castell Coch's most spectacular feature is the interior of the keep tower, where dazzling displays of romantic revivalism represent the height of Victorian fantasy. On the lower levels, visitors encounter the drawing room, an octagonal chamber crowned with an amazing two-story ribbed dome and embellished with brilliant colors and brightly gilded vaulting. Floral designs and a variety of birds, mice, lizards, monkeys, foxes, caterpillars, and butterflies adorn the walls and ceiling. Stars light up the painted skies inside the dome, while scenes from Aesop's fables and Greek mythology

CASTELL COCH. The gaily colored towers at Castell Coch (the Red Castle) in Glamorgan display the fantasies of the castle's restorers, the Marquess of Bute and his architect, William Burges, who rebuilt the structure on the foundations of its medieval precursor but embellished it with a flair that was all of their own imagination.

flourish in bold relief. This exotic room is filled with symbols of life and death, themes particularly meaningful to the Marquess of Bute. Lady Bute's bedroom was placed on the upper floor of the keep tower. As below, gay colors emboldened with gilding and mirrors illuminate the double-domed chamber. Painted birds, monkeys, squirrels, and mythological creatures grace the walls, while an elaborate arcade encircles the room with Moorish inspiration.

The gatehouse adjacent to the keep tower contains the windlass room and Lord Bute's bedroom. Initially, Bute had his bedroom on the level directly over the gate passage, but the commotion created from raising and lowering of the drawbridge and portcullis was so disturbing that he moved the winding mechanism into the lower room and hauled his personal belongings up to the second story. The windlass room contains the heavy mechanisms for moving the turning bridge and portcullis, and also a fireplace. The lord's bedroom features decorative wall stenciling, geometric designs, and floor tiling. The fireplace hood, the room's most notable feature, has a skilfully carved frieze running around the chimneypiece.

Ironically, once Castell Coch was finished in 1891, Lord Bute rarely stayed at his lavish Welsh residence. Stables, the chapel, and administrative offices were planned but never built. Bute did attempt a small vineyard on the slopes beneath the castle and apparently produced wine good enough for use in religious services, as it might have been in the Middle Ages.

CONCLUSION

Britain's castles were erected to symbolically emphasize the lord's military supremacy and control within the lordship. They flaunted the self-importance savored by their owners and symbolized their innate need to impress their rivals, their subjects, and anyone else who passed within visual range. Like their owners, castles exuded self-confidence, authority, and superiority. Their modern counterparts, in no way capable of military strength, likewise accentuated the wealth, power, and self-importance of their builders, men who compared themselves with medieval overlords and, at times, even portrayed themselves as such. Yet, they are mere imitations.

CHAPTER 5

Raglan Castle

A PROPERLY FORTIFIED MILITARY RESIDENCE

No one arriving at Raglan in the time of Sir William Herbert could fail to be impressed by this very public display of wealth, status and power.

> — John R. Kenyon, *Raglan Castle* (2003), 25

Commanding a ridge on the northern side of the A40 roadway near its junction with the A449 in southeastern Wales, Raglan Castle is a splendid monument to a late-medieval Welsh gentry family, the lords of Raglan, who played a key role in controlling the region and as Yorkist supporters during the Wars of the Roses. It also honors their successors, the Somerset Earls of Worcester, who completed the site's evolution into Wales' greatest and grandest late-medieval castle. Even in ruin, Raglan Castle exudes grandeur and power, two essential qualities expected of any influential leader, especially one destined to serve the monarchy.

A RICH MIXTURE OF MILITARY AND RESIDENTIAL COMPONENTS

Architecturally and historically, the glorious structure epitomizes the ideal medieval castle. Raglan Castle simultaneously served as the physical embodiment of the lordship, emphasized the owners' wealth and personal power, distinguished them both from subjects of lower status and their noble rivals (which was particularly important in an era when clashes between Yorkists and Lancastrians were increasingly common), and provided a grand venue for entertaining and impressing guests. Equipped with heavy defenses, including two great gatehouses, portcullises, and a virtually indestructible great tower, its builders ensured the castle would capably withstand a siege, whether it came from Lancastrian opponents, a resurgence of Wales' struggle for independence, or from some other foe. And, they also ensured the ostentatious fortress would house them in exceptional comfort and more than amply provide all the facilities needed for an upwardly mobile, highly affluent, aristocratic, native Welsh family and their successors.

FROM MANOR HOUSE TO MEDIEVAL CASTLE

Marrying Elizabeth (Blouet) Berkeley, "the lady of Raggeland," in 1406, William ap Thomas, a Welsh country squire, moved into the Blouet manor house at Raglan, which he occupied until his wife's death in 1420. Having fought alongside Henry V at Agincourt in 1415, ap Thomas had already begun to make a name from himself and was soon appointed as the steward of the lordship of Abergavenny. In 1426, Henry VI knighted the Welshman. Allowed to occupy the manor house after his wife's death in 1420, Sir William ap Thomas, "the Blue Knight of Gwent," was finally able to purchase the estate from his stepson-in-law, Lord Berkeley, in 1432. Within three years, he began the transformation of the manor house into a substantial masonry castle, one that matched his newly acquired status and his ambitions.

More than likely, the layout of the Blouet house influenced the plan of the castle that replaced it. There is some speculation that Sir William's great hexagonal keep originally occupied the site of a Norman motte castle, however, nothing survives to substantiate this theory. What does survive is an eye-catching combination of fortress and residence that suited the needs and conditions of the times—and the social inclinations of its owners.

In order to ensure his command of the region, which was challenged by the local unrest that ultimately led to the Wars of the Roses, Sir William ap Thomas began rebuilding his fortified residence with the construction of two powerful structures: the south gatehouse (the original entrance into the castle) and the imposing keep. His son and heir, William Herbert, completed the projects. Impressed by French castle architecture, the men fitted their Welsh castle with hexagonal and semihexagonal towers and the prolific use of machicolations, which not only performed a defensive function but also embellished the battlements on top of the great tower, the great gatehouse, and the spurred closet tower. Even now, the grimacing gargoyles watch for intruders, their mouths agape to guide rainwater off rooftops.

After Sir William's death in 1445, his son, William, inherited Raglan Castle and adopted the surname Herbert, supposedly to claim kinship with Henry I through Herbert ap Godwin, one of the king's illegitimate sons.[1] William Herbert soon became a man of tremendous import in the king's court. Knighted in 1452, Sir William Herbert began accumulating power, wealth, and status. He also chose to side with Edward, Duke of York, as he fought for the English throne. At the Battle of Mortimer's Cross in Herefordshire, Herbert joined the Yorkists in a resounding victory over the Lancastrians and received the titles chief justice and chamberlain of Wales for his service to the new king, Edward IV. He was also created the Baron of Raglan, selected as a Knight of the Garter, and had custody of a young Harri Tudor, the future King Henry VII, who spent 1462 at Raglan Castle. In 1465, the new lordship of Raglan was established, with Herbert at its Lord. Then, in 1468, in recognition for leading the capture of Harlech Castle, the last holdout against the Yorkists during the Wars of the Roses, Sir William Herbert received the title Earl of Pembroke and all the honors and responsibilities that accompanied it. He was the first member of Welsh gentry to become an English peer.[2]

Not surprisingly, Sir William Herbert also continued in his father's footsteps at Raglan Castle, adding the great gatehouse, the pitched stone court, kitchen tower, and the fountain court, which not only emphasized his personal clout and recently acquired wealth but also symbolically reiterated his support for the Yorkist cause.[3] Ironically, despite his accomplishments, Herbert's tenure at Raglan was short-lived. In 1469, after the Yorkist defeat at the Battle of Edgecote in Oxfordshire, he was captured and beheaded upon the orders of Richard Neville, the infamous "Kingmaker" and Earl of Warwick. Herbert's body was interred at Tintern Abbey, a short distance from his great castle at Raglan.

William Herbert's twin-towered gatehouse was a formidable obstacle. If attackers made it past the machicolations and across the drawbridge, they would then be confronted by defenders watching through spy holes and firing through gunloops, while barricading the gate passage with two portcullises and two sets of heavy timber doors. At one end of the passage,

RAGLAN CASTLE, GATEHOUSE. The machicolated twin-towered main gatehouse and adjoining hexagonal closet tower built by William Herbert in the late fifteenth century still command attention at Raglan Castle, Wales' finest late medieval properly fortified military residence.

a latrine chute opened into the moat; to either side, basement-level chambers provided access to the three upper stories. The first floor probably contained the constable's withdrawing room and a gallery, which may have contained a library; both were adorned with Tudor fireplaces. The chamber on the left side of the gate passage contained the porter's lodge or guardroom and the latrine block, which also served the adjoining state apartments. The similar chamber on the right contained a brick fireplace, an oven, and the caretaker's lodgings.

The lowest level of the semihexagonal closet tower, located at the eastern end of the gatehouse, may have functioned as the prison tower. On the first story, the presence of a fine fireplace and latrine implies that the tower may also have been the residence of a senior member of the household staff, such as the steward. Upper levels contain additional fireplaces, and small windows suggest that the chambers may have stored munitions.

Immediately to the rear of the great gatehouse is William Herbert's pitched stone court, a rectangular area dominated by large corner towers and paved with clumsy cobblestones. Comparable to an outer bailey, the courtyard formed an open area between the gatehouse, the all-essential hall block and its service buildings, and a wall of chambers that were apparently used as

RAGLAN CASTLE, Pitched Stone Court. The wellhead graces the pitched stone court at Raglan Castle, which occupied the area immediately behind the great gatehouse. Household staff, including the steward, worked and lived in and around this courtyard.

office space during the fifteenth and sixteenth centuries. All the domestic activities occurred inside this side of the castle. More than likely, the servants—residents of lesser status—slept in or near their work areas, whereas the steward maintained his own suite in the closet tower. The hexagonal, machicolated kitchen tower dominates the northern end of the pitched stone court. It contains a dank basement for cool storage (the wet larder), two huge, double-flued fireplaces and ovens (each fitted with a gunloop), and drains. The tower's upper levels had elaborate fireplaces and windows with seats and probably housed higher-status members of the household.

Before Sir William Herbert's untimely demise in 1469, he also managed to complete work on the fountain court, the castle's other bailey, which was originally accessed through the southern gatehouse built by his father and separated from the pitched stone court by the chapel and long gallery. Herbert's fifteenth-century chapel is now little more than foundations and a wall, which still supports the staircase to the upper-level gallery, where the lord and his family were provided with seating.[4] In its heyday, the chapel floor was adorned with brightly colored tiles, and the walls featured human-headed carved corbels. Little survives of the adjoining long gallery, which was added in the

RAGLAN CASTLE, statues in the ruined long gallery. Though now extensively decayed due to the ravages of time and weather, two skillfully carved statues, once believed to represent the Earl of Worcester and his wife, adorn the upper level of the long gallery at Raglan Castle.

sixteenth century, except for the impressive, though weatherworn, carvings of two figures. Once thought to represent William Somerset, the Earl of Worcester, and his wife, the figures were taken from Hugues Sambin's "La Diversite des Termes."[5]

Named for "a pleasant marble fountain in the midst thereof, called the White Horse, continually running with clear water,"[6] only the foundation survives of this pretty structure, which was actually added during the sixteenth century. However, clustered around the courtyard are the extensive remains of what once was a lavish series of apartments, three sets of which were probably reserved for dignitaries and other high-status guests and their entourage, while the fourth apartment range served the lord and his family. Entered via the elaborately decorated grand stair, a huge porchway gave access to two adjoining residential wings. At the rear of the stairway, a well-appointed latrine tower projected outwards from the castle and emptied human waste onto the ground outside the walls. The tower was later blocked when the exterior of the castle was transformed into a series of splendid terraced gardens. Each of the apartment blocks contained at least four rooms fitted with fireplaces, well-lit windows with seats facing both into and outside the castle, and additional latrines.

The lords of Raglan also maintained their own state apartments, which occupied the area between the entrance to the great tower (the keep) and the hall-and-chapel complex, and complemented the three other apartment ranges. Today, the extensively ruined chambers are difficult to distinguish from the other residences inside the castle; however, the lavishly decorated fireplaces and strategic positioning next to the great hall pinpoint their location. The suite of rooms is best recognized when looking back at the building from inside the great tower. Supplementing the accommodation provided by the great tower, the state apartments probably contained the parlor (or lord's withdrawing room), dining room, and state bedrooms.

TUDOR EXPANSION AND EMBELLISHMENT

In 1479, William Herbert's son, another William, lost his claim to Raglan Castle when King Edward IV seized it for his own son, the Prince of Wales, and forced Herbert to exchange it for the earldom of Huntingdon.

RAGLAN CASTLE,
Fountain Court.
Raglan Castle's
residential range
showcased the
splendor of life in the
late Middle Ages.
Now only the shell of
what would have
been luxurious
accommodation
survives near the
remains of the
fountain.

Over time, Herbert reasserted his position in South Wales and became chief justice under Richard III. In 1491, Raglan Castle passed to his daughter, Elizabeth, whose uncle, Sir Walter Herbert (William Herbert's brother), decided to possess and manage the property on her behalf. Once an avid Yorkist, Sir Walter Herbert took over his niece's estates and the castle at Raglan. Then, astutely switching allegiance to Harri Tudor, the Lancastrian who eventually became Henry VII, Sir Walter gained royal favor and feted the king's wife at the castle. After Walter's death in 1507, Henry VII granted the lordship of Raglan to the widow, Anne Herbert, who soon remarried. Then, Elizabeth Herbert, the rightful heiress, finally regained possession of her family's castle.

Majestic Raglan Castle promptly passed into the hands of Elizabeth's husband, Sir Charles Beaufort, the illegitimate son of Henry Beaufort, Duke of Somerset. An avowed Lancastrian, Sir Charles vigorously supported Henry VII and soon became his lord chamberlain. In 1504, he also became Baron Herbert of Raglan, Chepstow, and Gower by right of his marriage to the Herbert heiress. Having participated in Henry VIII's successful first campaign against the French, Sir Charles was created Earl of Worcester, a position with considerable status that allowed him to be buried in St. George's Chapel in Windsor Castle, not too far from his king.

RAGLAN CASTLE,
State Apartments.
When gazing at the
residential suites from
atop the great keep,
visitors can still
identify features that
pinpoint the location
of the lord's private
apartments, such as
this fireplace adorned
with skillfully carved
heraldic emblems.

William Somerset, Sir Charles' grandson and 3rd Earl of Worcester, initiated the final building effort at Raglan Castle, adding the hall, service block, and long gallery, rebuilding the Office Wing, and initiating the transformation of the surrounding grounds into elaborate walled terraces, knot and water gardens, and recreational facilities. Like his predecessors, Somerset played a key role in the courts of several monarchs, including Edward VI, Mary, and Elizabeth I, who dubbed him a Knight of the Garter in 1570. Raglan Castle became the Somerset family's showcase and one of Britain's finest late-medieval palatial fortresses. At Raglan, Somerset added the huge, multilevel pantry and buttery blocks that completed the building project probably planned by William Herbert. From the pantry and buttery, servants proceeded into the great hall, hoping to keep the meals from cooling down before they reached the diners.

The 3rd Earl of Worcester also erected the now-empty great hall between the castle's two courtyards. Accessed through a porchway opening in the pitched stone court, the hall still displays enchanting carvings and a massive fireplace. Originally, the great hall was embellished with wood paneling, which rose to window level and held stained glass; its timber ceiling featured a geometrical roof with a large cupola. Now, only the corbels survive. The raised dais still marks the spot where William Somerset entertained his guests beneath the finely carved heraldic plaque that proclaimed his selection to the Order of the Garter.[7]

After his father's death in 1589, Edward Somerset, 4th Earl of Worcester, lived at Raglan. Like his father, Edward courted royal favor. He served as Queen Elizabeth's Master of the Royal Horse, as Earl Marshal for the coronation of King James I in 1603, and as lord chamberlain for Charles I. Building upon his predecessors' efforts at Raglan, not only did the 4th Earl add the set of fireplaces above the buttery, he also extended his father's gardens, creating the fantastic water garden, or "parterre," and building the summerhouse at the northern end of the "great poole," formed by damming the Wilcae brook, which allowed a lake to flow behind the castle. Edward Somerset also developed the decorative moat walk, a grassy area at the foot of the great tower, and encouraged visitors to stroll past the fifteen brick niches that held the busts of several Roman emperors.[8] Perhaps, Somerset was hinting at a symbolic relationship between himself, his earldom, and his castle, and the great leaders of the Roman world. His spectacular castle at Raglan certainly emphasized the wealth, status, and self-importance of the Earls of Worcester.

THE GREAT TOWER AND THE ENGLISH CIVIL WAR

By far, the greatest structural achievement at Raglan Castle was the Twr Melyn Gwent, the Yellow Tower of Gwent, erected by Sir William ap Thomas. Standing on its own outside the main walls of the castle, the great hexagonal tower was a self-sufficient building capable of withstanding a lengthy siege which could function as a powerful refuge in the event that an enemy penetrated the rest of the castle. The sheer power of the imposing keep, which once stood five stories and had a machicolated roofline, is palpable. From its upper levels, soldiers would have had clear views of the surrounding countryside and, later, of the Civil War siege-works constructed just outside the main gate. Encircling the Tower of Gwent, an apron wall,

RAGLAN CASTLE, the great tower. Raglan Castle's Yellow Tower of Gwent, erected by Sir William ap Thomas, stands outside the curtain wall. The powerful late medieval keep stalwartly resisted the best efforts of parliamentarian troops to force its surrender, only falling to undermining after the end of the siege.

which dates to the late sixteenth or early seventeenth century, still leads to a well-preserved postern gate, a latrine turret, and five other turrets, which may have supported cannons. Seventeenth-century records claimed that in terms of its "height, strength and neatness," the Tower of Gwent "surpassed most, if not every other tower of England or Wales."[9]

Due to damage suffered during the English Civil War, the great tower now only stands four floors tall. Nevertheless, the shorter height in no way diminishes the Yellow Tower's visual impact, the enormity of which becomes obvious when standing on any of the upper levels. Like earlier medieval keeps, Raglan's great tower contained the lord's living quarters and all the necessary facilities to make life comfortable and secure. The basement level held the kitchen, with its great fireplace and fine latrine, and was equipped with gunloops and cross-slits. Quite possibly, the castle treasury was also located on this level. Fireplaces, latrines, and wide windows indicate that the upper stories were used for accommodation.

In 1628, Henry Somerset, 5th Earl of Worcester, inherited the earldom and Raglan Castle. While under the 5th Earl's control, Raglan Castle became a royalist stronghold and vigorously supported Charles I, who had played bowls in the terrace just outside the fountain court. Created 1st Marquis of Worcester in 1643, Somerset invested over £1 million to aid his king's cause,[10] spending about half that on refortifying Raglan. In the summer of 1646, parliamentary troops finally began besieging the castle, relentlessly pounding its walls with cannon fire, evidence of which is still visible in the curtain wall. Fitted with artillery bastions, the newly refortified castle stalwartly held out against the parliamentarians for over two months. Realizing the castle would not fall easily, the besieging army then constructed several siege-works to handle additional cannons and mortars, including the famous Roaring Meg.

On August 14, 1646, Somerset and his garrison finally initiated surrender. Most of the garrison was permitted to march freely from the castle "with their Horses and Armes, with Colours flying, Drums beating, Trumpet sounding."[11] The 1st Marquis, on the other hand, was seized and taken to London, where he died in December. Like his forebears, Henry Somerset was buried in the Beaufort Chapel at Windsor. Raglan Castle was forced to suffer a greater indignity—slighting by victorious parliamentarian troops. Ironically, the great Yellow Tower of Gwent proved a formidable foe to the end. The parliamentarians finally managed to damage the tower by undermining, but, even then, they only partly destroyed the walls. Among other losses were the castle's great library of books and manuscripts dating to the fifteenth century.

Despite the royalist defeat and his father's death in 1646, Edward Somerset, Lord Herbert and 2nd Marquis of Worcester, retained ownership of the castle and estates at Raglan. His most notable contribution to the castle was an invention he installed as a young man either inside the keep or in the adjoining moat. The device was Somerset's prototype of a "water-commanding machine," which could send a spout of water up to the keep's rooftop. During the 1640s, the machine was reportedly used to repel a group of local men who had hoped to seize the castle's weapons. The roar of the machine supposedly sounded so much like a lion that the intruders fled empty-handed.[12]

After the death of the 2nd Marquis in 1667, another Henry Somerset, 3rd Marquis of Worcester, began to reaccumulate his family's possessions; however, he did little to restore Raglan Castle to its former splendor. Instead, he rebuilt another ancestral home, Badminton House in Gloucestershire, and furnished the mansion with bits taken from Raglan Castle. An ornate chimneypiece and exquisitely carved paneling are among the items said to have once adorned the medieval castle. In 1682, the 3rd Marquis received the new title, Duke of Beaufort, and his descendants continued to live at Badminton House. Interestingly, in keeping with the resurgence of romanticism in Britain, Raglan Castle acquired a new, quite modern role as a popular tourist attraction before the end of the eighteenth century. It remains under the guardianship of Cadw and is regularly open to the public.

RAGLAN CASTLE: THEN AND NOW

In ruin as in its heyday, Raglan Castle has always been a stronghold of contrasts. Whereas the main entrance is still commanded by grandiose machicolated twin towers and a powerful, albeit partially broken-down, great keep, and two substantial corner towers dominate the pitched stone court, the rest of the buildings surrounding the two courtyards now only hint at their original grandeur. Yet, the elaborate carvings and heraldic crests, the unusual cobblestone courtyard, and the wide-ranging fountain court suggest that the interior was every bit as impressive as the castle's exterior. Coupled with what were once vast water gardens and ornate terraces, the entire site still creates an overwhelming awareness of power, wealth, status, and finery and boldly emphasizes the remarkable achievements of the lords of Raglan and their successors.

From the fifteenth through seventeenth centuries, Raglan Castle must have simply sparkled. Equipped in case of attack, the powerful fortified residence confirmed the status of the Welsh landowners who made their way up the social and political ladders to become the monarchy's most supportive advisors. The unique positioning of the great tower outside the curtain wall commanded the attention of anyone approaching the great gatehouse. The Yellow Tower of Gwent proclaimed its role as the lord's private residence and imposing stronghold, which towered over the heads of the rest of the castle, just as Sir William ap Thomas and his heirs stood head-and-shoulders above their countrymen. Even in ruin, Raglan Castle remains a classic example of a properly fortified military residence.

CHAPTER 6

What Is a Castle? Revisited

Despite the persistence of the notion that castles were first and foremost built to defend their inhabitants, this book has endeavored to place Britain's medieval castles in their larger, and more appropriate, context. True castles were built for several reasons, and not only to thwart sieges or unwanted intrusion. Indeed, I make the case that all castles were about aggression and power. Power and aggression go hand in hand, and the physical makeup of Britain's medieval castles necessarily and characteristically fulfilled these two overriding priorities. They were erected as offensive structures which at once established the primacy of an outsider, the lord, over the local population and acted as a base from which the lord could maintain control over the region and stage forays as needed to reiterate his power over his subjects. They were equipped with increasingly sturdy, innovative, and complex defensive structures, which not merely safeguarded the occupants but even more so ensured the continuation of the lord's dominion. As such, castles were primarily offensive buildings. That they protected their inhabitants was largely a secondary consideration.

At the same time, castles were private residences. Even though the lord might be away for a large portion of each year, the castle was always occupied on his behalf by a small yet permanent group of people, including the constable, who managed the military affairs, and the steward, who had control over the household and the surrounding estates. When the lord's family remained behind, the lady of the castle not only supervised the activities of the permanent staff, she also represented her husband in legal, ceremonial, and political matters. She could also be counted upon to be fully knowledgeable and to command a garrison during a siege. The castle itself provided accommodation for its residents—not necessarily the most lavish and comfortable facilities, but at the very minimum, a floor on which to sleep. Increasingly, the placement of structures within the castle delineated the social differences between its residents: the lord and his family living in the finest, most secure, and most spacious living quarters; and the lowliest servants occupied space wherever they could find it or to where they were assigned. One can make the case that even the residential capacity of the castle functioned in an aggressive—hence, offensive—way, heightening and reconfirming the lord's power, even within his own home.

THE CASTLE AND THE CHANGING
FEUDAL ORDER

The feudal system that dominated Britain during the Middle Ages gradually gave way to an economy based more on the exchange of money for services rather than on the exchange of personal services (such as knights' service or castle-guard) for land. The largely decentralized government, whereby the monarch depended on his lords for military support and to control the countryside on his behalf, had served its purpose. Lords and their knights found military service more and more inconvenient and preferred to pay for the privilege of land ownership. Money replaced land as the ultimate power symbol and drove the actions and ambitions of leading lords, monarchs, and men of lesser status. Tenants eventually bartered their services for wages, and trade, manufacturing, and agriculture took on new roles. Britain began moving toward capitalism and free-market competition.

Accordingly, the prevailing system of military service and land tenancy underwent major changes that ultimately led to the obsolescence of the heavily fortified military residence. The ability to create a permanent army of paid (or "indentured") soldiers encouraged fighting to move away from the castle and onto the open field. Castle sieges were no longer the focus of warfare. During the Wars of the Roses, which filled the decades between the Battle of St. Alban's in 1455 and Harri Tudor's victory at Bosworth Field in 1485, warfare involved the clash of armies on the battlefield, where major battles occurred at times and short skirmishes were the norm.[1] During the reign of the Tudor Dynasty, new fortifications were specifically designed to meet offensive and defensive purposes, and what had been the medieval castle's residential role was by and large confined to lightly fortified residences or newly constructed stately mansions.

As feudalism waned, Tudor England saw the rise of coastal fortifications, strongholds built solely to meet the military needs of the times. Elizabethan England experienced the spread of new architectural styles, which favored gothicized grandeur and abundant luxury over the harshness of the militarized lifestyle. Medieval castles received facelifts, which not only enhanced the quality of their owners' lives but also improved their image as weathly trendsetters. In West Wales, for example, Sir John Perrot added huge mullioned window frames and oriel windows to the facades on his castles at Carew and Laugharne to reflect his position as first lord of Munster (and later as lord deputy of Ireland) and also as a member of Queen Elizabeth I's privy council (he was also rumored to have been her half brother). Palatial masterpieces such as Hardwick Hall in Derbyshire and Burghley House in Lincolnshire soon surpassed medieval lordship castles as symbols of political power and social status.

In the 1640s, Britain's medieval castles experienced a renaissance of sorts during the English Civil War, when they were either refortified and garrisoned by royalists in support of King Charles I or occupied by his parliamentarian opponents, led by Sir Thomas Fairfax. Several castle sieges occurred, with both sides claiming victories. At the end of it all, the parliamentarians defeated the royalists, Charles I was executed, and scores of castles were "slighted" under the orders of the new Lord Protector, who wanted to ensure no castles could be garrisoned against him.

With the decline of feudalism and the changing sociopolitical temperament in post-medieval Britain, the wealthier classes no longer felt the urgency to occupy heavily defended strongholds. Many castles were altered over time into comfortable, often flamboyantly castellated homes, more palace than fortress. The one thread that tied medieval castles to later residences built and occupied by the upper class was that both building types showcased the owner's power, wealth, social achievement, and, in essence, superiority over other residents—and perhaps even over other lords or members of the gentry class. Today, relatively few "castles" still provide homes for Britain's upper crust. However, those that remain occupied are much more like stately homes than medieval castles. In many cases, even the castellation has been minimized.

Arundel Castle in West Sussex, however, retains its medieval fabric and also provides state apartments and more modern facilities for its noble residents. An outstanding example of a motte and bailey which evolved into a substantial stone enclosure castle, Arundel Castle remains a fitting home— and a stately castle—primed for England's premier duke and earl. Having

ARUNDEL CASTLE, the Quadrangle. Now more stately home than heavily fortified military residence, the great castle at Arundel in West Sussex not only retains its medieval character with the preservation of the motte, shell keep, and other early structures, but also provides a residential range of battlemented buildings designed to accommodate the Dukes of Norfolk in the style to which they have long been accustomed.

landed near Pevensey on England's southern coast to launch his invasion from France, William I recognized the value of fortifying the chalk spur on the River Arun, with its clear views of the English Channel that allowed easy detection of an inbound French invasion. In 1067, the new Norman king granted the land to Roger de Montgomery, Earl of Shrewsbury, who quickly constructed a substantial motte and bailey castle at Arundel. In time, the castle became the seat of the Fitzalan Earls of Arundel and their heirs, the Howard Dukes of Norfolk, the highest authority of state on royal ceremonial occasions, and transformed the earth and timber castle into a splendid palatial complex.

Tall enough to afford clear views to the English Channel, the grass-laden motte rose 70 feet high and had a basal diameter of about 250 feet. The massive mound was crowned with a well-preserved shell keep, which William d'Albini, one of Empress Matilda's supporters during her struggle with King Stephen for the English throne, completed in about 1138. Adorned with classical Norman zigzag and scrollwork designs, the battlemented oval wall measures 9 feet thick and stands about 80 feet by 70 feet round.[2] Inside, the keep still encloses fireplaces, roof timbers, and corbels, traces of the structure's former residential capacity.

By 1243, the male line of the d'Albinis had run its course. The "Castle and Honour of Arundel" passed to the Fitzalans when Isabel d'Albini married John Fitzalan. Initiating its conversion from a fairly primitive fortification into one of England's greatest treasure houses, their son Richard, the 1st Fitzalan Earl of Arundel, left a permanent mark on the Norman castle. Four hundred years later, Fitzalan's twin-towered barbican actually endured intensive pounding from parliamentarian cannons positioned on the roof of St. Nicholas' Collegiate Church, which forced the garrison's surrender in 1642. Fitzalan also added the Bevis Tower (named for St. Bevis), before which statues of the Norfolks' heraldic animals, the Howard lion and Fitzalan horse, stalwartly stand guard.

Two huge baileys occupy the land on either side of the great keep and complete the stone enclosure castle. Named for its reputation as a place for sparring or jousting, the bright green Tiltyard (formerly the outer bailey) still retains some of its original Norman foundations; it is now mainly used for private events. On the opposite side of the motte, the great Quadrangle, with its Victorian-era battlements, encloses the inner bailey with an impressive array of residential buildings, including State Apartments, a private chapel, and the armory.

In form, function, and symbolism, Arundel Castle embodies the classic British medieval castle. Interiors contain fine furniture, stained glass windows, tapestries and family portraits, and extravagant chimneypieces. Heraldic crests rim ornate ceilings. In the Victoria Room, named in honor of the Queen's visit in 1846, the stunning fireplace features lavish carvings, two heraldic flags, and a regal shield. Outside, precisely cut stone walls, battlemented cylindrical towers, and skillfully carved arches harken to the Middle Ages.

Erected in accordance with the terms of the will of Richard Fitzalan, the 3rd Earl, the Fitzalan Chapel occupies the eastern side of St. Nicholas' Church. Located on the same grounds as the castle, the former collegiate church still serves as the parish church and contains the impressive tombs of several Earls of Arundel and Dukes of Norfolk. Like other medieval lords, the Fitzalans sought a higher connection with the heavens, which was symbolically dramatized by the presence of the neighboring collegiate church. Today, the fortified ancestral residence of the Dukes of Norfolk continues to exudes status, power, and wealth and reminds all visitors that Arundel Castle not only houses a family of substance but one whose lengthy and historic pedigree sets them apart from the average citizen.

Arundel Castle, and its royal counterpart at Windsor, rank as two of England's greatest castles, both historically and structurally. Yet, the scores of other medieval castles performed the same essential functions: domination, subjugation, administration, and residence, and all symbolically (and very physically) exhibited the status, power, and self-importance of their builder-owners—some of whom ruled the kingdom, many more of whom ruled their little pieces of turf, the remains of which lay scattered throughout the countryside.

THE "CASTLES" OF HENRY VIII

During the reign of Henry VIII, the construction of artillery forts, which had originated in the late fifteenth century, began in earnest along England's southern coast. Generally labeled as "castles," Henry's coastal forts were just that—forts. They were built purely as military strongholds, strategically placed to defend against foreign invasion. They never centered a lordship, were not built to serve as a lord's private residence, and were not especially complex. They did, however, provide a response to the defensive needs of the times.

In the early 1530s, the Tudor king made the bold decision to rid himself of his first wife, Catherine of Aragon. When the Pope refused to authorize an annulment, Henry rashly responded by breaking all ties with the Church in Rome, dissolving monasteries throughout Britain, and creating himself as head of the new Church of England. In December 1538, the Pope excommunicated the English king and demanded that Europe's more pious leaders undertake a holy war to reestablish Roman Catholicism in England.

To secure the vulnerable coastline of his kingdom from what he perceived as an imminent attack, Henry systematically erected a series of fortresses. These coastal artillery forts and blockhouses (simpler versions that supported a single cannon and muskets) contained gun platforms that positioned tiers of cannons out to sea. The forts only provided living quarters for the soldiers who garrisoned them. Some were enclosed by ditches and an outer curtain.[3] Largely completed between 1539 and 1543, the formidable forts and blockhouses were placed at strategic points along the shores from Hull (almost 200 miles northeast of London) to Milford Haven (at the western tip of South Wales). Henry VIII built coastal forts at Sandown, Deal, Walmer, Sandgate, Camber, Southsea, Calshot, Hurst, Yarmouth, Portland, St. Mawes, and Pendennis, all of which were labeled as castles but were actually artillery forts. He also established blockhouses at Hull, Tilbury, Gravesend, Dover, Cowes, Sandsfoot, Brownsea, Harwich, Dale, and Angle (the latter two in Wales), and built numerous fortlets and bulwarks along the coastline.

"The Three Castles which keep the Downs"—Deal, Walmer, and Sandown—were among the first of Henry's coastal fortresses. Begun in 1539, all three were completed late the next year and formed a complex unit linked together by earthen ramparts, which no longer survive. They guarded a two-mile stretch of shoreline adjacent to the Downs, a shallow length of water just offshore that offered approaching ships a convenient, protected gathering place from which to coordinate an assault. With their concentric plans, their intentional resemblance to the Tudor Rose, and their strategic coastal placement, these three "castles" typified the Henrician fortress.

In fact, the physical layout of several of Henry VIII's artillery forts consisted of a series of circular bastions (projecting gun-towers) that surrounded a circular central tower. The entire structure was encircled by a curtain wall and ditch. Soldiers inside the forts were completely protected from view and could move throughout the castle without being detected by the enemy. Pendennis acquired a set of pointed bastions late in the sixteenth century, when Spanish adventurers began attacking ports in Cornwall after the defeat of the Armada.[4]

Deal Castle in Kent was the largest and most complex of the Tudor forts. Built with stone quarried from a nearby Carmelite Priory, Deal is "sixfoil" in shape. It features a tall central cylindrical tower surrounded by progressively shorter, semicircular bastions, six of which immediately adjoin the central tower, while six others link together to form the curtain wall. The design was intended to prevent blind spots, areas where firepower could miss an attacker. With this concentric, lobate shape, cannons could be positioned effectively and fired simultaneously without interfering with each other. A total of almost 200 gun ports penetrated the walls. Deal Castle also possessed several medieval defensive devices, including a portcullis, heavy double doors, and a series of five murder holes, and the enemy could be cornered inside one of several open areas, similar to a barbican, located between the

DEAL CASTLE. Erected by Henry VIII as part of a string of coastal fortresses, Deal Castle in Kent guarded England's vital southeastern shoreline from foreign invasion. Together, the rounded bastions resemble the Tudor rose.

curtain and the bastions. The self-sufficient central tower contained storage rooms, living quarters for the garrison, and the vital wellhead.

Ironically, Henry's massive coastal network was never put to the test, but some of the forts tolerated brief assaults. The anticipated invasion from across the English Channel never occurred. Only during the English Civil War did these forts see any real action. For five months during 1648, parliamentary forces besieged Pendennis Castle before the garrison surrendered, then only giving up after they had depleted the last of their supplies. St. Mawes Castle (Cornwall) surrendered without enduring any gunfire, but Deal Castle sustained considerable damage at the hands of the parliamentarians. And, even though Walmer Castle, in Kent, was later converted into the official residence of the Lord Warden of the Cinque Ports, it was never intended for use as a private residence. The last person to serve as Lord Warden was Queen Elizabeth, the Queen Mother. Since her death in 2002, the position has remained unfilled.

ADVANCING INTO THE ARTILLERY AGE

Even though the focus shifted away from fortified military residences to the new construction of gun forts for coastal defense, some medieval castles in England and Scotland were expanded and adapted to handle heavy artillery and withstand advanced firepower from attackers. In the wake of his divorce from Catherine of Aragon and second marriage to Anne Boleyn, Henry VIII felt an increasing threat from the Roman Catholic nations across the English Channel, mainly France, Germany, and Spain, and also from Roman Catholic Scotland. Consequently, Henry also fitted Carlisle Castle in Cumbria with casemates and emplacements for heavy artillery, such as the Half Moon Battery, and expanded the ramparts in anticipation of a Scottish invasion. The expected assault from Scotland never took place; however, during the late eighteenth century, when Napoléon posed a very real threat to England, and again in the nineteenth century, Carlisle Castle was strengthened, cannons were hauled into place, barracks buildings and a hospital erected, and an armory also raised. The King's Own Royal Border Regiment still occupies the castle, which now houses the county archives service and is open to the public.

During the sixteenth, eighteenth, and nineteenth centuries, Scotland's mighty Stirling Castle also moved from the age of the siege engines into the age of artillery. In 1559, when Queen Mary of Guise ordered the construction of an artillery platform known as the French Spur to bolster Stirling Castle against attacks from France and England, the castle still largely served as a royal residence. However, after the accession of James VI as

James I of England in 1603, the focus of the Scottish monarchy shifted to England. From then onward, Stirling Castle functioned primarily as a military establishment and acquired a variety of gun batteries, magazines, barracks, and casemates, which ringed the outer perimeter. The army garrisoned Stirling Castle until 1964, when it relinquished its control and transferred the castle to the capable hands of Ministry of Works, which consolidated the site and opened it to the public.

The military also maintains a presence at Edinburgh Castle, which was adapted to accommodate heavy artillery as well as a permanent garrison beginning in the 1570s with the construction of the Half Moon Battery, the Forewall Battery, and several other structures. New fortifications built during the seventeenth and eighteenth centuries included the Western Defences with the Butts, Argyle, and Dury's Batteries. The addition of the military prison, barracks, an ordnance storehouse, the governor's house, and hospital completed the building project and transformed the stronghold into heavily militarized facility.

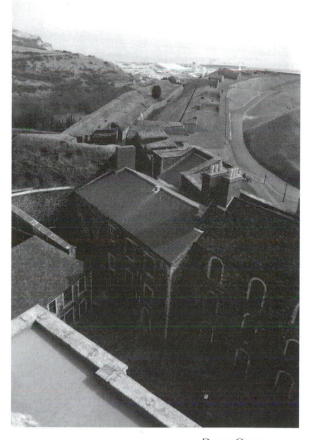

DOVER CASTLE, gun emplacements. Garrisoned by the military until late in the twentieth century, Dover Castle was repeatedly upgraded to keep up with advances in warfare technology. Gun emplacements now stand alongside medieval fortifications silently watching the action both inside the castle and outside, where Dover remains one of Europe's busiest ports.

Unlike any other medieval castle in Britain, Dover has stalwartly served the military needs of the monarchy, from its origins in the eleventh century well into modern times. Over the course of its lengthy history, the powerful concentric fortress has maintained a military presence on England's southeastern coastline. As technology changed, so did Dover Castle. Beginning in the mid-1700s, the army systematically demolished many of the original medieval fortifications to make way for artillery, gun batteries, bastions with underground facilities and caponiers (covered passages or bombproof galleries), and a new barracks in the event that France or Spain decided to stage an assault.

The Napoleonic Wars prompted further demolition at Dover Castle, along with the addition of more artillery bastions and gun platforms and the alteration of the medieval tunnels. Most of this construction took place from the 1790s to 1850s. The troops also added earthen ramparts, upon which they mounted cannons, while ditches fitted with caponiers acted as obstacles against direct attacks. In all, the castle was modified to accommodate some 231 guns.[5]

When other castles ceased to function or fell to ruin, Dover Castle persevered. During World War II, the historic fortress was still fully operational. In 1939, Vice-Admiral Ramsay used the stronghold as his headquarters and relied upon the lookout point, known as Hellfire Corner, to watch for enemy attacks. A year later, Dover played a key role in the evacuation of Dunkirk, which was directed from the castle.

Even though the army ended its official occupation of the castle in 1956, it remained in a state of readiness during the Cold War. In the early 1960s, the network of underground tunnels was refitted to serve as a Regional Head of Government in the event of a nuclear attack. Only in 1984 did the army finally decommission the castle's underground installations and relinquish them to English Heritage for public display. Nevertheless, one can only imagine that, if called into action, Dover Castle—now more military stronghold than fortified private residence—would capably fulfil its nation's demands. And, if circumstances required the monarch to flee London, Dover's great keep, which remains in outstanding condition, could be quickly restored to its original role as a well-defended home, albeit not necessarily a comfortable one, for its royal occupant.

BRITAIN'S CASTLES IN
THE TWENTY-FIRST CENTURY

Britain's medieval castles may now be distinguished between those that are still occupied and those enduring varying stages of ruin. Both types of structure provide a physical link between past and present. Both have histories that date to the Middle Ages. Both necessarily served as properly fortified military residences and were modified over time. Both had physical substance. They either fell into disrepair and suffered abandonment, the ravages of neglect or slighting, or they underwent a series of alterations instigated by successive owners intent upon modernizing defensive capabilities and living conditions, while also maintaining political control in the region. The changes displayed the superior power, status, and wealth of the owners, whether they belonged to the upper classes or the royal family or were upwardly mobile.

With some exceptions, Britain's still-occupied medieval castles have evolved into palatial residences, changing with the times to meet ever-changing social and political conditions. Now exclusively serving the residential (and status) needs of their owners, lordship castles in England that retain much of their medieval integrity include Berkeley, Arundel, Alnwick, Chillingham in Northumberland, and Raby in County Durham. England's two great royal castles, Windsor and the Tower of London, now rank among the world's best-known heritage attractions. Even so, Windsor remains a key royal residence and is an active castle occupied by an authentic military garrison trained both to protect the monarch and to perform ceremonial duties. Ironically, Britain's longest continuously occupied royal castle lacks much of a sense of its medieval past. The structures are there: the motte and shell keep, battlemented gatehouses and towers, and two baileys enclosed by residential ranges of buildings. However, the never-ending modernization programs and continual use of the castle as a private residence have overshadowed its medieval character. The restoration project undertaken by Queen Elizabeth II after the 1992 fire renovated the castle yet again, but distanced it even further from its medieval character.

Despite the daily throngs of visitors that descend upon the Tower of London, William the Conqueror's stronghold maintains a physical and sensory connection to its past. At first glance, the encroachment of modern buildings on both side of the River Thames and the presence of the London Underground within walking distance of the ditch and twin-towered main entrance seems to detract from the visual impact of the royal fortress. But, once on the property, awareness of the present dissipates. The Tower of London, with its broad array of architectural styles and its owners' historical impact on both Britain and the world, has the capacity to swiftly shift perception to the Middle Ages. Though still garrisoned and providing homes for dozens of employees, the Tower of London no longer serves as a royal residence. Like Dover, however, one can imagine that the castle could easily provide respite and a refuge for the monarchy if Buckingham Palace ever proved inadequate.

EARTHWORKS AND RUINS

Many more medieval castles survive in Britain than remain occupied. True, they are largely ruinous, fragments of what their builders originally intended, and often survive only as earthworks or rubble underneath the ground. Yet, earthworks and masonry ruins must be seen as castles and not piles of waste with no relevance to the past or the present. Their timber structures—ramparts, timber-framed halls, residential facilities, or stables—may have long since decayed. They may have been replaced during the Middle Ages by sturdier stone walls, towers, and apartment blocks. Regardless, archaeological and documentary evidence verifies the existence of such structures and substantiates all claims that these ruins were indeed operating castles. Even in decline, they are castles.

Motte and ringwork castles performed the same functions as masonry castles. Their lords erected them to demonstrate their conquest of an area and the establishment of a lordship. They were equipped with defensive features intended to thwart attack and perpetuate the lordship. They were private residences and also centers of bustling communities. They showcased the power and primacy of the lord and his subjugation of the local populace. What largely distinguished earth and timber castles from their stone counterparts was the choice of building material. Timber proved insubstantial and rotted easily. Stone provided strength and stability. Both were vulnerable to sieges and to the weather, and both were expensive and difficult to maintain in a state of ready repair. And, even though the stone castle prevailed in Britain, both types of castle were occupied until the fifteenth century. Furthermore, both types survive throughout the British landscape, in varying stages of repair to be sure, but each one provides ongoing physical proof that people of different social positions lived in, worked at, and fought to defend or destroy these sites. To discount mottes, ringworks, fragmentary ruins, and empty stone shells as true castles is to impose a set of cultural standards that dismisses the reality of the medieval era and the fact that the people living in them played an instrumental role in shaping the course of British (and world) history. As such, earthworks and ruins are rare, tangible, and invaluable links between the present and the past.

For over three hundred years, antiquarians, historians, archaeologists, and the public at large in Britain and abroad have endeavored to preserve castle remains. Governmental agencies, archaeological trusts, heritage societies, and amateur enthusiasts have all had a role in their restoration or in their clearance and consolidation. In an age where economic priorities are shifting, mottes have been quarried, ringworks ploughed over, and stone fragments allowed to collapse. In some cases, the very heritage agencies tasked to protect the sites either dismiss reports of vandalism or prohibit concerned landowners from making essential structural repairs. Some farmers who appreciate the historical and archaeological value of the earthworks and stone ruins on their properties have actually been prevented from removing trash, old tires, and rotting equipment from the medieval ruins. Consequently, these treasures from the past are rapidly losing their original fabric and their medieval character. In some ways, one can understand how some members of the public might fail to appreciate that mottes, ringworks, and ruins are indeed authentic castles, when officials, who should know better, ignore the plight of these sites to favor the preservation of modern structures or the construction of new airports and highways on top of archaeological sites. Perhaps, it is up to the public (and other heritage professionals) to take the lead in insisting the physical remains of the past do not vanish for good.

BUILDING RUINS FROM SCRATCH

Why anyone would intentionally erect a set of ruins seems unfathomable. Pride of ownership normally expresses itself in newly constructed buildings, often grandiose for the times and built with a flourish and the investment of a lot of money. Some two centuries after the end of the Middle Ages, a resurgence of interest in ancient and classical monuments occurred. New construction was modeled on Greek and Roman designs, which builders emulated as a way to symbolically link the present to the ancient past. This renewed regard for the past led young members of the elite upper class on Grand Tours of Europe, during which they explored and studied famed archaeological sites and gathered collections of fine artwork, paintings, and sculpture to exhibit at home. Their acquisitions displayed in a very visual way just how refined these world travelers had become.

Not only did the returning wanderers furnish their homes in grand style, the "Grand Tourists" also sought to re-create the architectural wonders they encountered in the landscape surrounding their stately residences. Miniature Greek or Roman temples and Egyptian-style pyramids began to dot country estates. At Wardour (Old) Castle, for example, Henry, the 8th Lord Arundell, added an unusual craglike grotto (an artificial cave) that used masonry taken from the ruined castle. He also moved a portion of what was reputedly an authentic stone circle from the landscape at nearby Tisbury and had it reconstructed near the grotto, along with two stone alcoves also constructed with stone from the castle. Arundell also built a mock-Gothic banqueting house on the opposite side of the grounds, which overlooked the Swan Pond and afforded views of his new "castle," located across the pond and to the rear of the heavily ruined medieval site. Inside the banqueting hall, the Arundells entertained their guests in style.

During the eighteenth and nineteenth centuries, the construction of these pseudo-architectural features—known as

FOLLY AT ABBEY CWMHIR. Known best as the traditional burial site for the late thirteenth-century Welsh hero Llywelyn ap Gruffudd, the "First and Last Prince of Wales," the remains of Abbey Cwmhir, in Radnorshire, sport an unusual folly—an artificial motte castle.

PENRICE CASTLE, sham ruins. High above the authentic medieval castle at Penrice on the Gower Peninsula, the sham ruins of a towered curtain wall create the ideal welcome for guests approaching the historic estate. Sadly, the castle itself is not accessible to the public.

"follies"—became something of a favorite British pastime. Essentially serving no real purpose, follies took on a myriad of forms. Indeed, many were sham ruins or earthworks. Two curious examples, which have the capacity to fool the most experienced castle explorers, are the "motte" at Abbey Cwmhir, in Powys and the "ruined" towered wall at the upper entrance to the grounds encompassing medieval Penrice Castle, on the Gower Peninsula. However, follies did—and still do—serve a purpose. They symbolically displayed their owners' individualism, ingenuity, cultural sophistication, and social status. After all, if someone could afford to put up purposefully built ruins, he or she must have plenty of spare cash to toss about!

The British landscape is a remarkable compilation of ancient, historic, and sham sites, which physically document the entire course of human occupation on the Isles. They connect the present to the past in a tangible, visceral way that enlivens the sites, regardless of whether they remain occupied or are little more than earthen mounds or chunks of masonry. Nonetheless, the difference between authentic medieval castles and their sham counterparts remains as profound as the difference between night and day.

AMERICA'S CASTLES?

Contrary to what popular television and some publications claim, there are no castles in the United States. Those buildings—including Hearst Castle in California, which incorporates architectural fragments from grand European residences, Belcourt Castle in Rhode Island, and Dick's Castle in New York—are not castles. Neither are Cinderella's Castle at Disneyland nor Mad Ludwig's Bavarian castle Neuschwanstein, upon which Cinderella's Castle was modeled. No matter how persistent their admirers and owners may be and no matter what they are called, these grand structures must be classified as palaces, palatial residences, stately homes, or mansions. They are not, nor were they ever intended to be, castles in the true sense of the word. Certainly, these fantastic places radiate wealth, personal achievement, and high status. They have housed their owners in remarkable splendor, which few of us can hope to afford. Yet, they were never intended to withstand a siege, center a lordship, or subjugate a population. By christening their fantastic homes as castles, the affluent owners intended to validate their position within social circles and to prove they were worthy of the reputations they ambitiously strove to achieve. Just as Henry VIII's "castles" were actually coastal forts and never intended as private residences, America's "castles" are more accurately characterized as mansions. And, Neuschwanstein? It was Mad Ludwig's turreted palace.

Epilogue

The erroneous but still widely held notion that castles were built primarily to defend the lord and his household undoubtedly has its origins in the interpretation of their structural nature. The rationalization for this point of view is that, logically, the most powerful and most enduring castles were those with the most complex defenses, thickest walls, and deepest moats, which were well positioned to thwart an assault with sheer cliffsides, inhospitable surroundings, and panoramic views of the countryside. Castles were erected, according to this belief, to dutifully and capably protect their residents from rampaging subjects or besieging armies. The better the defensive might, the greater the castle's capacity to keep an enemy at bay.

The theory seems sound, if one examines castles in a vacuum, removing them from their sociopolitical and historical contexts, their relationship to the historic landscape, the needs of the lords who ordered their construction, and the perceptions of their oppressed subjects. From the outside looking in, castles epitomized offensive power, not defensive assurances. The populace might be awed by the enormity of the stronghold or its unfamiliar appearance within the landscape, but they would have been even more likely to resent its physical presence and that of the overlord within. Like its lord, a castle was an intrusion into an area. Lord and subject understood this situation.

True, all castles were fortified to provide the inhabitants with at least a modicum of protection. And, over the centuries, castle defenses became increasingly complex, partly in response to technical advances in siege warfare, partly in response to the ongoing threat of rebellion or siege, and partly for symbolic and aesthetic reasons. But, the construction of a castle was an overtly hostile action and recognized as such from within and without the ranks. True, the castle's defenses were essential to survival, for surely no medieval lord would care to control an area or raise a family without a measure of security. Yet, to characterize castles as built primarily for defensive purposes distorts reality.

First and foremost, castles were built for offensive purposes—and they certainly offended many people. The aggressive actions taken after the Scottish Wars of Independence and the English Civil War suggest just how important it was to control castles. After the stunning Scottish victory over the English at Bannockburn in 1314, Robert Bruce, King of Scotland, ordered the deliberate destruction of his country's own strongholds, including powerful Stirling Castle, to prevent the English from retaking the castles and using them against the Scots. During the late 1640s and early 1650s, the parliamentary leader Oliver Cromwell, who governed England and Wales as "Lord Protector" after the defeat and execution of King Charles I, ordered the destruction of scores of castles. With this policy, known as "slighting," Cromwell intended to prevent royalist garrisons from re-manning their castles in order to maintain control of his newly acquired, but short-lived, protectorate. Many of today's ruined castles are the by-products of Cromwell's wrath.

Even today, some British citizens, particularly in Wales and Ireland, take offense at the ongoing presence of castles in the landscape. Viewing them as perpetual symbols of past (and, on occasion, present-day oppression), these people claim they would rather see demolition than careful preservation. This lingering resentment proves a point: despite their current state of impotence, castles remain as much the offensive weapons that their medieval owners originally intended them to be.

Notes

INTRODUCTION

1. Richard Muir, *The NEW Reading the Landscape: Fieldwork in Landscape History* (Exeter: University of Exeter Press, 2000), 236–237.

2. Richard Cavendish, *Prehistoric England* (London: Weidenfeld and Nicolson, 1983), 20–22.

3. Stephen Johnson, *Hadrian's Wall* (London: B. T. Batsford, 1989), 25–27.

4. Ann Williams, "A Bell-House and a Burh-Geat: Lordly Residences in England Before the Norman Conquest," in *Anglo-Norman Castles*, ed. Robert Liddiard (Woodbridge, Suffolk: The Boydell Press, 2003), 37.

5. Anthony Bradshaw, "The Burghal Hidage: Alfred's Towns," http://www.ogdoad.force9.co.uk/alfred/alfhidage.htm.

6. Anne Savage, *The Anglo-Saxon Chronicles* (London: Guild Publishing, 1988), 177–180.

7. D. F. Renn, "The First Norman Castles in England: 1051–1071," an abstract from *Chateau Gaillard* (1964), 128.

8. P. E. Curnow and M. W. Thompson, "Excavations at Richard's Castle, Herefordshire: 1962–1964," in *Journal of the British Archaeological Association* 32 (1969): 106.

9. D.J.C. King, *The Castle in England and Wales: An Interpretative History* (Beckenham, Kent: Croom Helm, 1988), 34.

10. Geoffrey Williams, *Stronghold Britain* (Stroud, Gloucestershire: Sutton Publishing, 1999), 102.

11. R. Allen Brown et al., *Castles: A History and Guide* (Poole, Dorset: Blandford Press, 1980), 16.

12. David Seller, "Farewell to Feudalism," in *Burke's Landed Gentry: The Kingdom in Scotland*, ed. Peter Beauclerk Dewar (Stokesley, North Yorkshire: Burke's Peerage & Gentry, 2004), http://www.burkes-peerage.net/Sites/Scotland/SitePages/page14e.asp.

13. Plantagenet Somerset Fry, *The David and Charles Book of Castles* (Newton Abbot, Devon: David and Charles, 1980), 9.

14. Brown, *Castles*, 98.

15. Robert Higham, "Timber Castles: A Reassessment," in *Anglo-Norman Castles*, ed. Robert Liddiard (Woodbridge, Suffolk: The Boydell Press, 2003), 118.

CHAPTER 1

1. Helen Clarke, *The Archaeology of Medieval England* (Oxford: Basil Blackwell, 1986), 109.

2. R. Allen Brown, *The Architecture of Castles* (London: B. T. Batsford, 1984), 27.

3. John R. Kenyon, *Medieval Fortifications* (Leicester: Leicester University Press, 1990), 7.

4. Trevor Rowley, *The Norman Heritage: 1066–1200* (London: Routledge and Kegan Paul, 1983), 46.

5. Robert Higham and Philip Barker, *Timber Castles* (Mechanicsburg, PA: Stackpole Books, 1995), 59.

6. Ibid., 49.

7. Richard Eales, "Royal Power and Castles in Norman England," in *Anglo-Norman Castles*, ed. Robert Liddiard (Woodbridge, Suffolk: The Boydell Press, 2003), 48.

8. C. J. Spurgeon, "Mottes and Castle-Ringworks in Wales," in *Castles in Wales and the Welsh Marches: Essays in Honour of D. J. Cathcart King*, ed. John R. Kenyon and Richard Avent (Cardiff: University of Wales Press, 1987), 37.

9. R. Allen Brown et al., *Castles: A History and Guide* (Poole, Dorset: Blandford Press, 1980), 14.

10. M. J. Jackson, *Castles of Cumbria* (Carlisle: Carel Press, 1990), 39.

11. O. H. Creighton, "Castles, Lordship and Settlement in Norman England and Wales," *History Today*, April 2003, 14–15.

12. Derek Renn, *Norman Castles in Britain* (London: John Baker Publishers, 1973), 32.

13. David Sweetman, *The Medieval Castles of Ireland* (Woodbridge, Suffolk: The Boydell Press, 2003), 17 (emphasis added).

14. Plantagenet Somerset Fry, *The David and Charles Book of Castles* (Newton Abbot, Devon: David and Charles, 1980), 130 (emphasis added).

15. English Heritage, *PastScape*, http://www.pastscape.org/homepage/index.html (2004).

16. N.J.G. Pounds, *The Medieval Castle in England and Wales: A Social and Political History* (Cambridge: Cambridge University Press, 1994), 52.

17. Michael Prestwich, *Armies and Warfare in the Middle Ages: The English Experience* (New Haven: Yale University Press, 2003), 207.

18. P. H. Humphries, *Castles of Edward the First in Wales* (London: HMSO, 1983), 5–10.

19. Arnold Taylor, *Rhuddlan Castle* (Cardiff: Cadw, 1987), 11.

20. Pounds, *Medieval Castle*, 182.

21. Derek Renn and Richard Avent, *Flint Castle/Ewloe Castle* (Cardiff: Cadw, 1995), 11.

22. Peter and Fiona Somerset Fry, *A History of Ireland* (London: Routledge, 1991), 124.

23. Ibid., 138.

24. Brian de Breffny, *Castles of Ireland* (London: Thames and Hudson, 1981), 177.

25. Plantagenet Somerset Fry, *Castles of Britain and Ireland* (New York: Abbeville Press, 1997), 229.

26. Brown, *Castles*, 16.

27. F.J.E. Raby, *Framlingham Castle* (London: HMSO, 1984), 5.

28. C. N. Johns, *Caerphilly Castle* (London: HMSO, 1978), 18.

29. A. J. Taylor, *Raglan Castle* (London: HMSO, 1970), 12.

30. Ibid., 10.

31. T. H. McK. Clough, *The Horseshoes of Oakham Castle* (Oakham: Rutland County Council, 1999), 7.

32. Chester County Council, "Chester Castle," http://www.chestercc.gov.uk (2005).

33. Arnold Taylor, *Conwy Castle and Town Walls* (Cardiff: Cadw, 1998), 25–26.

34. Pamela Marshall and John Samuels, *Guardian of the Trent: The Story of Newark Castle* (Newark: Newark Castle Trust, 1997), 10, 34–35.

35. R. Allen Brown, *Castle Rising* (London: HMSO, 1983), 16.

36. Jeremy K. Knight, *Chepstow Castle* (Cardiff: Cadw, 1986), 15. Also refer to the latest edition of the *Chepstow Castle* guide, updated in 2002 by Rick Turner.

CHAPTER 2

1. Tom McNeill, *Castles* (London: B. T. Batsford/English Heritage, 1992), 87.

2. Jim Bradbury, *The Medieval Siege* (Woodbridge, Suffolk: The Boydell Press, 1992), 2.

3. MacNeill, *Castles*, 91.

4. Bradbury, *Medieval Siege*, 308.

5. Mark P. Donnelly and Daniel Diehl, *Siege: Castles at War* (Dallas: Taylor Publishing Company, 1998), 53.

6. Bradbury, *Medieval Siege*, 326.

7. Philip Warner, *The Medieval Castle: Life in a Fortress in Peace and War* (New York: Barnes and Noble Books, 1993), 63.

8. Donnelly and Diehl, *Siege*, 68.

9. Frank Bottomley, *The Castle Explorer's Guide* (New York: Avenal Books, 1983), 28.

10. Bradbury, *Medieval Siege*, 271.

11. Bottomley, *Castle Explorer's Guide*, 156.

12. Ibid., 58.

13. Ibid., 120.

14. Donnelly and Diehl, *Siege*, 119.

15. Ibid., 243.

16. Bottomley, *Castle Explorer's Guide*, 15.

17. Ibid., 147.

18. Bradbury, *Medieval Siege*, 252.

19. Philip Warner, *Sieges of the Middle Ages* (London: Penguin Books, 2000), 30.

20. John Goodall, "Dover Castle and the Great Siege of 1216," *Chateau Gaillard*, XIX: Actes du Colloque International de Graz, http://www.deremilitari.org/goodall.htm (1998).

21. Bradbury, *Medieval Siege*, 141.

22. Warner, *Sieges*, 146.

23. Bottomley, *Castle Explorer's Guide*, 168.

24. Ibid., 28, 149.

25. Michael Prestwich, *Armies and Warfare in the Middle Ages: The English Experience* (New Haven: Yale University Press, 2003), 288.

26. Ibid., 76.

27. Donnelly and Diehl, *Siege*, 107.

28. Bradbury, *Medieval Siege*, 265.

29. Peter Vemming Hansen, "War Engines of the Middle Ages," *The Medieval Centre*, http://www.middelaldercentret.dk/english/us_home.htm (1998).

30. Goodall, "Dover Castle."

31. Bradbury, *Medieval Siege*, 142.

32. B. H. St. J. O'Neil, *Caerlaverock Castle* (Edinburgh: Her Majesty's Stationery Office, 1988), 6.

33. David Morrison, "The Siege of Caerlaverock," *Seanachaidh*, http://www.seanachaidh.org/siegeof.htm (2002).

34. Bradbury, *Medieval Siege*, 143.

35. Donnelly and Diehl, *Siege*, 167.

36. Bottomley, *Castle Explorer's Guide*, 71–72.

37. Prestwich, *Armies*, 61–62.

38. Ibid., 70–73.

39. Bottomley, *Castle Explorer's Guide*, 27.

40. Lawrence Butler, "The Origins of the Honour of Richmond and Its Castles," in *Anglo-Norman Castles*, ed. Robert Liddiard (Woodbridge, Suffolk: The Boydell Press, 2003), 96.

41. Oliver Creighton, "Castles, Lordship and Settlement in Norman England and Wales," in *History Today*, April 2003, 14–15.

42. Stephen Johnson, *Hadrian's Wall* (London: B. T. Batsford, 1989), 70.

43. Bottomley, *Castle Explorer's Guide*, 49.

44. Plantagenet Somerset Fry, *The David and Charles Book of Castles* (Newton Abbot: David and Charles, 1980), 33.

45. Derek Renn, *Goodrich Castle* (London: English Heritage, 1998), 6.

46. Mike Salter, *The Castles and Tower Houses of Northumberland* (Malvern: Folly Publications, 1997), 113.

47. Jeremy Knight, *The Three Castles* (Cardiff: Cadw, 2000), 27.

48. James Forde-Johnston, *A Guide to the Castles of England and Wales* (London: Constable, 1981), 63.

49. Arnold Taylor, *Beaumaris Castle* (Cardiff: Cadw, 1999), 9.

50. Bottomley, *Castle Explorer's Guide*, 127.

51. R. Allen Brown, *The Architecture of Castles* (London: B. T. Batsford, 1984), 63.

52. Sidney Toy, *The Castles of Great Britain* (London: William Heinemann, 1953), 240–241.

53. L.A.S. Butler, *Denbigh Castle and Town Walls* (Cardiff: Cadw, 1990), 33.

54. Toy, *Castles*, 236.

55. Ibid.

56. Bottomley, *Castle Explorer's Guide*, 12.

57. John R. Kenyon, *Medieval Fortifications* (Leicester: Leicester University Press, 1990), 81.

58. Bottomley, *Castle Explorer's Guide*, 135.

59. Forde-Johnston, *A Guide*, 300.

60. Stephen Friar, *The Sutton Companion to Castles* (Stroud: Sutton Publishing, 2003), 86.

61. Plantagenet Somerset Fry, *The David and Charles Book of Castles* (Newton Abbot: David and Charles, 1980), 212.

62. Ibid., 234.

63. Bottomley, *Castle Explorer's Guide*, 117.

64. Toy, *Castles*, 152.

65. Bottomley, *Castle Explorer's Guide*, 107.

66. R. Allen Brown, *Dover Castle: Kent* (London: HMSO, 1985), 9.

67. Kenyon, *Medieval Fortifications*, 72.

68. Bottomley, *Castle Explorer's Guide*, 190.

69. Arnold Taylor, *Conwy Castle and Town Walls* (Cardiff: Cadw, 1998), 43.

70. Derek Renn and Richard Avent, *Flint Castle/Ewloe Castle* (Cardiff: Cadw, 1995), 33.

71. Kenyon, *Medieval Fortifications*, 72.

72. Arnold Taylor, *Caernarfon Castle and Town Walls* (Cardiff: Cadw, 1993), 33.

73. Paul Barker, *Warwick Castle* (Warwick: Warwick Castle, 1990), 29.

74. Taylor, *Caernarfon Castle*, 42–47.

75. Brown, *Dover Castle*, 26.

76. Derek Renn, *Caerphilly Castle* (Cardiff: Cadw, 1997), 33.

77. Ibid., 36–39.

78. Ibid., 46.

CHAPTER 3

1. R. Allen Brown et al., *Castles: A History and Guide* (Poole, Dorset: Blandford Press, 1980), 118.

2. N.J.G. Pounds, *The Medieval Castle in England and Wales: A Social and Political History* (Cambridge: Cambridge University Press, 1994), 90.

3. Charles Coulson, *Castles in Medieval Society: Fortresses in England, France, and Ireland in the Central Middle Ages* (Oxford: Oxford University Press, 2004), 297.

4. Philip Warner, *The Medieval Castle: Life in a Fortress in Peace and War* (New York: Barnes and Noble Books, 1993), 195.

5. Tom McNeill, *Castles* (London: B. T. Batsford/English Heritage, 1992), 22.

6. John R. Kenyon, *Medieval Fortifications* (Leicester: Leicester University Press, 1990), 101.

7. Adrian Pettifer, *English Castles: A Guide by Counties* (Woodbridge, Suffolk: The Boydell Press, 1995), 92.

8. Francois Matarasso, *The English Castle* (London: Cassell, 1993), 122.

9. Jeremy K. Knight, *Chepstow Castle and Port Wall* (Cardiff: Cadw, 1991), 25.

10. John R. Kenyon, *Raglan Castle* (Cardiff: Cadw, 2003), 34.

11. The National Trust, *Corfe Castle Dorset* (London: The National Trust, 2000), 35.

12. Robin Mackworth-Young, *The History and Treasures of Windsor Castle* (London: Pitkin-Britannia, 1982), 14.

13. Plantagenet Somerset Fry, *The David and Charles Book of Castles* (Newton Abbot: David and Charles, 1980), 11.

14. Kenyon, *Medieval Fortifications*, 39.

15. Fry, *David and Charles Book of Castles*, 212.

16. Kenyon, *Medieval Fortifications*, 39.

17. Derek Renn and Richard Avent, *Flint Castle/Ewloe Castle* (Cardiff: Cadw, 1995), 27.

18. David M. Robinson, ed., *Tretower Court and Castle* (Cardiff: Cadw, 1990), 4.

19. Fry, *David and Charles Book of Castles*, 180.

20. T. L. Jones, *Ashby de la Zouch Castle* (London: English Heritage, 1999), 11.

21. Diane M. Williams, *Gower: A Guide to Ancient and Historic Monuments on the Gower Peninsula* (Cardiff: Cadw, 1998), 42.

22. Kenyon, *Medieval Fortifications*, 161.

23. Ibid.

24. Stephen Friar, *The Sutton Companion to Castles* (Stroud, Gloucestershire: Sutton Publishing, 2003), 91.

25. David Thackray, *Bodiam Castle East Sussex* (London: The National Trust, 1995), 49.

26. McNeill, *Castles*, 81.

27. Fry, *David and Charles Book of Castles*, 129.

28. Oliver Creighton and Robert Higham, *Medieval Castles* (Princes Riseborough, Buckinghamshire: Shire Publications, 2003), 17.

29. Williams, *Gower*, 31.

CHAPTER 4

1. P. H. Humphries, *Castles of Edward the First in Wales* (London: HMSO, 1983), 10.

2. Frank Bottomley, *The Castle Explorer's Guide* (New York: Avenal Books, 1983), 103.

3. Ibid., 102.

4. N.J.G. Pounds, *The Medieval Castle in England and Wales: A Social and Political History* (Cambridge: Cambridge University Press, 1994), 261.

5. Ibid., 262.

6. Robin Mackworth-Young, *The History and Treasures of Windsor Castle* (London: Pitkin-Britannia, 1982), 36–42.

7. Pembrokeshire Coast National Park, *Carew Castle* (Haverfordwest: Pembrokeshire Coast National Park Authority, 2002), 9.

8. Peter Furtado et al., *The Ordnance Survey Guide to Castles in Britain* (Twickenham: Country Life Books, 1987), 142.

9. Oliver Creighton and Robert Higham, *Medieval Castles* (Princes Risborough Buckinghamshire: Shire Publications, 2003), 20.

10. Derek Renn, *Kenilworth Castle* (London: English Heritage, 1999), 7–8.

11. Nick McCann, ed., *Berkeley Castle* (Derby: English Life Publications, 1997), 17.

12. Charles Kightly, *A Mirror of Medieval Wales: Gerald of Wales and His Journey of 1188* (Cardiff: Cadw, 1988), 8–9.

13. Peter Hammond, *Her Majesty's Royal Palace and Fortress of the Tower of London* (London: Historic Royal Palaces, 1993), 33–34.

14. Historic Tours (Wales), *Ludlow Castle* (Caernarfon: Historic Tours (Wales), 1987), 8.

15. Ibid., 11, 14.

16. English Heritage, *Farleigh Hungerford Castle* (London: English Heritage, 1998), 4.

17. St. George's Chapel, http://www.stgeorges-windsor.org/history/hist_stgeorges.asp (2005).

18. R. Allen Brown et al., *Castles: A History and Guide* (Poole, Dorset: Blanford Press, 1980), 117.

19. Royal Commission on Ancient and Historical Monuments in Wales, *An Inventory of the Ancient Monuments in Glamorgan*, vol. 3, Part 1b, *Medieval Secular Monuments: The Later Castles from 1217 to the Present* (London: HMSO, 1991), 165.

20. Tom McNeill, *Castles* (London: B. T. Batsford/English Heritage, 1992), 51.

21. Ibid., 57.

22. Ibid.

23. Ron Shoesmith, *A Guide to Castles and Moated Sites in Herefordshire* (Almeley, Herefordshire: Logaston Press, 1996), 113–115.

24. McNeill, *Castles*, 60.

25. Pounds, *Medieval Castle*, 274.

26. James Forde-Johnston, *A Guide to the Castles of England and Wales* (London: Constable, 1981), 282.

27. Ibid.

28. David Thackray, *Bodiam Castle* (London: The National Trust, 1995), 39.

29. Matthew Johnson, *Behind the Castle Gate: From Medieval to Renaissance* (London: Routledge, 2002). Johnson presents a thought-provoking look at the symbolism behind the construction of castles, focusing on Cooling, Bodiam, and Kenilworth Castles.

30. John R. Kenyon, *Raglan Castle* (Cardiff: Cadw, 2003), 54.

CHAPTER 5

1. John R. Kenyon, *Raglan Castle* (Cardiff: Cadw, 2003), 9.

2. Ibid., 10.

3. Anthony Emery, "The Development of Raglan Castle and Keeps in Late Medieval England," *Archaeological Journal* 132 (1975): 176.

4. Ibid., 41.

5. Kenyon, *Raglan Castle*, 42.

6. Ibid., 40.

7. Ibid., 38.

8. Ibid., 17.

9. Ibid., 50.

10. Ibid., 19.

11. Ibid., 21.

12. Ibid., 18.

CHAPTER 6

1. N.J.G. Pounds, *The Medieval Castle in England and Wales: A Social and Political History* (Cambridge: Cambridge University Press, 1994), 250.

2. James Forde-Johnston, *A Guide to the Castles of England and Wales* (London: Constable, 1981), 73.

3. Plantagenet Somerset Fry, *The David and Charles Book of Castles* (Newton Abbot, Devon: David and Charles, 1980), 158.

4. Ibid., 160.

5. R. Allen Brown, *Dover Castle: Kent* (London: HMSO, 1985), 42.

Glossary

allure: wall-walk

angle-spur: pyramid-shaped projections rising at the corners of towers, intended for added support and to prevent collapse from undermining

apsidal: D-shaped

arrowslit: vertical slot in castle walls used for firing crossbows from inside castle; also called "arrowloop"

ashlar: building stone neatly trimmed to shape; stone with cut, flat surface

aumbry: a cupboard for storing valuables

bailey: defended courtyard or ward of a castle; open area enclosed by the castle walls; a ward

ballista: siege engine shaped like a giant bow, which fired iron-tipped arrows or stone missiles

barbican: fortified outwork defending the gate of a castle or town

bar-holes: holes behind doors placed to receive timber bars, which were used to bolt the doors closed

barmkin: Scottish term for defended courtyard of a castle; also, the wall enclosing such an area

barrel vault: a vault in the shape of a half barrel split lengthways

bartizan: an overhanging corner turret

basement: a secure storage space at ground level or below

bastion: an open projecting work placed at the corner or along the wall of a fortification that acts as an added firing platform

batter: inward and upward slope of an external wall, normally located at its base

battery: gun emplacement

battlement: jagged stonework protecting the wall-walk, consisting of crenels and merlons; also known as "crenellation"

bawn: walled enclosure

besiege: to surround a castle in order to cut off its supplies, stage an assault if necessary, and force its surrender

bratticing: wooden housing erected on top of walls; known as "war-head" when erected on towers; see "hoarding"

bretasch: wooden tower or wooden defense

burh: Saxon defended settlement

buttery: storeroom where wine and other drink were dispensed from barrels; the "bottlery"; usually located between the hall and the kitchen

buttress: thickening of a wall or projecting masonry added for strength and support

capital: head of a column

caponier: covered connecting passageway

casemate: vaulted chamber embedded in ramparts or walls and equipped with a gun emplacement; passageway within thickness of a curtain wall that leads to gun and musket ports

castellan: individual in charge of the castle; castle custodian

castellation: battlements; implies use as a decorative feature

castle: a properly fortified military residence; from the Latin, "castellum"

cat: hide-covered framework that protected miners during a siege

cesspit: a depression in the base of a tower or in the ground that collected human waste

chamberlain: individual responsible for the great chamber and for the personal finances of the castellan

chancel: part of church or chapel containing the altar

chancery: medieval high court that presided over cases of common law and equity; chancellor's court or office

chapel: chamber for religious services

chatelaine: lady of the castle; wife of the castellan

cobbled: paved with cobblestones, large rounded stones

comitatus: county court

concentric: having two parallel lines of defense, the lower outer wall closely surrounding the higher inner wall; a walls-within-walls design; circles within circles

constable: governor of a castle

corbel: projecting stone (or timber) feature on a wall used to support an overhanging parapet, platform, turret, or timber beams

crenel: the openings between the upright sections of crenellation

crenellation: toothlike protective stonework rimming the top of a castle wall; fortification, including crenels and merlons; battlements

cross-wall: a stone wall that creates a barrier between two chambers or forms part of a passageway between two structures

curtain wall: defensive wall which encloses a bailey, courtyard, or ward, generally constructed in stone; links towers, the main gateway, and other structures

custodian: manager of castle in absence of lord

dais: a raised platform for the high table, located at the end of the great hall, where the lord and his guests dined

donjon: keep or great tower, the main citadel of a castle

dormer: a window located partly in the wall and partly in the roof

dovecote: medieval pigeon house, often associated with castles or monasteries; building with pigeon holes used to breed doves for food supply

D-plan: semicircular design of towers; apsidal

drawbar: sliding wooden bar used to secure a door in the closed position

drawbridge: a timber or stone bridge or roadway across a moat or ditch that lifted or pivoted to prevent unwanted access into the castle

drum tower: a completely round tower

dungeon: castle prison

embankment: earthen wall or slope that enclosed an area or formed the walls of a ditch

embrasure: splayed opening in a wall or parapet; slits cut into the merlons

enceinte: enclosure or courtyard wall

escalade: assault on a wall or palisade using scaling ladders

exchequer: individual tasked with collecting revenue

fee: land held by a knight or other landowner in exchange for the military service of a single knight

feudalism: a political and economic system under which land was granted by a landowner to a person in exchange for military service or other duties

fief: a feudal estate

forebuilding: projecting defensive work that screened the entrance to keep

fossatores: miners

foundations: the masonry substructure of a building; often the only surviving remains of a castle or its inner structures

garderobe: usually the latrine chute, privy, or castle toilet; sometimes, a room to store personal items; a wardrobe

garrison: a group of soldiers stationed at a castle

gatehouse: strong multistory structure containing a fortified gate, the portcullis chamber, and accommodation for the castle constable

gothic: architectural style developed in northern France that is characterized by pointed arches

great hall: entertainment center of the castle, where guests were feasted; also used as the main administrative chamber

guardroom: room used by guards when on duty; normally located in the castle gatehouse, often on either side of gate passage

gun emplacement: platform or defended position providing a place to secure cannons or other guns

gunloop: opening in a wall for firing a gun, often a modified arrowslit; also called a "gunport"

harrying: harassing with destructive raids

hearth: open fire in center of chamber

hillfort: a large hilltop enclosure surrounded by one or more earthen ramparts

hoarding: wooden fighting platform fitted to the parapet of wall as extra protection for defenders that provided extra space from which to fire down on an enemy

hornwork: earthwork barrier usually set before an entrance to impede attackers

inner ward: interior courtyard; hub of castle where daily activities took place

keep: the main citadel or great tower of a castle; a fortified tower containing living quarters and used as the last line of refuge in a siege; a self-sufficient tower; the "donjon"

lancet-headed: pointed arches at the peaks of narrow windows

latrine chute: an open channel in a tower or wall through which human waste passed into a cesspit or outside the castle walls into the moat

license to crenellate: official permission from the monarch to erect a fortified building or fortify an existing structure

lifting gaffs: mechanical arms used to raise drawbridge

light: compartment of a window

loophole: vertical slit for air, light, or firing through

machicolation: carved projections located along a wall or above an archway through which defenders could drop or shoot missiles vertically onto attackers below; functioned similar to murder holes

magazine: chamber for storing ammunition, arms, and provisions

mangonel: stone-throwing siege engine consisting of a heavy frame that supported a long arm with a cup or sling at the free end, worked with ropes stretched between upright posts

mantlet: stretch of land running along the outer side of a curtain wall

marches: borderlands or frontier, especially associated with the border between Wales and England

merlon: the "teeth" of the battlements rising between the crenels or embrasures; high sections of battlement

meurtrieres: murder holes

mint: where coins were produced

missile: a large stone or other object thrown at an enemy through murder holes or by a siege engine

moat: water-filled ditch encircling the castle; a body of water around the castle, as at Caerphilly

motte: artificial or improved natural mound on which a timber tower or shell keep was built

mullion: vertical bar of stone or wood dividing a window into smaller openings

multilobed: having several curved or rounded projections

multivallate: having more than one rampart

mural: within the wall

murder holes: openings in the ceilings of gate passages through which missiles and liquids could be dropped onto attackers or fires

newel stair: circular or spiral stair within a wall or tower

Normanized/neo-Norman: architectural features imitating Norman style

oratory: a small private chamber for prayer

oriel: a large projecting, curved or polygonal window supported on corbels

oubliette: tiny cell where prisoners were left to die; secret chamber; pit-prison

palisade: timber fencing, normally erected on top of earthen ramparts or motte

parapet: a protective, battlemented wall located on the outer side of the wall-walk

parliamentarian: supporter of Parliament against King Charles I during English Civil War in 1640s

partibility: system whereby a deceased person's property is divided equally among his sons

pele tower: similar to a tower house, but on a smaller scale

piscina: stone basin with drain hole for the priest to wash hands or vessels

pit-prison: underground cell accessed through a hatch or trapdoor in ceiling; dungeon; bottle dungeon; oubliette

plantation: deliberate settlement of a group of people from outside the area

plinth: projecting stone platforms upon which keeps or wall towers were raised to prevent undermining

portcullis: heavy wooden, iron, or combination grille protecting an entrance, raised and lowered by winches (the windlass) located inside the gatehouse; grooves visible in gate passages

postern: secondary gateway or back doorway used for quick escape or to take in supplies

putlog holes: square holes that supported timber scaffolding

rampart: battlement or protected fighting platform for castle defenders; a defensive bank of earth or rubble, topped with timber fence

range: a group of associated buildings

revetment: an outwork or embankment faced with a layer of timber or masonry

revetting: stone or timber facing applied to a wall or bank

ringwork: an earth and timber fortification similar to a motte but where the summit is dished to some degree, encircled with earthen banks and then topped with timber palisades

royalist: supporter of monarchy (King Charles I) during English Civil War in the 1640s

rubble: walling of rough, undressed stones; fill stone

sacristy: room used to store sacred vessels and vestments

salient: part of a fortification that points or angles outward

sally port: small door or gate, usually some distance from main entrance of castle or ward, which allowed defenders to discreetly enter and exit castle without detection; related to "sally forth"

sapper: miner

sedile: priest's seat in chapel

seigneurial: of or related to a feudal lord

seneschal: individual in charge of a lord's feudal estate

serf: a member of the lowest feudal class who is bound to the soil and subject to the lord

shell keep: a stone ring wall encircling the top of a motte which held domestic chambers, the hall, and other facilities

shire: an administrative subdivision similar to a county

shire hall: building used to conduct the administrative business of the shire

shutter: movable device for closing the crenel or other wall openings

siege: attacking a castle in order to cause surrender

siege engine: a machine for firing missiles at castle or for scaling walls; includes trebuchet, mangonel, ballista, and belfry

siege-work: an earthwork raised for the protection of a force besieging a castle

slighting: the process of rendering a castle useless to prevent its future use; dismantling a fortification accomplished by breaching walls, undermining walls, and, later, by blowing them up with gun powder; a policy enforced by Oliver Cromwell to ensure all castles were unable to oppose his authority after the English Civil War

solar: the lord's private living quarters, usually adjacent to great hall; a withdrawing chamber

splay: an aperture that widens as it progresses inwards, normally associated with windows

steward: individual who took care of the estate and supervised the castle's household and events in the great hall; the "seneschal"

string course: horizontal projecting molding or band of masonry running along the face of a wall

stronghouse: a horizontally oriented Irish tower house, that often had five stories, but was wider than it was tall; dates to the sixteenth and seventeenth centuries

tower house: a significantly fortified residence built to thwart brief assaults rather than prolonged sieges; architecturally similar to a rectangular keep

trebuchet: stone-throwing siege engine worked with counterweights

triforium: a gallery forming the upper story in the aisle of a church

turning bridge: early form of drawbridge, operating on seesaw principle

turret: a small tower, often an add-on to a larger tower

twin-towered: describing a gatehouse with matching drum towers flanking either side of the gate passage

undercroft: plain chamber underneath a medieval house or castle, most often used as storage and barrel-vaulted

undermining: digging a tunnel at the base of a curtain wall or tower, which is then propped up with timber beams and set alight to bring down the foundations overhead

univallate: having a single rampart

vassal: a feudal tenant

vault: an arched ceiling, usually of stone

wall-walk: interior walkway along a wall top, protected by a parapet

ward: courtyard or bailey enclosed within castle walls

wicket: small gate or doorway, part of the portcullis

windlass: mechanical device used to raise and lower the drawbridge or portcullis

yett: gate made of intersecting iron bars penetrating each other vertically and horizontally; Scottish variation of portcullis

Bibliography

Barker, Paul. *Warwick Castle*. Warwick: Warwick Castle, 1990.

Bottomley, Frank. *The Castle Explorer's Guide*. New York: Avenal Books, 1983.

Bradbury, Jim. *The Medieval Siege*. Woodbridge, Suffolk: The Boydell Press, 1992.

Bradshaw, Anthony. "The Burghal Hidage, Alfred's Towns." http://www.ogdoad .force9.co.uk/alfred/alfhidage.htm, 1999.

Brown, R. Allen. *The Architecture of Castles*. London: B. T. Batsford, 1984.

———. *Castle Rising*. London: HMSO, 1983.

———. *Dover Castle: Kent*. London: HMSO, 1985.

———. *English Medieval Castles*. London: B. T. Batsford, 1954.

———. *Rochester Castle, Kent*. London: English Heritage, 1986.

Brown, R. Allen, et al. *Castles: A History and Guide*. Poole, Dorset: Blandford Press, 1980.

Butler, L.A.S. *Denbigh Castle and Town Walls*. Cardiff: Cadw, 1990.

Butler, Lawrence. "The Origins of the Honour of Richmond and Its Castles." In *Anglo-Norman Castles*, edited by Robert Liddiard. Woodbridge, Suffolk: The Boydell Press, 2003.

Cavendish, Richard. *Prehistoric England*. London: Weidenfeld and Nicolson, 1983.

Chester County Council. "Chester Castle." http://www.chestercc.gov.uk, 2005.

Clarke, Helen. *The Archaeology of Medieval England*. Oxford: Basil Blackwell, 1986.

Clough, T. H. McK. *The Horseshoes of Oakham Castle*. Oakham: Rutland County Council, 1999.

Coulson, Charles. *Castles in Medieval Society: Fortresses in England, France, and Ireland in the Central Middle Ages.* Oxford: Oxford University Press, 2004.

Creighton, O. H. "Castles, Lordship and Settlement in Norman England and Wales." *History Today*, April 2003, 14–15.

Creighton, Oliver, and Robert Higham. *Medieval Castles.* Princes Riseborough, Buckinghamshire: Shire Publications, 2003.

Curnow, P. E., and M. W. Thompson. "Excavations at Richard's Castle, Herefordshire, 1962–1964." *Journal of the British Archaeological Association*, 3rd ser., 32 (1969).

De Breffny, Brian. *Castles of Ireland.* London: Thames and Hudson, 1981.

Donnelly, Mark P., and Daniel Diehl. *Siege: Castles at War.* Dallas: Taylor Publishing Company, 1998.

Eales, Richard. "Royal Power and Castles in Norman England." In *Anglo-Norman Castles*, edited by Robert Liddiard. Woodbridge, Suffolk: The Boydell Press, 2003.

Emery, Anthony. "The Development of Raglan Castle and Keeps in Late Medieval England." *Archaeological Journal* 132 (1975).

English Heritage. *Farleigh Hungerford Castle.* London: English Heritage, 1998.

———. *PastScape.* http://www.pastscape.org/homepage/index.html, 2004.

Forde-Johnston, James. *A Guide to the Castles of England and Wales.* London: Constable, 1981.

Friar, Stephen. *The Sutton Companion to Castles.* Stroud, Gloucestershire: Sutton Publishing, 2003.

Fry, Peter, and Fiona Somerset Fry. *A History of Ireland.* London: Routledge, 1991.

Fry, Plantagenet Somerset. *Castles of Britain and Ireland.* New York: Abbeville Press, 1997.

———. *The David and Charles Book of Castles.* Newton Abbot, Devon: David and Charles, 1980.

Furtado, Peter, et al. *The Ordnance Survey Guide to Castles in Britain.* Twickenham: Country Life Books, 1987.

Goodall, John. "Dover Castle and the Great Siege of 1216," Chateau Gaillard, XIX: Actes du Colloque International de Graz. http://www.deremilitari.org/goodall.htm, 1998.

Hammond, Peter. *Her Majesty's Royal Palace and Fortress of the Tower of London.* London: Historic Royal Palaces, 1993.

Higham, Robert. "Timber Castles: A Reassessment." In *Anglo-Norman Castles*, edited by Robert Liddiard. Woodbridge, Suffolk: The Boydell Press, 2003.

Higham, Robert, and Philip Barker. *Timber Castles.* Mechanicsburg, PA: Stackpole Books, 1995.

Historic Tours (Wales). *Ludlow Castle.* Caernarfon: Historic Tours (Wales), 1987.

Humphries, P. H. *Castles of Edward the First in Wales.* London: HMSO, 1983.

Jackson, M. J. *Castles of Cumbria.* Carlisle: Carel Press, 1990.

Johns, C. N. *Caerphilly Castle.* London: HMSO, 1978.

Johnson, Matthew. *Behind the Castle Gate: From Medieval to Renaissance.* London: Routledge, 2002.

Johnson, Stephen. *Hadrian's Wall*. London: B. T. Batsford, 1989.

Jones, T. L. *Ashby de la Zouch Castle*. London: English Heritage, 1999.

Kenyon, John R. *Medieval Fortifications*. Leicester: Leicester University Press, 1990.

———. *Raglan Castle*. Cardiff: Cadw, 2003.

Kightly, Charles. *A Mirror of Medieval Wales: Gerald of Wales and His Journey of 1188*. Cardiff: Cadw, 1988.

King, D.J.C. *The Castle in England and Wales: An Interpretative History*. Beckenham, Kent: Croom Helm, 1988.

Knight, Jeremy K. *Chepstow Castle*. Cardiff: Cadw, 1986.

———. *Chepstow Castle and Port Wall*. Cardiff: Cadw, 1991.

———. *The Three Castles*. Cardiff: Cadw, 2000.

Mackworth-Young, Robin. *The History and Treasures of Windsor Castle*. London: Pitkin-Britannia, 1982.

Marshall, Pamela, and John Samuels. *Guardian of the Trent: The Story of Newark Castle*. Newark: Newark Castle Trust, 1997.

Matarasso, Francois. *The English Castle*. London: Cassell, 1993.

McCann, Nick, ed. *Berkeley Castle*. Derby: English Life Publications, 1997.

McNeill, Tom. *Castles*. London: B. T. Batsford/English Heritage, 1992.

Muir, Richard. *Castles and Strongholds*. London: Macmillan, 1990.

———. *The NEW Reading the Landscape: Fieldwork in Landscape History*. Exeter: University of Exeter Press, 2000.

The National Trust. *Corfe Castle Dorset*. London: The National Trust, 2000.

Norman, A.V.B., and Don Pottinger. *English Weapons and Warfare: 449–1660*. New York: Barnes and Noble, 1992.

O'Neil, B. H. St. J. *Caerlaverock Castle*. Edinburgh: Her Majesty's Stationery Office, 1988.

Pembrokeshire Coast National Park. *Carew Castle*. Haverfordwest: Pembrokeshire Coast National Park Authority, 2002.

Pettifer, Adrian. *English Castles: A Guide by Counties*. Woodbridge, Suffolk: The Boydell Press, 1995.

Pounds, N.J.G. *The Medieval Castle in England and Wales: A Social and Political History*. Cambridge: Cambridge University Press, 1994.

Prestwich, Michael. *Armies and Warfare in the Middle Ages: The English Experience*. New Haven: Yale University Press, 2003.

Raby, F.J.E. *Framlingham Castle*. London: HMSO, 1984.

Renn, Derek. *Caerphilly Castle*. Cardiff: Cadw, 1997.

———. *Goodrich Castle*. London: English Heritage, 1998.

———. *Kenilworth Castle*. London: English Heritage, 1999.

———. *Norman Castles in Britain*. London: John Baker Publishers, 1973.

Renn, Derek, and Richard Avent. *Flint Castle/Ewloe Castle*. Cardiff: Cadw, 1995.

Robinson, David M., ed. *Tretower Court and Castle*. Cardiff: Cadw, 1990.

Rowley, Trevor. *The Norman Heritage: 1066–1200*. London: Routledge and Kegan Paul, 1983.

Royal Commission on Ancient and Historical Monuments in Wales. *An Inventory of the Ancient Monuments in Glamorgan*, vol. 3, Part 1b, *Medieval Secular Monuments: The Later Castles from 1217 to the Present*. London: HMSO, 1991.

Salter, Mike. *The Castles and Tower Houses of Northumberland*. Malvern: Folly Publications, 1997.

Savage, Anne. *The Anglo-Saxon Chronicles*. London: Guild Publishing, 1988.

Seller, David. "Farewell to Feudalism." In *Burke's Landed Gentry: The Kingdom in Scotland*, edited by Peter Beauclerk Dewar. Stokesley, North Yorkshire: Burke's Peerage and Gentry, 2004.

Shoesmith, Ron. *A Guide to Castles and Moated Sites in Herefordshire*. Almeley, Herefordshire: Logaston Press, 1996.

Spurgeon, C. J. "Mottes and Castle-Ringworks in Wales." In *Castles in Wales and the Welsh Marches: Essays in Honour of D. J. Cathcart King*, edited by John R. Kenyon and Richard Avent. Cardiff: University of Wales Press, 1987.

St. George's Chapel. http://www.stgeorges-windsor.org/history/hist_stgeorges.asp, 2005.

Sweetman, David. *The Medieval Castles of Ireland*. Woodbridge, Suffolk: The Boydell Press, 2003.

Taylor, A. J. *Raglan Castle*. London: HMSO, 1970.

Taylor, Arnold. *Beaumaris Castle*. Cardiff: Cadw, 1999.

——. *Caernarfon Castle and Town Walls*. Cardiff: Cadw, 1993.

——. *Conwy Castle and Town Walls*. Cardiff: Cadw, 1998.

——. *Rhuddlan Castle*. Cardiff: Cadw, 1987.

Thackray, David. *Bodiam Castle East Sussex*. London: The National Trust, 1995.

Toy, Sidney. *The Castles of Great Britain*. London: William Heinemann, 1953.

Vemming Hansen, Peter. "War Engines of the Middle Ages." *The Medieval Centre*. http://www.middelaldercentret.dk/english/us_home.htm, 1998.

Warner, Philip. *The Medieval Castle: Life in a Fortress in Peace and War*. New York: Barnes and Noble Books, 1993.

——. *Sieges of the Middle Ages*. London: Penguin Books, 2000.

Williams, Ann. "A Bell-House and a Burh-Geat: Lordly Residences in England Before the Norman Conquest." In *Anglo-Norman Castles*, edited by Robert Liddiard. Woodbridge, Suffolk: The Boydell Press, 2003.

Williams, Diane M. *Gower: A Guide to Ancient and Historic Monuments on the Gower Peninsula*. Cardiff: Cadw, 1998.

Williams, Geoffrey. *Stronghold Britain*. Stroud, Gloucestershire: Sutton Publishing, 1999.

Index

About the Author

LISE E. HULL is an independent researcher who has spent twenty years researching Britain's castles. She is the founder of Castles Unlimited, an organization dedicated to promoting appreciation and preservation of these masterpieces of military engineering. She is the author of *The Castles of Pembrokeshire* (2005) and numerous magazine articles.